Teaching Hitting

Teaching Hitting

A Guide for Coaches

Dirk Baker

FOREWORD BY MIKE EASLER

McFarland & Company, Inc., Publishers
Jefferson, North Carolina, and London

LIBRARY OF CONGRESS CATALOGUING-IN-PUBLICATION DATA

Baker, Dirk, 1969–
Teaching hitting: a guide for coaches / Dirk Baker ; foreword by Mike Easler.
p.   cm.
Includes index.

ISBN 0-7864-2049-9 (softcover : 50# alkaline paper) ∞

1. Batting (Baseball)   2. Youth league baseball — Coaching.
I. Title.
GV869.B28   2005   796.357'26 — dc22   2005004473

British Library cataloguing data are available

Cover photograph ©2005 Brand X Pictures

Manufactured in the United States of America

*McFarland & Company, Inc., Publishers
Box 611, Jefferson, North Carolina 28640
www.mcfarlandpub.com*

To my family for making me into the person I am today.
To my teachers for inspiring me to write.
To my coaches for teaching me the game of baseball.
To my teammates for pushing me to excel.
To my players for making every practice and game
the best part of my day.

Acknowledgments

The photographs are used with thanks to Rex Baker, Steve Berg, Rudy Winston, Tim Hardison, Neal Portnoy, John Meany, Dave Morris and Bruce Baker.

Also, thanks to Dan Donato, Chris Aufiero, and Jack Janasiewicz for appearing in many of them.

And thanks to Shannon O'Connor.

Table of Contents

Foreword

by MIKE "THE HIT MAN" EASLER

Baseball has so many disciplines. Players have to hit, field, throw, run, jump and slide. But of all the skills, none is more difficult than hitting a baseball.

To be a good hitter, one must first learn the basics. No one can just walk on the field and hit, or even coach for that matter. You have to read up on the fundamentals, because if the coach doesn't know how to teach proper balance, the hitters certainly won't learn it.

This book is one of the best guidelines for coaches and hitters to learn how to hit a baseball. It's full of concepts and theories to use on the field.

I was a world champion as a player with the Pittsburgh Pirates in 1979. I played with great hitters like Willie Stargell, Don Mattingly, and Wade Boggs. They all knew and practiced the basics of hitting.

I've also coached hitters of every age. I still tell my hitters to keep everything simple. Many coaches try to teach in a way that makes them sound professional and smart. The key to coaching is keeping complicated theories simple, so the kids can learn and do it for themselves. This book does that.

My keys to hitting are balance and flexibility in the stance and in the swing. I call my video *The A, B, Cs of Hitting:* *See, Read and Explode* because hitting should be taught in a simple manner. Kids need to understand the concepts being taught to them. Hitters should see the ball out of the pitcher's hand, read the ball as it's coming to the plate, and then explode on the ball. Any kid who wants to be the best can work to do so.

This book is ideal for coaches of all levels, because it gives coaches the opportunity to chart a hitter's success from the grip, to the swing, to batting practice. It's all here.

This book is perfect for kids as well as coaches to help them learn, and become better at what they do. It has everything a hitter of any age needs to know. And the keys to the book are its positive attitude and readability.

Hopefully this book will find its way to thousands of baseball nuts around the country. Every reader will learn something to improve his or her own team. The coaches will be more confident in teaching hitting, and that will most certainly carry over to the kids.

In conclusion, baseball is like life. There's a lot of winning and losing out there. But it's how hard you work during life that people remember. Hard work distinguishes winners. You have to read, experiment, watch, and learn from other coaches and other players.

Hitters need to do everything it takes to be the best. No one can ever just walk up to the plate and hit for the cycle. You have to work, work, work. And that goes for coaches as well.

Be confident and positive. Have fun. And enjoy your baseball experiences. Good luck to all the hitters and coaches out there.

Introduction to Teaching and Coaching

"Tell a ballplayer something a thousand times; then tell him again. Because that might be the time he'll understand something."
— Paul Richards, former major league manager

There are four basic rules to teaching: explanation, demonstration, correction and repetition. Successful coaches must be able to effectively communicate these concepts to their players on a consistent basis. Work hardest in practice, and let the kids play during games. Coach and teach at the same time. Love what you do, and have fun.

The concepts in this book can be adapted for any age group. Watch the Little League World Series. These kids are learning big-league concepts, playing on national TV and in front of thousands of people. If they can handle curveballs, an in-depth signaling system, and double-session practices, so can your team. So read this book, ask questions, challenge your kids, and work hard.

Have Fun

Make baseball fun to play. Breed a positive attitude. Without the cheering, laughing, team work, sweating, and enjoyable sides to baseball, the game itself is lost. You're responsible for motivating, teaching, and even comforting the players. Be their leader. Make them want to improve. If they love what they're doing, they'll love playing for you. To coach a sport or teach a subject, one must thoroughly enjoy it. Read, talk, watch, learn, write, dream about it. Winning teams play loose, so don't be tight. And treat the game as the best part of your day.

Help Your Players Climb the Ladder

Know the basics of hitting, and then transmit those skills to the team. Learn and practice the fundamentals, because those skills must travel to each higher level of baseball. Climbing the ladder involves starting at the bottom and working up to the top. With each rung get higher and more advanced. If the team gets too high for its abilities, go back down a few rungs to regain their confidence and good work habits. Even when reaching the top, keep reinforcing the basics.

Focus on being fundamentally sound, and keep theories simple. If this is done the hitter can carry these princi-

Surround yourself with good people. (Bruce Baker)

ples over to the game. The prepared and refined hitter is a successful one.

Listen and Watch the Players

Not only do players have to listen to their coaches, but coaches have to listen and watch as well. This goes for the positives and negatives. Coaches may just learn something. You may leave a successful .400 hitter alone, for example, because any feedback may not help or might even conflict matters. The coach must know, through experience, when and when not to help a player. Teach specific philosophies and theories to everyone, and offer assistance to each player. But don't coach just to hear yourself speak.

Some hitters may have the worst stance and swing, fundamentally speaking, but constantly hit the ball hard and for base hits. Leave this type of player alone (especially during tryouts). Tryouts should be the place where hitters show their capabilities to the coaches with only limited instruction. See if a kid can do the job. Simply watch and learn, and then analyze their strengths and weaknesses. Ask yourself, "What can this kid do to help the team win?" Heighten the positives, and work to improve the negatives. Both the player and coach will benefit more.

A player who has lost confidence may not come directly to you for assistance. Look for such clues, especially when players are down. Recognizing these signs may rescue a person's confidence. Some baseball concerns go further than the field. Troubled players invariably take that slump home and to school. Be there for the kids, and be able to get them out of the doldrums. Work and speak with them. Don't wait to correct a flaw in someone's swing. The better they feel about approaching you, the more they will inform you of their highs and lows. Always be there for them, and take the initiative to fix a problem — hitting or personal. Moreover, while you're not their friend, never ask the players to do anything which you wouldn't do yourself. Whether it's washing uniforms, raking the mound, making sandwiches, or throwing batting practice, you'll motivate the team more by doing the exact same duties you ask of the players.

Get Your Message Across — and Be Sure It's One You Should Be Sending

Communicate face to face as opposed to email or voicemail. And remember that no one wants to play under someone they fear. Many coaches spend too much time doing the Xs and Os when they should be interacting with the players. Coaches are father or mother figures, and even role models for some. Show your human side. Baseball is supposed to be fun — not boot camp.

There are two types of players: the coachable and the coach killer. Tell someone once, and the message should get across to them; tell them twice, and it should become a part of them. Everyone must follow the same rules. But do give kids second chances to redeem themselves, and show them where they went wrong. Part of growing up is learning from one's mistakes.

Communicate through positive reinforcement, even during a negative confrontation. Show caring by giving confidence and motivation. Positive reinforcement is often viewed as a reward. However, support means much more

than external rewards such as money, awards or statistics. Verbal signs could be "Nice going," "Way to go," or "Like to see it." Be consistent, keep terms simple, don't generalize, and be honest. Sometimes the truth hurts, so tell it like it is. Have guts. And never lie to a player in fear of hurting his or her feelings. Players need to know where they stand.

Interaction is almost as much nonverbal as verbal. Basic nonverbal signs (facial expressions and body language) include using the hands when speaking, a high-five, slap on the butt, hug or handshake. A stern glare can go a long way to get a message across. You can use constructive criticism by showing how selfish play or lack of hustle, for example, are detrimental to the team. For mental or fundamental mistakes during games, run full sprints around the bases afterward. Five mistakes equals five sprints. This self-teaching method illustrates that baseball is a team game, and that mistakes won't go unnoticed.

Expect Steady Effort

Good coaching is not achieved overnight. Teaching and coaching involve knowledge and love of the subject, communication skills, time management, discipline, and innovative ideas. Kids must be interested and on task for virtually every minute. It's an amazing responsibility. But coaches and teachers love to teach and interact with young people — making them love and enjoy learning.

Ask your players for three things: (1) hard work, (2) a willingness to listen, and (3) a willingness to change. Encourage them to give 100 percent effort and compete for the entire game. Then, with a winning attitude and a coach who takes risks, good results will happen.

Help Your Players Achieve Consistency

Hitters and coaches need consistency. Don't be a chameleon by changing your attitude, personality, or coaching style according to the score or team's record. Being a chatterbox may work for some and not for others, but effective communicators speak directly to the players. Talk to them one on one. Address positives and negatives in the dugout and between innings. With big leads, treat the score as if it were 0–0. With a deficit, try to manufacture one hit, one run at a time. If a team is rallying against you, have poise under pressure (i.e. bend but don't break). And being behind in a game warrants positive coaching qualities more than any other time in a season.

Players will respect you for who you are, not someone playing the role of a particular moment. Be consistent in mannerisms, lineup selections, game strategy, work habits, and approach to the game. Respect from the players will push them to compete at their best.

Know the Game

Two points about coaching: (1) The greatest hitter of all time may not be a good communicator and (2) reading all of the hitting books in the world is worthless without knowledge of the fundamentals. Gain the knowledge and transmit it to the players, so they can improve and succeed. Remember, all players and coaches don't know everything. New ideas are being developed and refined even at this moment. So adapt to the changing times. Read those books, watch other coaches and videos, attend clinics and seminars, and try to learn something at every stop. Moreover, learn the history of baseball (see Ken Burns's epic nine-part series *Baseball*), and know the rules of your particular league.

Create Organization

Practices decide the fate of a successful baseball team. Every practice must have drills and stations, constant productivity, and proper use of space and equipment. Speak slowly and in general, applicable terms; use conditioning to increase speed, quickness, power and stamina; and have a purpose for everything. Practices should be more than just batting practice, infield/outfield, and a few sprints. Every hitter should have a goal of 100 to 200 swings a day, sprints and distance running, tee work, soft toss, live BP, and even swings without a ball. And that's not even considering the defensive aspects of a practice.

Use Photographs

Show the kids what the major leaguers are doing. Find newspaper or magazine photos of the stance and swing. Cut them out and put them into a photo album. Arrange the photos just as this book is organized: bat size, grip, different stances, focus points, stride, weight shift, swing, full extension, head down, follow-through, and even mistakes. This photo book is perfect for teams, clinics, and summer camps. See it and do it. Remember, if the pros practice and repeat the fundamentals, so can the Little Leaguer.

Demonstrate How Together Everyone Achieves More

Emphasize personal sacrifice for the benefit of the team. Recognize the contributions of each player for the overall goal of being successful as a group. A sacrifice bunt looms just as important as the home run. Never get caught up in the glories of winning, because baseball has a way of bringing us down just as quickly. Enjoy the game for more than just the final result.

Since baseball is a game playable by all members of your team, attempt to

---

Game Day Assignment Chart

DATE:
GAME #:
OPPONENT:
Game Time:
6, 7, or 9 Inn:

Game Day Assignments (write in player names):
STARTER: RELIEF:
BULLPEN CATCHER:
PITCHING CHART: (DH-Game 2 starter)   *# of pitches to Coach each inning
SCOREBOOK: (inning/game totals)   *Chart people sit next to Coach
STATS PAGE: (opponent's stats, note key players: batting average, steals, Ks)
BP BUCKET: Previous Game Starter
FOUL BALLS:
FUNGOES: Pitchers
OF FUNGOES:
OF WARM-UP:
STRATEGY: (watch/yell for steals, squeeze/bunts, pick-offs, signals, sun balls)
BATS (carry/setup):   (make sure bats/helmets come to away games)
BALLS: (game balls unwrapped and rubbed)
HELMETS/TEES: (carry and setup)
WATER/FOOD:
TRASH: (dugouts, bleachers, parking lot)
LAST MAN:

Home Game	*TIME BEFORE GAME*	*DURATION*
Run, Stretch, Calisthenics, Throw	2 Hours Before	30 Min. [If Home, then Later]
WSC BP [May be 45 min. at Home]	1½ Hours Before	30 Min.
Visitor BP	1 Hour Before	30 Min.
Equipment Break Down, Rake IF	30 Min. Before	5 Min.
Home IF/OF	25 Min. Before	10 Min.
Visitor IF/OF	15 Min. Before	10 Min.
Sprints, Gr. Rules, Anthem, Huddle	5 Min. Before	5 Min.

Home Game Duties and Postgame
BP SETUP (turtle, mats, screens/chair): OF
INFIELD RAKING: Back-up IF
BASES/PLUGS (1 Each): Starting IF
PLATE RAKING, TAMP, TARPS: Catchers   *DHs=Duties Required Between Games
MOUND RAKING, TAMP, TARPS: Starting Pitchers *DHs=Duties Required Between Games
BULLPEN RAKING, FUNGOES: Relievers
SOUND SYSTEM/PA/ANTHEM/TABLES/CHAIRS/PROGRAMS: (setup/breakdown)
NOTE: Before leaving all players help to put gear away and attend final team meeting

play everyone. Every player can make a contribution. Being fast, strong, agile, or large are not baseball requirements. All that's needed are a bat and ball. Reward each player's self-worth.

No one enjoys sitting on the bench, but kids must understand that starting positions are earned in practice via hard work and performance. Even with a late pinch hitting or field appearance (know that kids would much rather hit than play the field), at least that kid can go home and say, "I played today."

Develop your own practice and game day duty list, so everyone has a chore for that particular day (rotates game to game).

Be Aware of Game Conditions

Since so much is happening during the game, it's a good idea to have an assistant or assistants. One individual can't do everything. Even youth teams need a scorekeeper, someone to do the lineup, call signals, move infielders and outfielders, give encouragement, and even carry the equipment. Designate coaching roles early in the season to avoid squabbles later on. Delegate responsibilities to each player, coach, or team manager. Time the pregame workouts. Keep a notebook. Stay calm and smile. Always think safety first before planning or doing any activity.

Make every situation a safe one. Are hitters wearing helmets at the plate? Are bases tied tightly to the ground? Does anyone have asthma? Do players know how to slide properly? Are players old enough to throw and catch real baseballs? Is the diamond (i.e. wet field) safe enough for practice and games? And where's the nearest phone in case of emergency?

Allow one batter in the on-deck cir-cle away from the rest of the bench players. Watch the action going on. When doing swinging drills as a team, spread hitters apart with plenty of room in between, so no one gets hit by the bat. Moreover, during team hitting drills have a command for "bats down" before players rotate to the next station. No one should ever swing a bat when you're talking. Wear helmets whenever a ball is being pitched, especially in the batting cage and during BP (players throwing BP in a cage should also wear a helmet). During on-field BP, focus on the hitter at all times, and also be aware of players running the bases and those retrieving balls. Make a point for players to be aware of batted balls, and never walk directly next to the batting cage net.

Try to be certified in first aid and CPR. Have a med kit at every practice and game. Coaches are essentially physical education teachers who need to be informed of these medical care. Knowing the correct action for sprains, strains, and breaks enables you to react with proper care when such unfortunate events occur. And when kids play hard, injuries may happen. Proper procedures to handle these shortcomings make your job even more valuable.

Make Sure Players Play and Coaches Coach

Since baseball is so mentally draining, you need players who are concerned with only the game. Players should be thinking about hitting a curveball, not who should be in the starting lineup. This side of coaching is often overlooked. Being prepared can mean the difference between little problems and big headaches. No task in baseball is menial, but all should be done without you having to ask. Winning teams realize the importance of these chores (listed below), while losing teams lose balls and leave equipment at the field. Assume all responsibilities. Tips for games and practices include:

- Check for all equipment, scorebook, lineup cards, pens and pencils.
- Assign a player(s) to each set of gear.
- Pack an extra hat, uniform, belt, stirrup socks, and shoelaces.
- If the home team, put the bases in early and line and drag the field.
- Have the scoreboard, sound system, PA, and music set up before the players arrive.
- Bring a rake to manicure the batter's box and pitching mound.
- If the away team, check the bus or cars/vans for enough gasoline.
- Print up directions to all away games and leave them in each vehicle.
- Use a motorcade for all away games.
- Assign a "last person" to check the dugout for equipment before leaving a field.
- Take a player count going to and from away games.
- Assume a practice/game is always on no matter what the weather.
- Set up a phone list (email or phone chain) for cancellations.
- All team members need an answering machine.
- Call a day before if unable to attend a practice/game.
- Make photocopies of the practice and game schedules, and give a copy to the parents.

Making Cuts

The coach will inevitably have to make cuts. No one enjoys doing it. The best way to trim a roster is to examine the talent of the current club and foresee a player's contribution to the success of the team. There are many facets to baseball. Few master all of the skills: pitching, fielding, throwing, hitting and running. Thus, you may be able to include an extra pinch hitter or runner, a reliever who throws hard, or a strong arm in the outfield. When evaluating talent, players should try out for their best position. There may be three tremendous shortstops who can all hit. If so, convert some into other positions. Good hitters are always needed.

Evaluate in practices and scrimmages. A test for hitting ability is to count the number of swings in one minute. This isn't a test of how many times a kid can swing the bat. Watch for quality, not quantity. Analyze bat speed. Does the kid take aggressive swings? Watch the approach to hitting (before the swing), balance, and proper fundamentals. Fatigue after swinging the bat for a minute is a tell-tale sign that the player hasn't worked on his or her bat speed.

Evaluate how a player dresses for tryouts (look for those dressed for success), stretches, warms up, walks to the plate, and carries him or herself during dead time. Take notes during tryouts. Learn every kid's name. If a confrontation does arise later on, have sufficient evidence of the player's performance. Offer a private conference with the cut player and provide tips and drills to improve on weaknesses. Encourage kids to stay in shape, attend games, play summer baseball, and try out next year.

Be honest and specific, and refrain from speaking in generalities. Tell them why they didn't make the team. Remind everyone that you put the best nine players on the field. Some kids expect to make the team no matter who is playing their position.

When naming the team, ask those kids to stay afterwards or call them at home; and possibly list identification numbers on a school bulletin board rather than names of those players making the club. This ensures privacy and no embarrassment from peers.

I got cut as a freshman at Boston University. But I didn't give up. I pestered the coach and athletic director for another tryout. I lifted weights every day, snuck into the team's indoor batting cage, and played over the summer. I made the JV team as a sophomore and started as the platooning DH as a junior. As the starting DH as a senior I was named captain and made All-Conference. Then as a fifth year player in 1992 I finally became the everyday left fielder. Dreams come true for those who work hard and gut it out.

Look for Potential

Categorize positions, ages, birth dates, and player classes. Focus on developing talent, and look for potential physical makeup in future seasons. And never discount those feisty first year players. A rookie has started for me every year since 1996.

Interact with Parents

Dealing with parents, fans, and umpires can sometimes be a nightmare. Only people directly associated with the

Play hard and good things happen. (Dave Morris)

team should be on the bench. All parents want their children to play and start. Understand that all fans love a winner. Be honest with parents, fans, and media just as with the kids. Never treat these involvements as an argument. Stay calm and cool. Adults may not approve of your reasons behind the team selection or lineup, but you have to make the final decision on all matters. Sometimes this takes the fun out of coaching, but enjoyment will begin once the roster is set.

Develop a Coaching Philosophy

A coaching philosophy is both mental and physical. This must apply to game strategy, attitude, work ethic, and personality. Write down your philosophy and goals for each new season. Explain this philosophy to the team along with the goals to be achieved. If players know who the coach is, they can know what to expect. Make them believe and trust the system. There's a saying, "Do it my way, or you will be replaced by someone who will." At Worcester State we offer three ideals: (1) Players will represent the college, team, and their families with class, (2) players will graduate, and (3) every WSC ballplayer will have an opportunity to play for a championship. The following is a guide to coaching baseball at any level:

Team: "Us" and "we," not "I" or "me." Faith, family, academics, baseball — in that order. Don't do as I say — do as we do. Never look for what you'll get, but what you'll contribute. Togetherness is excellence. Care about each other. Treat others as you would want to be treated. Study like a champion, play like a champion, be a champion. Set goals. Have fun.

Attitude: Good things happen to those who work hard. Be proud of your accomplishments. Never make excuses. Respect the opponent. Take risks. Ask questions. Self-educate. Be a positive force in society. Proper attitude equals greatness. Make the players better.

Winning: Winners sacrifice. Do what is right. Do your best. Success is earned. Winners never quit. Winners aren't born — they decide themselves. Be a leader. Don't let life pass you by. Never be satisfied. Always be prepared. Overcome adversity. Pay attention to detail. Be fundamentally sound.

1

When to Start

"I believe the youth idea is great with some minor leagues: Put an eight-foot board fence around the playing area and only let the kids inside; take away all uniforms and let the kids wear street clothes; let them choose teams by the one-potato, two-potato system; let them play until it gets dark or until the kid with the ball goes home."

— David Gey, Educator

The First Bat or Glove

Every newborn should be fitted with a bat and glove. Have them learn to throw with both hands, and start swinging the Wiffleball bat from both sides of the plate. Seriously, a child should be brought into baseball as soon as the parent sees fit. Since organized leagues don't start until around age six, the parent is the motivating factor in a child's life before the start of competition.

Ages and Leagues

The following is a league guideline for parents and kids. Avoid skipping a league. Children will develop better and play more by staying two years in each league up to age 13. Most states have different brackets for ages 13 to 18. For example, a kid may play one year in Junior League (age 13) or two years in Babe Ruth (13 to 15; high school freshmen-sophomores) and then two years in Senior Babe Ruth (16 to 19; high school juniors-seniors). Whatever league it is, a kid should be out there playing. *Note:* In 2003 American Legion and Senior Babe

Ruth increased the age limits to include 19-year-olds.

6 to 8: Tee-Ball or Pony League*
9 to 10: Minor League
11 to 12: Little League or Major League
13: Junior Little League or Babe Ruth
14 to 15: Senior Little League or Senior Babe Ruth
16 to 19: Freshmen–JV–Varsity HS/ American Legion/Senior Ruth/Connie Mack
18 to 21: College/NCAA Sanctioned Summer Leagues

*Depends on the first year of baseball. Kids could begin as early as age 5. Birthdays after August 1 may allow a child to spend an extra year in L.L. and/or play against similar-aged kids or younger. This especially helps those in Senior L.L. or Senior Babe Ruth who have just completed their sophomore high school seasons yet can still compete in summer all-star competition.

The First Taste of Baseball

The first baseball experience should come within the family. Parents and siblings playing catch or hitting the ball around the yard puts the child in a familiar and comfortable setting. Parents should stress correct techniques and learning through failure. Trying is much better than worrying about a mistake. Lastly, in reading about the changes in kids as they grow up, coaches and parents must understand that the number one aspect to youth sport competition is participation.

Age 4

By age four, most children start to play with other kids their age. The first level of organized baseball should be Tee-Ball. Kids at this age have little patience or understanding of organization. Motor skills (coordination and balance) develop as well as hitting, throwing, catching and running. Children should be exposed to a variety of activities. Keep in mind that player's motor skills develop at different rates.

Age 7

Fundamental changes occur to children here. They become more self-aware and less prone to temper tantrums. Coordination is improving, and intuition rises. Baseball skills should improve. Be concerned with how kids deal with failure and fear. For some hitters that first toss from a pitcher can be a traumatic experience.

Ages 8 to 10

Kids are now honing newly acquired physical skills. Concentration on fundamentals, rules, and strategies is getting better. Being part of a team is very important. An interest in contact sports may be a motivation for some. Parents and coaches should be concerned about stresses on the throwing arm (i.e. curveball) at least until the growth plates have developed.

Ages 11 to 12

Children are now examining their own performance and comparing that to others. Achievement looms large. Many may drop baseball from a feeling of inferiority to their counterparts. Kids are focusing on a specific position (i.e. infielder, catcher, pitcher or outfielder). Stress the importance of playing many positions. Being versatile makes one more valuable to one's team. Little League is a glorious time for children. For many first-time all-stars, baseball is now more than just something played in the back yards. Game scores, names, and highlights may also begin appearing in the newspapers.

Ages 13 to 15

Between the ages of 12 and 16, a large majority of children drop out of sports due to lack of playing time and criticism from peers. This is also the start of high school and competition on the freshman, junior varsity, and varsity teams. Some players may not be able to make the proper adjustments to the major league-sized diamond. Teenagers are beginning to show physical maturity. With so many activities today, interests are also becoming more diverted from baseball. Perhaps the number one reason why kids drop out of sports at any age is the lack of fun.

Ages 16 and Up

Kids are now being considered adults. Many want to be treated as such. Winning is a key component. For some who have played since first grade, high school may be the last level of competitive baseball. Playing sports can only happen with passing grades. Athletic scholarships are awarded to a select few

(11.7 total for most Div. 1 schools), and less than 1 percent of the population sign pro contracts. High school athletes must balance sports and schoolwork in order to get into college. College ballplayers must maintain a B-/C average or better to remain eligible.

Ages 15 to 22 should consider playing in the spring, summer and even fall, and stay in tip-top shape year-round. Always emphasize baseball fundamentals. Be aware of the kids who think they "know everything." Instead look for players who'll contribute anything.

The First Game

Hopefully everyone remembers something about their first baseball game. Parading around in the flashy new hat and uniform is as wonderful as opening presents on Christmas morning. As a coach or parent, photograph or videotape these cherished moments. Those pictures or tapes are great for the moment, and you'll probably file them away somewhere in the desk shortly thereafter. Take it from me, go find those old childhood photographs. You'll be glad you did.

Parents should attend their child's games. It's your kid out there, so be there for support during the good times and bad. A shoulder must be present to cry on sometimes. They'll always remember that, and so will you.

Size of a Ballplayer

Baseball players come in all shapes and sizes. But for some reason, people assume that the smaller the ballplayer, the harder that person has to work to succeed. Assume the competition is working 24 hours a day. No one will ever hand someone a .400 batting average. The batter has to earn it through conditioning, lifting weights, and refining skills.

Heart Determines Ability

Talent can be an advantage for some, but desire and having fun can mean just as much. Every player has a skill to call his/her own and different from everyone else. Sometimes it may be only one skill, but use it whenever possible. Encourage players to try hard, hustle to bases, sprint onto the field, run out home runs and walks, and cheer from the bench. Cherish these great moments on and off the field.

Role of the Coach

The year a child begins playing isn't the problem. It's combining playing *and* winning at an early age that has become such a dilemma. Youngsters can begin hitting and throwing at ages four or five, but they should be left alone to be kids. Refrain from stressing the score and instead emphasize the practice of fundamentals. Teaching and learning — not necessarily winning.

Variety of Sports

Baseball is a spring activity. Kids should be encouraged to play a variety of sports and especially lifetime hobbies (i.e. fishing, tennis and golf). It all comes down to time management, having fun, and desire to be the best.

Stay Fit

Children of today are much heavier and less fit compared to those of the past. Kids who rarely exercise run the risk of obesity and a lifetime of poor fitness and eating habits. The trend is to stay indoors to play. Many factors of modern society can be blamed for this: threat of crime and drugs, lack of playgrounds and fields, video games, the internet, and TV. Sports are fun and keep us in shape. So get kids out to the diamond, YMCA, playground or gym. Staying active provides higher energy and enthusiasm. And remember to laugh once in a while.

2

Bat Size

"Speak softly and carry a big stick."
— Theodore Roosevelt, U.S. President

Selecting the Correct Bat

Selecting the right bat is the same as purchasing a mattress. To get a good night's sleep one needs a bed that is comfortable. The same goes for a bat. Don't encourage a kid to use the flashy new bat or the same one someone else hits well with. The hitter succeeds with proper

Bat size test. (Steve Berg)

equipment. This goes for bats, cleats and gloves.

Test a bat's weight by holding it out front with the dominant hand for 30 to 60 seconds. If the youngster is unable to hold it steady, the bat is probably too heavy. Also, hold two bats of choice (one heavier than the other) out front with both hands for a few seconds. Experiment with the bats to see which one feels better, and then switch hands.

Another way is to take an aggressive cut and attempt a check swing before the bat head crosses the front of an imaginary plate. It's not easy. A bat, with proper weight distribution for the individual, will only be suitable for a hitter who can check his/her own swing. This drill reinforces the light bat phenomenon. Swing the bat; don't let the bat swing you.

Quicker the Better

The laws of physics apply to choosing a bat. The shorter the bat, the more control and bat speed, but less power. The longer the bat, the more power, but less control and bat speed.

Good bat speed means going from the stance to contact with the ball in the shortest amount of time. Preach "hands to the ball as quickly as possible." Many power hitters use a heavier bat to drive the ball long distances. Youngsters should concentrate on bat speed rather than power, because bad habits form from swinging upwards to reach the fences. Choose a bat that enables the individual to get across the plate quickly and efficiently (i.e. hit the ball square and hard). If anything, select a lighter bat.

The process of choosing a bat should continue each season. As players grow, gain weight and change in bat speed, it may become necessary to change bat size and length. Once comfortable with one, stay with it the rest of the season. Consistency is a necessity. Changing what works can only lead to confusion. Slumping hitters usually want to change bats. Nine times out of ten, the problem has to do with basic mechanics and not the bat size or weight.

Pick a quick bat. (Steve Berg)

Bat Size Chart

Here's a general guideline for selecting a bat according to length and weight. Practice with different bats before finalizing the one of choice for games. As in life, every decision depends

on the situation. While the normal-sized 12-year-old may use a 29-inch, 22-ounce bat, a larger kid of the same age may be able to swing a much heavier bat. So test, experiment, and practice.

Age	League	Bat Length	Bat Weight (in ounces)
5–6	Tee-Ball	25–26	17–18
8–9	Minors	27–28	20–22
10–12	Majors	28–30	22–24
13–15	Seniors	30–32	24–28
16–18	High School	32–33	28–30
18–21	College	32–34	28–30
21–up	Pro	33–36	30–up*

*Wood bats weigh more than aluminums of similar length.

Note: Ounces may vary for the specific make of bat.

Cracks and Dents

Check for cracks in the older bats. Even the smallest cracks shorten the distance of a ball hit on contact, because the hitting surface isn't solid. It's like letting air out of a balloon. Constant use may also make a bat simply lose its "pop." Test for this by banging the bat handle on home plate. If the bat doesn't make a nice "pinging" sound or simply sounds "dead," it may be time to use a new one. At Worcester State alone, we cracked or

Don't lose your pop. (Steve Berg)

deadened five aluminum bats between 2002 and 2003. Our kids simply hit all the time and year-round, so the wear and tear is immense.

Most bat companies have a warranty on defective bats, so check with a sporting goods store for similar details. Aluminum bats break/crack just as the woods. If a wooden bat breaks, tape it up and use it for soft toss or team-swinging drills. Lastly, if a team has the necessary funds in the budget, purchase a couple new bats for a playoff run.

Also check for dents or depressions. These dents come from constant hitting and overuse. Some may not be visible by the human eye. Gently rub the hitting surface every so often. Feel for areas not completely smooth to the touch. Hitting on a dent won't drive the ball solidly. It's like skating on a bump or crack in the ice.

Advantages of the Aluminum Bat

Hitting and/or getting jammed with an aluminum bat doesn't hurt the hands as much as the wooden. The sting of a bat, especially in cold weather, may last an entire inning or game. Just shake or blow on the hands. And keep the fingers moving, so they don't stiffen up.

In 1999 the NCAA handed down new rules for the aluminum bat: two and five-eighth inches in diameter and a length-to-weight differential of three (i.e. a 33-inch bat must weigh 30 ounces). The ruling came about after numerous players were hit by line drives and some absurd scoring in the Div. 1 ranks. The rules, in an attempt to lessen the exit speed of the ball, are now seen in high school baseball as well.

Did the new ruling change college baseball? In 1998 the Worcester State baseball team hit .380 (fourth in the NCAA) with the then "lethal" minus-5 bats. In 1999 WSC hit .373 (fifth NCAA), 2000 .341 (29th NCAA), 2001 .363 (seventh NCAA), 2002 .379 (second NCAA), and 2003 .348 (15th NCAA). I guess if you can hit, it doesn't matter what type of bat you use.

Best Makers of Bats

The makes of aluminum bats are basically the same. Hillerich and Bradsby's Louisville Slugger TPX and Worth's Tennessee Thumper are popular for younger players (ages five to 10). Little Leaguers (ages 10 to 12) and high school players (ages 14 to 17) seem to prefer Easton bats. Worth and Nike are also popular. Again, kids shouldn't use a new bat in competition without first swinging it in practice.

Popular wooden bats include Hillerich and Bradsby, Rawlings-Adirondack, Cooper and Worth. Barnstable Bats are a major supplier to the Cape Cod Summer League. Hillerich and Bradsby has been making the Louisville Slugger for over 100 years. There are fewer than six companies in the wooden bat business, but many individuals have started their own wood bat sales. One popular wooden composite bat (with a fiberglass coating) is the Baum Bat (maker Steve Baum). Worcester State has used the composite bat in the fall and spring preseasons every year since 2000. Composites are a terrific investment for practice, because the bats seldom break. Bats now come completely covered in the fiberglass, just the handle, and even with a rubberized sleeve (similar to taping the "sweet spot") to protect the hitting area.

Sweet Spot and Meat of the Bat

The "sweet spot" and "meat" of the bat are locations where the greatest force is generated. Gravity, leverage, and force all apply to hitting the ball solidly. The "sweet spot" is four-to-six inches from the top of the bat (aluminum: between the "S" and "N" of the word "Easton"; wood: just above the label). When using a wooden bat, with a hitter eyeing the label in the 12 o'clock position, hit the ball at three-or-nine o'clock. Rotate the bat in the hands to make contact in the correct area. Also, look for knots, which add thunder to the bat.

"Meat" of bat. (Steve Berg)

The "sweet spot" is technically a single point, and studies show that a ball struck by a major league-quality wood bat in that spot will go farther than one struck by an aluminum bat in the corresponding spot. But an aluminum bat has a larger area of high performance. To test for the "sweet spot" try tapping the bat against a telephone pole.

Aluminum Versus Wood

Before the 1970s, wooden bats were used by everyone. Woods are now exclusively used in the Cape Cod and Alaskan Leagues (hotbeds for professional prospects) and in just over a dozen other amateur summer leagues. For the hitter looking to swing a heavier bat, using the wood in practice can increase bat speed and muscular strength.

Kids today have the advantage of using the aluminum bat. Little League started using it in 1972, and college legalized the metal in 1974. Because an aluminum bat weighs less (hollow interior) than a wooden bat of the same length, a hitter can generate better bat speed.

Aluminum bats seldom break, which is the economic cause of their popularity. Moreover, the ball comes off metal harder and faster upon contact (i.e. trampoline effect). Watch a hitter get jammed with an aluminum, yet the ball can be flared into the outfield; not so often with the wood, which may also result in a splintered shaft. Advantages to the metal bat include narrower handles (better grip for "whipping" the bat through the hitting zone), wider hitting surface ("meat" of the bat), and virtually no bend to it when meeting the ball (for more solid contact).

Everyone Should Swing the Wood

The wood bat is used in certain collegiate leagues: the New Jersey Athletic Conference (Div. 3) and the Northeast 10 (Div. 2) to name two. While Massachusetts was the first state to bring the wood back into high school competition (2003), the results were mixed. Yes, batting averages and home runs were lower than in past years. But not all teams used the wood (some inner-city schools continued to use metal for budgetary reasons). While woods weren't required until the state playoffs, virtually every team used the wood bats throughout the year to gear up for the postseason. Metal returned to competition in 2004.

Swinging the heavier wooden bat develops stronger wrists and forearms, better bat control, and promotes keeping the bat head up in order to swing down on the ball. It's more difficult to hit with the wood; thus concentration and focus have to be better. One's hands and stride must go to the ball, and the hitter has to be more aggressive. Nothing good is ever achieved by swinging easy.

Facts About the Wooden Bat

The following are some wooden bat tips:

- Experiment with different sorts of bats until you get the right feel. Every bat has its own identity since every tree is different according to its grain, hardness and feel.
- Try to stay with the same bat make. Look for bats with less grain. The less the grain means the harder the bat and less chance of cracking or splintering.
- Contact hitters may want a thicker bat handle and power hitters a thinner one (this all depends on better contact or bat speed, respectively).
- Separate game bats from BP models. Splintered bats can be taped or glued, but always take care of the "gamer."
- Before a game, use tape or rub pine tar on the handle for a better grip (area above the hands). Shave the handle down (for a thinner handle) using sandpaper or a bottle cap.

Most wooden bats (a quality one costing $35–$40) come from the white ash tree. In 1999 a bat made of maple appeared in the majors. While maple is heavier than ash, some players claim that the maple bat is more durable. And someday you'll likely see a baseball bat made out of cherry, probably the heaviest wood in the forest. A hitter may also look for a bat with the greatest amount of winter growth in the wood (dark-colored) and least amount of summer growth (light-colored). Winter growth is hard and recoils less on contact.

Hitters who want to decrease the bat weight can order a "cupped" bat (concave shape). A lathe can take extra weight from the top while maintaining the same bat length. Hitters can also "bone" the wood. Select a large and cleaned leg bone from the butcher. Rub the bone along the hitting surface. This hardens the "sweet spot" by closing the pores and strengthens and protects it. Rubbing a glass bottle also makes the bat harder and decreases the chance of splintering.

To protect a practice bat, tightly wrap the middle with duct tape. Then wrap white athletic tape around the "sweet spot," so the hitter knows where to hit the ball each time (i.e. line up the "sweet spot" before hitting balls off the tee). In cold weather (even for metals), try black electrical tape underneath the regular grip to thwart those stinging sensations.

Conclusion

What's the single most important ingredient to hitting? It's the bat. Swing a quick and brand new stick each season. Have your hitters try the following: 1) Give the bat a name. Be original. 2) Talk to it before each at-bat. Use positive reinforcement. The bat should feel confident before hits and even after outs. 3) Keep the bat warm at night. Place it next to the heater. To get into a hot streak, the bat should arrive at the game nice and cozy. 4) Arrange the bat behind the backstop. It should get an early look at the competition.

In all seriousness, refrain from banging dirt out of the spikes with the bat, leave the field with it in the bat bag, and never throw it after an out. The bat is a hitter's best friend.

3

Grip

"I never smile when I have a bat in my hands. That's when you've got to be serious. When I get out on the field, nothing's a joke to me."

— Hank Aaron, all-time home run leader

Introduction

The basic fundamentals are the same for everyone. Use language that kids can understand and relate to. Hitting isn't easy, but reading about it and having the kids do it themselves is what this book is all about. We'll start with the grip, move to the stance and swing, and progress into different aspects of drills and ways to improve. Read, take notes, ask questions, and keep swingin'.

Comfort and Feel

The key to proper grip is comfort and placement. Kids need to hold the bat at the base of the fingers. Imagine holding it the same way as a pencil — with relaxed fingers. Understand that for a left-handed batter, the left hand rests on top of the right hand; vice versa for a right-handed batter.

Knuckles

To grip the bat the hitter should lean over with the bat resting in the fingers. With one hand over the other, simply grasp the bat and come up. The thumbs wrap around the index fingers for stability.

Many coaches say to line up the middle knuckles on both hands. Don't worry about kids doing so exactly. Grip the bat so that it feels comfortable. Be loose at first, then firm upon swinging. As long as the bat is gripped with the fingers (not the palms) and proper wrist turnover is accomplished, a hitter should be able to generate a near level swing each time. Upon contact, the middle knuckles should be aligned with the bat head parallel to the front of the plate. *FYI:* Grasping with only the fingers locks the wrists, and with just the palms cuts down on bat speed along with wrist flexibility and proper turnover after contact. And there should be virtually no space between the bat and hands.

Grip with the fingers. (Steve Berg)

Lean over with the bat. (Rex Baker)

Also try the "roll grip." First grasp the bat with the top hand by rolling the top of the fingers underneath the handle. Roll the fingers around until the hand surrounds the bat. Then line up the middle knuckles of the bottom hand with the top.

Anything new takes time to get used to. Don't worry. Have the kids experiment and strive for comfort, balance, and the bat feeling good in their hands. Keep working on it, because proper grip (just as in throwing) is just as important as any other aspect to hitting.

Relax the Hands

Players need to relax when holding the bat. Tense hitters grip too tightly and will fail. Tension restricts a fluid swing. Pitchers hate to face those batters who appear totally at ease. The key to hitting is a loose body and relaxed mind. Grip the bat as if holding a puppy. Just before the swing begins, the grip tightens naturally as in clenching a fist. And those hitters with a tight grip should wiggle the fingers before the pitch.

Know that the bottom hand leads the swing, because it's the first one to the ball. Thus, this hand should hold the bat more firmly than the top (pressure on the thumb and pinkie). Left-handed hitters with a dominant right hand do have an advantage here. That's why ballplayers should work to strengthen both hands (i.e. fingertip pushups, wrist curls, handball, and even boxing).

The Knob Grip

Younger hitters should rest the bottom hand on the knob, so the bat doesn't come flying out after contact. However, hitters need bat control, and the knob effect tends to produce top-heaviness (bat head dips under the ball). Moreover,

Side view of the grip. (Steve Berg)

Other grip variety. (Rex Baker)

the knob constricts proper wrist turnover and flexibility, because the bottom hand doesn't have free movement. Try it and feel how the bottom hand runs into the knob.

During my career, I wrapped my pinkie around the knob. It just felt comfortable hitting this way and gave me a little bit more bat length to my 32-inch bat. I could stand off the plate and still drive the outside pitch. Again, this promotes the leading of the bottom hand to the ball, better bat leverage, control and comfort. Again, younger hitters should stay on the knob, but the above point illustrates how an individual can slightly alter his/her grip for an added advantage.

Mature hitters, once comfortable with their swing (mentally and physically), should leave a half-inch space between the bottom hand and knob (choke up a bit). This allows for smoother wrist turnover without interference from the knob.

Choking Up

For better bat control, one can choke up some two to three inches from the knob. This will, however cut down on power. But you want to hit the ball hard; not necessarily hit home runs. Bat control allows one more time to get the

Leave space between the hands and bat. (Steve Berg)

bat through the strike zone compared to the knob grip. Power hitters, who swing hard to drive the ball, usually keep the hands on the knob for a better pushoff and to prevent bat slippage.

Youngsters should choke up with two strikes. "Guard the dish" by slapping the ball somewhere in play. Imagine hitting with the "Little League Strike Zone," so anything close will be swung at. Preach contact in every at-bat, and never take a called third strike. Aggressive hitters make for aggressive-hitting teams. Ground balls put pressure on the defense and annoy those strikeout pitchers (case in point: long at-bats with frequent foul balls). Preach "never go easy," and "don't let the ump call you out." By putting the ball in play, the hitter has more confidence, the team will reach base on errors, and a two-strike base hit totally frustrates the pitcher.

Players with quick hands may want to choke up with a heavier bat. This adds more bat control with added "pop" or distance to the ball. For example, Worcester State's Jason Akana, even though a "tiny" five-foot-four, choked up on a 34-inch bat in 1996. With superior bat speed, he proceeded to lead the NCAA in batting at .514.

Tape, Rubber and Leather Grips

There are three types of grips for the bat. The common rubberized grip has two advantages: (1) Stickiness for the bare hands when pine tar isn't available, and (2) protection against the vibrations of an aluminum bat during cold weather. Many sporting goods companies can easily apply this grip with a machine at low cost.

The tape grip is a favorite of those who use wooden bats. The tape gives the hands something to hold onto (all wooden handles have a natural surface). Try rolling up lines of athletic tape under the regular tape for a "hockey stick" feel (tape arrangement at the end of hockey sticks). The tape grip doesn't protect against the bat vibrations as well as the rubber. For aluminum bats with thick rubber grips, hitters can remove the grip and apply some tape.

The leather grip came out in the early 1990s. It lasts much longer than the rubberized grips and doesn't get as sticky. The leather strip can be purchased in sporting goods stores and can easily be applied by hand.

Ways to Check for Proper Grip

First, organize a station to check for proper grip. Have each player show their hands in position on the bat.

Second, design an Axe Bat to test for proper hand alignment. Simply glue

Axe bat. (Steve Berg)

Types of grips. (Steve Berg)

an axe handle into the middle of a sawed-off wooden bat. Swing as if chopping a tree. Also use an axe handle to illustrate this point. For youngsters learning the grip for the first time, stress the importance of lining up the middle knuckles (at least for hand position on contact), leading with the bottom hand, swinging level, and extending the arms. Players can hit with the Axe Bat during drills in the first week of practice.

Third, point the index fingers. A proper grip should have both fingers pointing straight out and directly underneath one another.

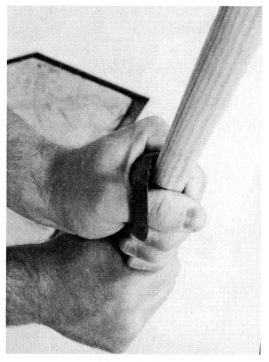

Direct protect. (Steve Berg)

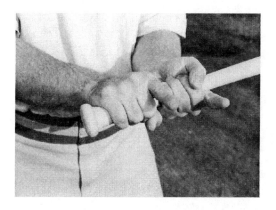

Point the fingers. (Rex Baker)

A way to improve and maintain a proper grip is to purchase the rubber thumb device called Direct Protect. The device: (1) Improves proper bat grip and position, thereby increasing bat speed, power, quickness and control, (2) gives the top thumb space between the index finger, and something to rest on and then pushoff of, and (3) when jammed gives the hitter extra protection against the sting, shock, or bone bruises from bat vibrations. So if Direct Protect helps with any of the above, try it out.

Direct Protect is also popular for switch hitters where grips may be altered during changing stances. While a stance may vary, the swing should be the same from either side of the plate.

Hitting to the Left and Right Sides

To be the "grip master," there are three grips for hitting to left, center, and right field. The wrist can be angled towards the most desirable direction.

For center field, use the traditional grip (i.e. lining up the middle knuckles), but make sure the bottom wrist follows in a straight line with the forearm. This keeps the hands aligned to hit the middle portion of the ball and towards center field. For the opposite field, bring the hands closer to the body. Turn the bottom wrist slightly toward that side (left or right depending on a right- or left-handed hitter). This creates a desirable angle to hit the inside half of the ball, thus towards the opposite field.

For the pull side, place the hands away from the body. Now angle the bottom wrist towards the pull side of the field. This angle better enables the hitter to get around and pull the ball (portion farthest from the body). Situations which may call for hitting to a particular portion of the field include moving a runner to third with zero outs, an infielder moving to a spot in the infield, or repeated tendencies of a pitcher locating to a certain area in the strike zone.

4

Stance

"Always look forward in life. That is why God put two eyes in front of our head rather than behind — so we can see where we're going, rather than where we've been."
—Lou Holtz, college football coach

Be Yourself

Many kids copy the stance of their favorite major leaguer. When I was 12 years old, I thought if I could bat like Reggie Jackson, then I could hit like Mr. October. Suffice to say, I hit only two Little League home runs.

Be ready to hit. (Bruce Baker)   Front view. (Steve Berg)

Side view. (Bruce Baker)

Just as every snowflake is different, every hitter's stance is unique. In one respect, that's the beauty of baseball. But every stance should promote a level swing and proper mechanics. So elements of different stances (wiggling of the bat, placement of feet, etc.) all make that particular batter comfortable. In proceeding to the stance, remember the following throughout the entire hitting phase: relaxed grip, balanced stance with the weight back, two eyes on the pitcher, aggressive swings at strikes, head down, good extension, and a complete follow-through.

Plate Coverage

Hitters must design a stance that allows the bat to cover the entire plate. This is called plate coverage. Get into the batter's box. Hold the bat out with both hands, bend the knees, and stretch to touch the outside part of home plate. Where the feet are when the bat reaches the edge of the plate is where one should stand. This shows that any strike located over the plate can be hit hard. Remem-

Be able to hit every pitch. (Rex Baker)

ber the "sweet spot" when working on this. Plate coverage should be assured before every pitch (yet another aspect of a consistent approach to hitting).

During the game, plate coverage can be altered slightly. A pitcher may have a tendency to throw inside or outside, or your team may anticipate a particular pitch coming in certain counts. Good hitters make adjustments during the game to gain an offensive advantage.

Feet

Once you've determined the proper distance off the plate, decide how far forward of back to stand in the batter's box. Kids should have their front foot (one closest to the pitcher) either in line with the front or middle of the plate in order to hit the ball directly in front of it.

The feet, both pointing to home plate, should be about shoulder width apart (i.e. proper balance). Don't be too wide or too closed. Once comfortable (stay with the basic stance to start out), practice with this stance. Look for con-

Be balanced. (Steve Berg)

Pigeon-toed stance. (Rex Baker)

sistency in kids, so that when doing drills they can work from one proper and comfortable stance. A batter can keep the front foot slightly closed (pointing towards the plate) to keep the swing from flying open too much. And speaking of the feet, when striding (next chapter) make sure to step directly to the pitcher. *Other*: For purposes of balance, hitters also use the pigeon-toed stance, pointing their feet inward with the knees closer than normal.

Balls of the Feet

Good hitters stand on the balls of the feet. Have your hitters jump up and down, so that they get a feel for what this means. Then have them rock back and forth on the balls of their feet. Repeat it over and over. They'll find their balance point in the stance. Have them lean over a little bit. The front foot heel should be slightly elevated off the ground. The rear foot should be balanced but not flat-footed. This alignment keeps the weight back on the rear leg. Then get your hitters into the batting stance ready to attack the ball, never sitting back on their heels.

Stay back. (Steve Berg)

Even, Closed or Open

With the even stance (parallel feet), the feet are shoulder width apart and even with each other. With the closed stance, the lead or front foot is closer to the plate than the rear foot. Moving closer to the plate with the lead foot enables the hitter to better cover the outer half of the plate. The open stance, where the back foot is closer to the plate, is becoming more prevalent. Even though it appears that the hitter is far off the plate and may never be able to reach the outside pitch, make sure the front foot lands in the exact same area as in the other two stances—directly towards the pitcher. Power hitters use the open stance to better pull the ball by getting around the inside pitch.

The individual should develop his or her own style of stance or seek a coach to work with. Whatever the stance, make sure of complete plate coverage, balance, and emphasize the basics of hitting.

Start kids with an even stance and work from there. By keeping it simple, one can maintain balance and control without complicating matters through the closed or open stances.

Coil Stance

The coil stance is yet another variation. It emphasizes power, weight on the back leg, and explosion. Hitters cock the front leg in the air just as the ball arrives at the plate.

This stance keeps the lower body in motion. Just as in the movement stage before the pitch (discussed later on), this

Closed and open stances. (Steve Berg)

Coil and drive. (Steve Berg)

leg-cocking initializes the stride. All good hitters have balance and movement in the stance so that they can use their entire body. Moreover, balancing with the leg high in the air allows the hitter more time to read the ball.

Body Alignment

The hitter needs to be balanced and relaxed, or tension will foul up a correct and smooth swing. Practice proper body control and alignment. These techniques must be repeated each day, so the body can automatically perform the necessary hitting movements. Once these habits become natural and fluid, each swing will be similar.

Knees

The knees should be slightly bent. This balances and relaxes the body. Stiff knees aren't flexible and won't initialize proper body and hitting mechanics.

Legs

Body weight should be back and resting on a firm rear leg (60 percent of the weight on the back leg and 40 percent on the front). The rear leg should be almost straight up and down, with the front leg angled back.

Chest

The torso (chest area) should be slightly bent. This allows for a balanced and relaxed body. Plus, it shows the pitcher that your hitters own the plate. Instead of being straight up (don't be a robot), the body is bent and thus able to drive the ball down (we'll get into this theory later on). With a bent chest and

Legs. Lean over the plate. (Rex Baker)

knees, weight distribution from the back to the front is more effectively utilized. Try to push a hitter backwards when in his/her stance. If you're able to push them over, the hitter isn't properly balanced.

Hips

One's hips and bellybutton should be facing the plate. This allows the weight to be shifted back just before contact. If the hips and bellybutton aren't facing the plate, the hips are either rotating too early or too late. This hinders proper weight transfer. Moreover, pulling the hips open too early may jerk the head and front shoulder out (poor mechanics).

Hands and the Treasure Chest

The hands should be three to five inches away from the body in an area I call the "Treasure Chest." This placement should show an imaginary rectangular box from the back to front shoulder, down to the front elbow near the middle of the chest, over to the back elbow through the hands, and back up to the back shoulder. The box should be small and compact.

The hands should be under the back shoulder and in line somewhere between the chin and back shoulder. Keeping the hands too high (above the back shoulder) may drive the ball into the ground and not on a line. Keeping the hands too low (near the waist) may pop the ball up. Proper hand placement enables the hitter to find the treasure, which is a solid base hit.

Check the hands. (Rex Baker)

Shoulders

With the back shoulder level, the front shoulder (which is facing the pitcher) should be slightly lower than the rear. This is a key to swinging down if everything else is done properly. Remember the hands start high in the stance and proceed down to the pitch (i.e. swinging down).

Ike to Mike

Ike and Mike designate the shoulders in the stance and upon contact. Ike is the front shoulder. The chin should be resting or almost touching Ike. This keeps the head and both eyes looking at the pitcher and front shoulder closed. Mike is the back shoulder. The transfer is made from Ike to Mike. This classi-

Treasure chest. (Steve Berg)

Shoulders. **Angle is down. (Rex Baker)**

fication attempts to keep the head/eyes on the ball, a compact swing with a closed front shoulder, and proper hip rotation. The old saying goes, "You can't hit what you can't see."

Elbows

The front elbow (closest to the pitcher) should be pointed slightly downward at 45 degrees (diagonal line down). It should be relaxed and about four to six inches away from the rest of the body. The rear elbow (farthest from the pitcher) should be almost level or parallel to the ground (horizontal line). This allows the hands to go through to the ball without having the body tie up the hands.

While many coaches call for a firm/level back arm, just make sure the hitter is comfortable and relaxed. Instead of being so focused on a stiff back arm, focus on driving the front arm down to the location of the pitch. Remember that whenever the back elbow drops, a fly ball will probably occur. Good hitters swing down. If the front elbow leads the swing and the rear elbow stays relatively level, the bat should go correctly through the hitting zone.

Head

"Two eyes are better than one." Do you make sure that every hitter has both eyes fixated on the pitcher? Many youngsters take the "Robin Hood approach." As if shooting a bow and arrow or even a rifle, they tilt the head sideways and focus with only one eye. That's why the closed stance screws up the vision of so many youngsters. Hitters should rotate the head until both eyes are focusing on the pitcher (and not looking over the nose). It may feel uncomfortable at first, but it's a must for seeing the ball from the pitcher's hand until contact is made.

Have the kids play catch with two eyes then with one eye closed. The depth perception changes. Plus, if a hitter ever moves his/her head (up, down or forward) during the swinging phase, depth perception of the pitch changes dramatically. Everything must be in sync (level and balanced) for the mind to tell the body what to do in the swing. Kids must also be taught not to blink at the oncoming pitch. Some are also afraid of the ball. Talk to them about this fact and check to see what they do.

Soft and Hard Focus

Soft and hard focus comes from former big-league batting coach Mike

Hard focus. (Steve Berg)

proper eye movement (tracking the ball) from the pitcher's hand to the bat hitting the ball. Remember, soft focus on the pitcher's head, and then the ball above the throwing shoulder and upon release (hard focus), track it as it comes from the mound, see if it's a strike or ball, then decide to swing or not. The longer one sees the ball equals more time to do some damage.

Bat Position

Now take a look at the stance. Don't worry too much about the bat angle. Just make sure it's behind the head and more or less pointed straight up in the air. Some hitters like to angle the bat back on a 45-degree angle with the goal of hitting on a downward plane (ground ball/line drive swing). But make sure the bat is in the best possible launching position. The bat is a hitter's rocket, so get it ready to explode on the ball.

Those who want to increase contact potential may try the "flat bat." Instead of the bat behind the head, hold the bat at an almost level plane. This action quickens the swing. Power may be decreased, but better contact is maintained.

Soft focus. (Steve Berg)

Easler. By first keying on the pitcher and especially his/her head (soft focus), one can react better to the thrown ball. Focus only on the pitcher. Don't be distracted by surrounding sounds or movements.

Hard focus is concentrating on the ball when it's released from the pitcher's hand (the arm is shaped like the letter "L"). Here the hitter picks up rotation of the ball and can distinguish between pitches. Focusing with two eyes on the pitcher, and then on the ball, leads to

Bat behind the head. (Rex Baker)

This is also a good two-strike stance to put the ball in play somewhere.

Other Things to Consider

Once hitters get a feel for the different pitches, they may want to move up or back in the batter's box. For example, with two strikes, move up and closer to the plate to hit curve balls, for example, before they break across the plate. But for most hitters, preach the same stance and mentality for every count. Obviously strategy comes into play, but more often than not, don't change a thing. Think offense even on 0–2. One is basically swinging at anything close, so don't make the pitcher better by simply chopping at the ball.

Jeff Wood of Worcester State demonstrates proper stance. (Bruce Baker)

With a hard-throwing pitcher, power hitters like to move back in the box so they have more reaction time. However, being farther back (near the rear chalk line) may increase the number of foul balls. But power hitters like that extra split second to recognize the fastball, so they can drive it for a home run. And for those soft throwers who are barely reaching the plate (also for pitchers getting the low strike), get up in the box and rip!

Try moving closer to, or away from, the plate with a 3-0 count (take sign is on). This may confuse the catcher calling and catching the pitch and even the umpire, who may be used to calling pitches from the previous stance. With a 3-0 count don't just stand there and take a strike. Do something productive, and possibly distract the pitcher with a fake bunt. After deciding who the best disciplined hitters are, 3-0 can be a favorite count in which to swing.

5

Swing

"It's easy to hit .300 with your swing. Try doing it with mine."
— Dave Valle, career .230 hitter, to former superstar teammate Ken Griffey, Jr.

It Ain't So Easy

In tennis, badminton, racquetball, and squash, a moving ball is struck by some flat-surface instrument that is large in relation to the ball. The hockey stick has a flat blade, and a cricket bat has three plane surfaces from which to hit the ball in any direction. The flat golf

Stance. (Rudy Winston)

club is designed to hit a stationary ball, and even in billiards (non-moving object), the tip of the cue stick is relatively flat. Not only does a base hit in baseball have to land in fair territory, but it must be struck almost perfectly square in something less than half an inch.

Consider the math: A baseball's diameter is 2.868 inches; the bat, at its fattest part, can't exceed 2.75 inches. The ball weighs five ounces while a youth bat may weigh 20 ounces, for example. To hit the ball, obviously the batter must decide and then swing before the ball arrives. That said, the batter has less than a second to decide if it's a ball or strike, high or low, type of pitch, make any necessary adjustments, make contact, hopefully somewhere on the "sweet spot," put the ball in fair territory and in a place beyond the reaches of the defense. Never mind the situation, pressure, weather, talent of the pitcher, and possibility of getting hit. Then consider the velocity and moment of a pitch plus different pitchers each game and day.

How does one hit, anyway? Physicists would probably admit that hitting appears to be an impossible scientific act, something like a race car driver who has to make split-second decisions on

Stride. (Rudy Winston)

Swing. (Rudy Winston)

whether to pass, slow down, advance, pit stop, or simply survive a 400-lap race. That's why major league hitters are so praised for their offensive talents. So many try; so few excel. Think about the thousands of swings a Sammy Sosa has taken in his lifetime. The tee work and soft toss of an Edgar Martinez. The adjustments, BP, spring training, regular season, and playoff games of a Cal Ripken, Jr. The concentration and mental preparation of a Tony Gwynn. And the weight work, proper nutrition, consistency, and all-around skills of a Barry Bonds. Truly awesome!

To witness in person the 2003 Home Run Derby in Chicago reinforced the admiration of the truly amazing talent of MLB hitters. Seeing Garret Anderson, Jim Edmonds, and especially Al-

bert Pujols in action was incredible. These athletes perform such skills every single day from March to October. So go to the cages with a brand-new wooden bat, crank up the pitching machine, and see the results. Then think about a Roger Clemens fastball underneath the chin, or trying to hit Randy Johnson with the bases loaded and 35,000-plus people on their feet cheering. But remember that hitting in Little League is just as special for the kids.

Theories on Hitting

Since hitting has so many variables and interpretations, every coach has an individual opinion on what the batter should be thinking and doing. Some let hitters be themselves, and others are strict about techniques for each team member. Others teach a specific discipline (i.e. taking a lot of pitches), and some analyze output through statistics as opposed to philosophy.

Take bits and pieces from every theory. Remember Rome wasn't built in a day. Aim for a comfortable stance and smooth swing that works for the individual. Games are won by scoring runs. Runs are scored by hitting fair balls. So get your team out there and mash!

Two Types of Swing

To dissect every hitter's swing would take dozens of books. There are two basic types: top-hand-released version (perfected by former MLB batting coach Charley Lau) and the two-handed swing (a la Ted Williams). These men wrote two of the best hitting books around, and both should be read by anyone wanting to know hitting (*The Winning Hitter* and *The Science of Hitting*, respectively). Read as many books as you can. Use what works for your team and each hitter. Hitting is about making adjustments, hard work, and execution. But explain these theories so the hitter can understand, go out on their own to work on it, and then perform in a game. Scientific lingo is for physics class. Don't be out to impress just to look good or sound like a big-league hitting coach. If a kid can go home and practice shoulder-to-shoulder work (Ike to Mike) and realize it helps with keeping his/her head down, then you've done the proper job. Use simple terminology, and yet again: Get a balanced stance, swing for strikes, be aggressive, and keep the head down.

I was lucky enough to have great youth coaches. But I also outworked the opposition. I made my L.L. All-Star team, hit over .500 in high school (with school records for batting average, RBIs, and doubles in a season), over .400 in Legion, and over .330 during my senior year at Boston University (school records for home runs and walks in a season). The problem was no arm and no speed, but boy could I hit. My nickname was "The Machine," because I hit endlessly in the electronic batting cage.

Even though I was shorter and smaller than most of my competition, I used every bit of my body to hit that round ball with a round bat. I crowded the plate (to reach the outside corner), kept my weight back, kept my body moving, ready to explode, used my lower body (hips and legs), shifted my weight and stride into the location of the pitch, swung hard at strikes, used my eyesight and bat speed, went with the pitch, and finished with a proper follow-through. I worked at hitting and spent hours with the BU strength coach. I was confident, aggressive and disciplined. I worked on bunting and varying game day strategies. I did drills over and over, and hit off left- and right-handed pitchers. Repetition, hard work, and performance equaled success.

Since I became a coach, Worcester State has been among the top offensive leaders throughout the country — every year since 1996. We believe in the fundamentals, but every hitter is different, so the approach to each athlete is slightly different, not only speaking to him but also in the drills and things to work on in practice. We preach the top-hand-released swing upon contact (for better plate coverage, less wrist turnover tie-ups, and for a more fluid swing), but we also let the kids prove to us what they can do. This starts in the fall and continues into the preseason, throughout the spring and over their careers. The results have been tremendous:

Worcester State Team Batting
Averages and Rankings
in the Conference and Nation

1996 (.335) — 3rd MASCAC and 31st NCAA
1997 (.348) — 3rd MASCAC and 28th NCAA
1998 (.380) — 1st MASCAC and 4th NCAA
1999 (.373) — 1st MASCAC and 5th NCAA
2000 (.341) — 1st MASCAC and 29th NCAA
2001 (.363) — 1st MASCAC and 7th NCAA
2002 (.379) — 1st MASCAC and 2nd NCAA
2003 (.348) — 2nd MASCAC and 15th NCAA

In 2000 and 2002 Worcester State Led
New England in Team Batting Average
4 Conference Batting Champs —
"We Hit Till Our Hands Bleed"

1996 — Jason Akana (.514 — 1st NCAA)
2000 — Eric Swedberg (.500 — 4th NCAA)
2002 — Swedberg/Matt Heenan (.442 —
33rd NCAA)

.400+ Hitters Every Year Since 1996

1996 — Jason Akana (.514), 1997 — Mike
Cantino (.412),
1998 — Jason Piskator (.462), Tim Leonard
(.449), Jason Richards (.429), Jeff De-
coteau (.400),
1999 — Shawn McNamara (.442), Richards
(.414),
2000 — Eric Swedberg (.500), 2001 — Swedberg (.462), Andy Sebring (.436),
2002 — Swedberg/Matt Heenan (.442), Dan
McTigue (.428), 2003 — Bear Dunn
(.440)

The Swing in Simple Swingin' Terms

Bat and Grip: First select a bat that
is right for the individual: light enough
to control yet heavy enough for a hard
swing. Gently grip it at the knob with
both hands (try to line up the middle
knuckles). Hold the bat with the base of
the fingers, not the palms.

Stance: Stand straight up in the
batter's box and face home plate. Be bal-

Overhead view. (Steve Berg)

anced with the feet about shoulder width
apart. The front foot should be placed
near the plate's midpoint. Bend the
knees, lean over slightly, and turn the
head to face the pitcher. Put the hands
near the back shoulder with the bat behind the head. The rear arm should be
level or relaxed while the front arm is
shaped like the letter "L." Tilt the front
shoulder down slightly. Focus on the ball
as it's released from the pitcher. Start
with most of the weight on the back leg.

Stride and Cock: As the pitch is
coming, cock the hands back and rotate
the front shoulder in slightly. Take a
small step forward. Place the front foot
down on the big toe. Think motion back.

Swing: The basic two-handed
swing is a powerful yet fluid movement.
While starting the hips towards the
pitcher, shift the weight from the back
leg to the front. Direct the bat straight
down to the ball. Extend the arms, and
forcefully swing at strikes located from
the knees to the middle of the chest. Aim
to make contact in front of home plate.
The bat should be almost level on contact with a firm front leg (foot pointing
at the plate) and bent back leg (heel off

the ground). The hips should rotate around with the bellybutton facing the pitcher. Keep the head still and both eyes fixated on the ball throughout the swing. Instead of guessing, react to the location of the pitch.

Follow Through: After contact, the top-hand wrist turns over the bottom. Allow the bat to come completely around and hit the backside. The batter should be balanced straight up and down. After hitting the ball, drop the bat near the plate and sprint towards first base. In normal situations concentrate on making contact and hitting the ball hard. Progress to hitting inside pitches to the pull side and outside pitches to the opposite field.

Swingin' Checklist

- Maximize the strengths and minimize the weaknesses of an individual hitter.
- Be flexible, patient, and positive in regard to theory and implementation.
- Have a game plan and purpose for each at-bat.
- Be balanced and relaxed in the stance and after contact with the ball.
- Move the body and bat before the pitch (don't be a flat-footed statue).
- Start with the weight back (think 60 percent back and 40 percent forward) with the front foot heel slightly off the ground.
- Have the hands up and back to start, then drive them directly down to the pitch.
- Stride directly to the pitcher.
- Use the hips and legs for power and quick hands for bat speed.
- Keep two eyes on the ball throughout (head down), go with the pitch (be able to hit strikes over the whole plate), hit the ball in front of the plate, and completely finish the swing.
- Use either swing: top hand released upon contact or the two-handed version.
- Swing the same way each time (hands

Focus on the ball. (Bruce Baker)

simply go to the location of the pitch), be aggressive, and only swing at strikes.

- Practice hard, do the many drills, and take it one pitch, at-bat, and game at a time.

The Actual Swing

Certain actions and movements occur for all successful hitters. Begin with a fundamental approach. Break down each phase, and progress according to the abilities of the hitters and team.

Balance

Let's start from the ground up. A proper swing starts with balance. Think of a hitter as a table. With four legs the table stands; three legs the table falls over. Balance involves the reflexes and coordination plus vision — and the brain. Balance starts in the stance and moves to the swing and making contact. With proper balance, a hitter can maximize his/her entire body and impact into the ball. The bat (one a hitter can get around with) adds leverage and momentum achieved through a forceful and level swing.

One's center of gravity, different for everyone, is vital to stability and coordination (i.e. fundamentally sound stance and swinging so one doesn't fall over). It can be drawn straight down from the head, through the chest, between the legs, and to the ground. Look at pictures of the pros and assess their balance points (stance, then swing).

Movement

The hitter needs bat and body movement. Why? Because it takes less than a second to decide and then swing at a pitch. As Isaac Newton said: Things in motion tend to stay in motion. Thus, move the bat and whole body: the bat, arms, torso, hips and legs. Think of the difference for a boxer punching or a football player tackling an opponent. Is it better to use the whole body or just the arms? Hitters need to move and be ready to attack. Don't just stand there waiting for something to happen. The batter is an idling car engine ready for the light to turn green.

Movement in the stance, once ready in the box, is accomplished in two stages. First, before one takes the actual stance, the batter should circle the bat towards the pitcher. This relaxes the body and gives the pitcher a good view of the hitter's weapon. In a game of mental discipline and always looking for an edge, the bat circles aim to distract the pitcher from attempting to focus on the catcher's signs. Plus, it shows that one is ready for action, not just standing there like animal prey!

Second, the hitter should tap the front foot up and down or back and forth (i.e. pushing off from the back side). This mimics what the body is going to do when weight is shifted from the back side into the pitch. It's a tricky subject to describe. Think about the foot-tapping as "stepping on thin ice." Do this once the pitcher comes to the set position and continue throughout the wind-up phase. With a firm back foot and weight on the big toe of the front foot, lift the front foot up and down slightly while keeping the weight back on the rear leg. This adds balance before attacking the ball.

Once in the launching position (movement phase), some hitters also wiggle the bat back and forth or bounce it gently off the back shoulder. Movement with the front leg and bat should be slow, and relaxed. Kids should not be too jumpy. Flinging the bat around behind one's head before the pitch may result in poor bat angle (the moment before swinging, the bat should be in the same position each time). The instant before the stride, hold that weight on the back leg. The swing then continues into the cocking and swinging actions.

Stride

The stride initializes the swing. The front foot should be lifted up one to two inches and land some 5-to-10 inches directly towards the pitcher. The front leg should remain straight. The front foot should be closed throughout (pointing towards the plate). An open foot prematurely initiates hip rotation and leads to an opening of the front shoulder/head and dropping of the hands.

When striding, emphasize weight being balanced on the ball of the back

foot and weight on the front foot big toe. A flat-footed hitter automatically bends the front knee and thus shifts the weight too soon. A stiff front leg ensures maximum balance and strength on contact. Once the front foot touches down, the back knee should bend slightly. Since power is initiated from the rear leg (like a pitcher driving off the rubber), think about a balanced center of gravity with 60 percent of the weight on the inside of the back foot.

Have kids strive for a short stride, landing on the big toe of the front foot at the same time as the hands are cocked back. Landing on the big toe keeps the weight back. The shorter the stride (with weight back), the more patient a hitter can be in battling those nasty off-speed pitches. And never lift the back foot off the ground.

Mature hitters can attempt to stride towards the actual pitch: at the pitcher for middle/inside pitches and slightly outside for pitches located on the outer half of the plate. This can be accomplished through soft toss and tee work. Especially with a widening strike zone and pitchers throwing to the outside corners, kids need to practice and hit all types of pitches in varying locations. And think for a moment: If a hitter

Use the feet. (Steve Berg)

Go the other way. (Rex Baker)

doesn't practice the outside pitch (loves to hit those home runs on inside pitches), and the pitcher knows this and throws to the corners (away from the hitter's hands) — don't you think the pitcher has an even greater advantage? Take notice: Think about hitting pitches up the middle and to the opposite field. Any hitter worth his/her stock can hit the inside fastball. A good hitter hits to all fields and drives off-speed pitches the other way.

Lastly, many power hitters land on the heel of the front foot. This is done naturally in order to drive underneath the ball for a possible home run. Sluggers live and die by the fly ball. Be concerned more with thinking and swinging down. Good things happen when you put the ball on the ground and into the gaps.

When to Stride?

The front of the pitching rubber is 46 feet away (60 feet, six inches for high school and up) from the back point of home plate, which in turn is 17 inches wide and long. Pitchers throw at varying speeds and from different angles and arm lengths. The importance here is striding directly to the pitcher with the weight back. The stride should start upon recognizing the pitch coming out of the pitcher's hand. It should be the same for a ball and/or strike. On seeing the pitch type and location, the hitter can then use his/her hands, body, and bat to drive the ball.

Think of everything occurring in a straight line: The pitcher striding directly towards home plate, the hitter (focus on the even stance for now) stepping to the pitcher, and hands forcing the bat directly to the pitch. Practice the stride with or without cocking the hands

and even without a bat. Think of it as the latest dance craze: not the electric slide but the striding slide.

Weight Shift

After a batter recognizes a strike, weight should transfer from the back side to the inner thigh of the front leg. Don't lunge too far forward. On contact keep a stiff front leg angled straight back. Weight shift means generating power from the lower body in accordance with the upper torso and bat. With everything working together, one can use the entire body to drive the ball. Practice the stride and weight shift without a bat. Do it over and over until comfortable.

To practice weight shift, have the kids lean over and rock back and forth with their hands on their thighs. Feel the weight moving from the back to the front parts of the body.

Overstriding

Weight shift may be the most common flaw in the swing: too soon, too long, or too late. Overstriding (bringing the front side too far to the pitcher) means improper weight shift forward. When a hitter keeps his/her weight back, proper power can be used to hit line drives. Shift too far up, and you'll see those weakly hit ground balls and pop-ups. To stay back means to hit right. To lunge forward means death to one's batting average.

Think about widening an overstrider's stance and concentrating on a shorter stride. Keep the weight back on the rear leg. And make sure that back heel stays dug in. A lot of coaches teach the no-stride technique, and some hitters simply pick the front foot up in the air without a stride (i.e. pick it- up and put it down). As long as a hitter can stay back, while still cocking the hands and hips, proper hitting techniques won't be compromised.

Many youngsters have stride problems because they don't have a clue what weight shift means. They want to hit those long homers over the fences. They lunge into pitches impatiently. Work on the stride and weight shift even without swinging. Look non-strikes into the mitt. Practice this to see if a hitter's hands and weight are indeed back. Also watch for those who wrap the bat improperly towards the pitcher. Keep the bat behind the head in the stance/stride sequence before forcefully thrusting it towards the pitch.

Lastly, if a slugger doesn't stay back (the time needed to distinguish the pitches plus strikes vs. non-strikes), he/she will undoubtedly see more and more breaking pitches (the late break fools hitters in to falling forward) and not hit as many homers. No stride is the same. But all hitters need to keep their weight back until the last possible moment before deciding to swing hard.

Motion Back

The hands should be back near the rear shoulder during the stride. Front-foot hitters make the mistake of bringing the hands and weight forward. Even if fooled by a breaking pitch, keeping the hands back enables the now lunging hitter to drive the ball with the hands — preferably to the opposite field.

Fundamentally sound hitters all have the hands back (near the back shoulder) and bat (behind the head) in the exact same area just before the front foot hits the ground. Some cock the hands back while others don't. Try some type of motion back (hands, front shoulder and front hip) to initiate the swing — just like cocking a pistol. Cocking adds momentum to the swing. One needs to get the body moving just before the pitch arrives to counteract its velocity, movement and location. Think back to the "treasure chest," though; make sure the hands stay in the vicinity of the back shoulder. Don't cock too far back or below. Cocking, just like the stride, is a subtle motion (not slow-motion) just before the explosion of the swing.

Contact

On contact the shoulders should rotate from Ike (front) to Mike (back). The head shouldn't move at any time during the swing. Follow the ball with the eyes. A stationary head keeps the front shoulder

Ike to Mike. (Steve Berg)

from flying open. See the ball hit the bat, just as in bunting. Too many hitters watch where they want the ball to go (back to that awful pull mentality) and essentially don't see the ball as well as they could.

Always focus on the ball. How many coaches stress this point? If a hitter doesn't see it early enough, track it, and watch the ball the entire time while it travels to the plate — how does one expect to hit at all? When we say "keep the head down," don't confuse this with looking down at the plate. Think about a teacup on the head. Don't swing too hard or the tea cup might spill. Don't lunge forward or the cup might fall. Keep a steady head throughout. I always wanted to rig up a helmet dangling from a basketball hoop. The hitter would wear the helmet and swing. If the head moves so does the rope. Swing until the rope stays still.

Here's an example to illustrate keeping the head still throughout the swing. Place a hat on the ground serving as home plate. The hitter should swing and look at the hat. Try this on a sunny day with the hat inside the shadow of the head. Take a regular swing. Swing until the shadow of the head stays in the hat. Then gradually progress to keeping the head still throughout the swing while focusing on the pitched ball. Be smooth and look for that aggressive yet in-control swing. The swing should appear effortless. Don't swing like a snake trying to come out of its skin.

See the Ball

Think about depth perception for a moment. If a hitter moves his/her head on a curveball, the perception upon release from the pitcher's hand is different from the ball appearing on contact. Effective curveballs should drop some one to two feet before reaching the front of home plate. No matter the stance or swing, keep the head and especially two eyes from moving too much in any direction. This goes back to proper balance and working within the parameters of a straight line. Striding to the pitcher, keeping the head still, two eyes on the ball, hips and hands working together in the direction of the pitch, moving the body as a single unit, full extension, and a complete follow-through. That's hitting, baby! And when it all works together and produces a frozen rope — there's nothing like it in sports.

Good mechanics come from seeing the ball. Follow its path and watch it hit the bat. Visualize this action in slow-motion. Imagine the ball coming and slow the swing down piece by piece. Keep the head down on contact and never blink.

Preach the basics without the flash, crazy gimmicks, or funky stances. Don't be out to impress. Results (not looks) mean the most. So do things that are proven effective. Keep the head down and swing for strikes.

Shadow drill. (Steve Berg)

Rotate the Hips

The hips should rotate around fully upon contact. Have the "bellybutton say hello to the pitcher." Maximum power must be thrust into the pitch. Rotate the hips simultaneously with the weight shift and actual swing. The hitter should still be leaning out over the plate.

To work on hip action, hit off a tee with a long hockey stick wrapped behind the hitter's back. Swing the hips around, and hit the ball with the end of the stick. This triggers the back hip into going with the pitch.

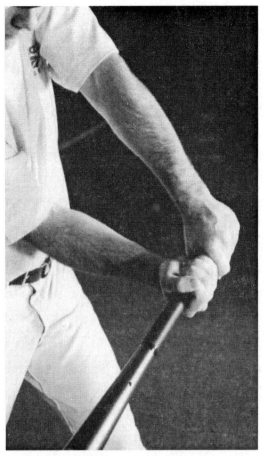

Level swing. (Steve Berg)

Twist and rip. (Rex Baker)

Palm-Up Palm-Down

On contact have the kids attempt to fully extend their arms and hold the bat firmly. This action absorbs shock and avoids bat recoil. Most times the top-hand arm is slightly bent, but make sure the bottom-hand arm is fully extended. The "flat bat" should be almost parallel to the ground but angled downward. This ensures for a level/downward swing and proper wrist alignment before the hands turn over. The hands should be directly behind the bat and located somewhere over the front knee. To hit the ball solid in front of the plate, the hands have to be situated in accordance with proper weight shift. Everything must flow together. For example, throwing the hands too far in front induces improper and early weight shift. Now, while the wrists are unbroken at impact, the hands

Palm-up palm-down. (Steve Berg)

L-to-I. (Rex Baker)

should be "palm-up palm-down" with the bottom-hand palm facing the ground and the top facing the sky. *Note*: Coaches preach a "level swing." There's really no such thing as a level swing. The hands start up with the bat, move down to the ball, and with full extension on a slightly downward plane to the bat meeting the ball.

"L to I"

The closest distance between two points is a straight line. Thus, the quickest distance (i.e. bat speed) deals with the hands reaching straight downward to the ball. The "L to I" theory begins without a bat and the hands within the "treasure chest." The lead arm starts off shaped like the letter "L." Have the kids fully extend this arm downward. When straight the arm is now shaped as the letter "I." Drive into the ball—not down

first and then around it. This position promotes a downward swing since the lead-arm forearm is on the same horizontal plane as the ball. Perform "L to I" first in slow-motion, at regular speed, then use both hands, and top if off with swinging a bat with and even without a tossed ball.

Throw the Hands

Mike Easler came up with "Slap the Midget." Kids really relate to this phrase. Tell them a mean midget is standing on home plate with his tongue sticking out at them. Have the youngsters slap him silly. First with the bottom hand and then the palm of the top hand, "throw the hands" at the midget just as one would at the pitch. Do it one hand at a time. Then extend one hand, come down and slap the two hands together, and follow through. Then mimic a swing with just the hands.

First, realize that the bottom hand initiates and leads the swing. Second, straight arms on contact maximize arm strength. Third, this action promotes wrist turnover (top hand rolls over the bottom after contact). Now "throw the hands" at the location of the pitch. At full extension make sure the chin is located between both shoulders. As the hands go, so does the swing. *Note*: Slap tape balls wearing batting gloves. Throw each hand at the ball. First, the bottom hand. Second, the top hand. Third, the bottom followed shortly thereafter by the top. Fourth, both hands together as in a real swing. The balls should travel in the direction of the toss. Also, hold a ball in each hand (in the stance) and throw them in the direction of a certain pitch: inside, outside, high, low, and up the middle. Demonstrate this by actually letting go of the bat while facing the backstop. Take a mental note of the hand position upon releasing the bat for different pitch locations.

Throw the Hands. **Extend for the outside pitch. (Rex Baker)**

Good extension. (Bruce Baker)

Stay Low

The batter's rear leg should be bent and shaped like the letter "C." As the back leg bends, weight should explode from the rear side into the ball. A firm front leg (like a log) and bent rear knee keep the weight back along with a balanced and coordinated body. Feel the difference in bending both knees. A bent front knee forces the weight too far forward (i.e. if fooled by a breaking pitch).

Some kids lift the back leg off the ground upon swinging. Hitters need a firm base in the stance and upon contact. Lunging into the pitch only causes problems. Stay back, drive off the back leg, use a short stride, shift the weight forward and into the pitch, and hit the ball in front of the plate.

Mash the Bug

When contact is made, the majority of weight should be placed on the rear big toe. Rotating the back foot up and then back gives the hitter maximum leg power and weight into the swing. With weight on the biggest toe, the body is better balanced and stable. This is why hitters should lean slightly over the plate — not simply to relax the upper body and reach outside pitches, but also to send a message to the pitcher, "This is MY plate."

Look to "Mash the Bug." Think about a nasty bug just a few inches in front of the front foot (i.e. landing pad for the stride). Kids should "step on that bug and squish it into the ground." Do it over and over. This action promotes a short stride, hip rotation, and good weight transfer. Moreover, once the front foot lands, both of the heels should be turning into the plate. Remember, all of this turning should be happening together in unison: heel turn, hip rotation, hands to the ball, and shoulder turn. Repeat it until it does.

Follow Through

By habitually keeping the head down after the swing, the rest of the body is trained to do what it's suppose to do. This action forces the eyes to focus on the ball for every pitch. The brain is better equipped to adjust to errors in perception from the instant the pitch is released. If fooled by a curveball, a hitter whose hands are back and head is down may be able to shoot the ball to the opposite field; if nothing else he can put the ball in play. Power may be lost, but a base hit may still be achieved.

Head down and end high. (Rex Baker)

Full Rotation and Extension

The back shoulder should be slightly higher than the front. This action drives the ball down and on a line. Remember Ike to Mike. The hips should now be rotated to their maximum capacity with the belt buckle facing the area of actual contact.

For both the two-handed and top-hand-released-on-contact swings, the top hand does forcefully rotate over the bottom. At this point the middle knuckles should be aligned properly (think back to the Axe Bat). Hitters shouldn't concentrate too much on when wrist turnover should occur. The top hand rolls over naturally. Swing with two hands, make contact in front of the plate, and if one decides to release the top hand, do so after the ball is hit.

The key to the follow-through is lead arm extension and a complete finish with the bat and arms. The lead arm must initiate the swing without interference from the top hand. With the top-hand-released swing, arm action must continue after contact or it might jeopardize maximum force on the ball and possibly straining or pulling muscles. For example, a punch isn't thrown in midflight. Continue the whole way through.

The front leg should be firm and rigid throughout the follow-through. This drives the body's weight into the ball and promotes the most power. The back leg makes a "C" (just as in contact), but a hitter should concentrate on pushing the weight into the baseball. The front foot should still be closed. Weight should have been shifted from the back side into the ball. Lastly, beginners want to run to first base as quickly as possible. Some forget to finish the swing and are running when they should still be following through. Have them wait that extra split second.

Two-Handed Versus Release of the Top Hand

To illustrate the dichotomy of the two-hand versus top-hand-released-on-contact controversy, very few hitters before 1980 ever released the top hand after contact. Now hundreds of hitters do so in the major, minor, and youth leagues across the country. For years people thought that this swing cut down on power. But one can still hit home runs by releasing this hand. In fact, the two-handed version almost ties up a nice fluid swing, especially when trying to reach those tricky outside pitches.

The front arm initiates and leads

Be able to hit every pitch. (Rex Baker)

the swing — not the back arm. Trying to reach an outside pitch with two hands on the bat is hindering. Moreover, avoid rolling the top-hand wrist over too soon (i.e. premature contact). The two-handed swing needs a dominant top hand during the follow-through. With the one-handed swing, extension is a more natural motion. So try it with your team, and see if it's comfortable for them.

Too many youngsters try to pull home runs with the two-handed swing. They step outside and come off the ball (lean backwards), pull their head and front shoulder out, and invariably hit a fly ball. Try an extension exercise. See how far one can reach with the two- vs. one-handed finish; even drop the bat on the ground to see where it lands. The two-handed swing just doesn't appear to get as far out as the one-handed. And in baseball, every advantage counts.

Some long-armed hitters stand off the plate for added reach. Others use both varieties: top-hand-released for pitches down the middle and on the outside corners, and the two-handed version for inside pitches. Most youth hitters should stay with the same swing each time. Yes, there are adjustments and things which come up in a game, but consistency counts most in honing a swing that works.

Top-Hand-Release Drill

The following is a slow-motion drill to teach release of the top hand on contact:

(1) Swing down with a level bat on contact. (2) Turn both wrists over. (3) Release the top hand off the bat with the five fingers spread apart. (4) Bring both arms completely around. The forceful swinging of the top arm turns the hips. The top arm should now be hugging the chin. Finish high with the bat above the head.

Verbal commands should be: (1) Swing down, (2) turn over, (3) release, and (4) follow through. It's a new concept, so work on it before using it in a game. This drill is also excellent for teaching the swing to switch hitters.

The Magician

The moment the top hand is released from the bat, this hand turns over but not over the bottom hand. In actuality the wrists are aligned side by side just after contact (palms facing the ground), and then separate from one an-

Do some hocus-pocus. (Rex Baker)

other shortly thereafter. Imagine a magician performing some hocus-pocus. The fingers should be extended after contact with the arms circling up towards the head during the follow-through.

Finish High with the Bat

The bat should end high (above the shoulders), and somewhere in the vicinity of where it started (the stance). This action assures for the complete circle and momentum of the swing; just as in throwing a baseball (make a circle with the arm).

The follow-through is an interesting phase. Why does it matter if the ball has already been hit? Just overemphasize the continuation of the arms and bat until unable to do so any longer. This may result with the bat grazing the backside on the two-handed swing. The top-hand-released swing, with an extended bottom arm, should form the letter "V" (bat and arm).

Lastly, watch the slap hitters. Most stop their swing at the moment of contact. Their hits are sprayed and not driven. The swing isn't smooth. A complete hitter finishes the swing every time.

Swing Through the Ball

Encourage kids to think about hitting a series of imaginary baseballs, one after another, from the time a ball is hit, after contact, and during the follow-through. Emphasize the point of swinging aggressively, down at the pitch, full extension on contact, through the im-

Hit every ball. (Rex Baker)

pact zone or location of the pitch, and a complete finish. This "swinging through the ball" allows the bat to be in the strike zone longer and is an advantage if one makes a mistake in timing the pitch.

Afterthought: The Body

The body should be balanced with a good center of gravity upon completion of the follow-through. A vertical straight line should be maintained down the middle of the body from the head, through the middle of the chest, both legs, and to the ground. Hitters have to be centered in the stance, upon contact, and on the follow-through. Some common flaws here include pulling the head to the side or being too far in front or back.

It's a positive trait if a hitter falls into the plate area after the swing. This cuts down on the time needed to get to first base, but this falling inward reinforces the aggressive swing theory. Gravity simply takes over. If anything, never fall backwards or away from the plate. Be balanced to start (stance) and end (follow-through).

Drop the Bat

Most hitters unconsciously drop the bat after contact. Remember three points. First, kids should drop the bat after completion of the swing somewhere in the vicinity of home plate. Second, bend at the waist and sprint to first base. Third, never hold onto the bat on the way down the base line. Too many young hitters treat the bat as a security blanket. The bat is indeed the hitter's weapon, but after contact leave it for the bat boy. Include a drill for swinging hard, finishing the swing, dropping the bat, and working on a quick first step out of the batter's box.

Teach kids not to throw the bat after contact. Tee-ballers may crush the ball yet be called out for throwing the bat. Some even fling the helmet off while running bases. Leave the helmet on for safety reasons (hit by the thrown ball or protection from hard tags or collisions).

Speed to First Base

Obviously the left-handed batter is closer to first base. But right-handed hitters are actually quicker down the line, because they fall towards first base after the swing. Left-handed hitters (especially those who crowd/lean over the plate) sometimes even fall towards third base after swinging. Don't make a major deal about which hitter is quicker down the line. Again, practice a proper swing and a good first step out of the box. For some reason baseball made the bases even distances apart (60 feet in Little League and 90 feet for high school and up), and this distance has maintained that a routine ground ball fielded, thrown, and caught correctly equals an out for the defense 99 percent of the time. Have the kids focus on running in a straight line to first, run through the base like a sprinter at the finish line, and turn right after making contact with the bag. And never slide into first — it'll slow the runner down and may cause an injury. *Note*: Even where leading is not allowed, L.L. coaches should continually preach aggressiveness on the bases, which can spawn a productive running/bunting (and beyond) game.

Field of Dreams Chart

Focus on the "field of dreams" (best areas for a base hit). Obviously the hit-

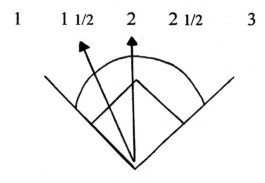

Left-Handed Hitter

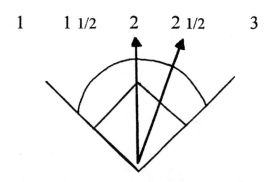

Right-Handed Hitter

ter should go with the pitch — never guess or aim to hit to a certain spot unless for a hit-and-run or moving a runner over to third base with no one out. I don't even like swinging up to hit a sacrifice fly. Bad things happen when one swings under the ball or tries to reach the fences. But all hitters should attempt to use the whole field and adjust to the pitch location. Thus, don't try to pull an outside pitch. In practice focus on hitting up the middle and to the opposite field.

Pitchers, generally not known as good fielders, are the only defenders against a base hit up the middle. Plus, if an outfielder moves in any direction it's usually to a hitter's pull side (more so for left-handed batters). So have kids look to drive the ball up the middle, and go with pitches to the opposite-field gaps. The majority of home runs come to the pull side, but batters shouldn't practice hitting them. The inside pitch is easier to hit, because of its close proximity to the hands. The outside pitch is more difficult to hit; thus many players don't want to work on it. The good hitter really only needs to refine the inside pitch during drills and BP.

Ground Balls vs. Fly Balls

Practice hitting line drives and at least ground balls. Fly balls mean outs. Whether it be running laps for every game day fly ball or sitting people down for refusing to swing down, winning teams put the ball in play and put pressure on the defense. In BP or soft toss, throw the high strike (at the "letters") where the hitter must swing down enough, so the hands are above the ball. And expect this type of pitch when down in the count.

A ground ball out requires one person fielding the ball cleanly, that person throwing the ball cleanly, and a second person catching the ball cleanly. A fly ball out only requires one person making the catch. Look at a game, a week of games, or an entire season. Line drives and ground balls will equal a much higher on-base percentage than pop-ups or fly balls. And never have a kid go up to the plate thinking about hitting a dinger.

Check Swing

Against contrary belief, the check swing isn't in the hitter's best interest. It takes away from aggressiveness, pulls the front shoulder and head out, and leaves the bat in a susceptible position to be hit by the pitched ball. Hitters usually check their swings on off-speed or borderline pitches. If a player hits the ball on a check swing, which happens more than you think, the result usually is a slow dribbler. Checks swings result from difficulty in picking up grip, spin and location. These hitters guess and are undecided. Once the hitter has decided to swing (less than a second), it's better to swing through rather than checking. Good things happen when hitters attack the ball. And never check a swing in a RBI situation, especially with a runner at third and fewer than two outs.

For an indecisive team, practice this "swing for a borderline strike" discipline in live BP. Try and locate pitches in and around the hitter's strike zone. Hitting perfect pitches in practice (yes for game day BP, so hitters can get their timing down) doesn't simulate game conditions, so be aggressive in this drill. One must see pitches coming from both arms, with different grips and locations, and from numerous distances. Swinging through a pitch, instead of checking the swing, gives the hitter a chance to hit the ball. A check swing never results in a line drive.

Ground Ball   Fly Ball   Line Drive   Inside Pitch   Outside Pitch

It's one thing to be disciplined, but another to take called strikes right down the middle. Preach aggressiveness along with knowledge of the strike zone. Bring a local umpire in to work your scrimmages or hitting/pitching sessions. Many times the umpire will call a strike on a check swing, often for the larger/ stronger hitter. If one thought about swinging, it probably was a strike in the first place. Since power hitters generate so much bat speed (to drive the ball long distances), it's much more difficult to hold the bat back. Umpires get paid to call strikes and outs, not balls and safe calls. Umps invariably call a check swing strike when, the wrists turn over, bat head exceeds the front of the plate, and the front shoulder opens up. If a hitter knowingly is unable to hold the bat back and prevent a called strike, never glance at the umpire for the pitch call. Admitting a strike usually results in a called one.

Look in a mirror. (Steve Berg)

Ways to Check for a Proper Swing

Have kids swing in front of a mirror. Photograph and videotape the stance, stride and swing. Break the swing down into individual phases. Talk about it, demonstrate, drill, practice, and prepare players to play. And work on individual weaknesses, because no one hits 1.000.

A check swing means indecision. (Rex Baker)

6

Drills and Station Work

To Be Legit … You Hit.

Introduction

Emphasize the importance of drill work to increase strength, speed, and flexibility, and localize a specific discipline. Taking the same aggressive swing with proper fundamentals (key on "fun") in practice forces the body to do the same in a game. Since teams don't face a sufficient amount of BP, good hitters get their swings during drills provided in this chapter. For example, in BP, it's difficult to break down flaws in seven to 10 swings. However, taking 25 to 30 step-hit swings (discussed later) may show a hitter lunging at the ball. Drills are a must for understanding the many facets of the swing. Every club should be a well-drilled unit.

Don't go crazy with drills that have little or nothing to do with game situations. Do what works for the particular age group, and don't put too much into the kids' heads. Always focus on the fundamentals, and practice drills the kids can do on their own.

Drills

Soft Toss

Soft toss perfects the precise timing in which to swing. The philosophy here is to practice different aspects without the ball being pitched from a normal distance. This breaks the swing down into separate disciplines. Soft toss strengthens a portion of a hitter's swing and corrects noticeable weaknesses. Use soft toss drills at every practice and before games. Use a mock home plate (i.e. hat or towel) in accordance with mental preparation (eyeing the pitcher and ball, location of the pitch, stride, etc.).

Soft toss and other drills should include different equipment (i.e. bats, balls, stance, situations, etc.). Most every drill can be done indoors or out, against a net, backstop or chain link fence, or on the regulation diamond. *Note*: All soft toss drills should work the whole plate (i.e. inside, outside, middle, high and low). Repeat the different locations with different pitches. The complete player needs to be effective at hitting all types of pitches.

Soft toss. (Steve Berg)

1. Normal Stance

BATTER LOCATION: Take a normal stance in the batter's box.

STYLE OF TOSS: The toss should be a straight line drive, so the batter can hit the ball on a line (simulates game conditions). Don't lob it too much, but make sure the hitter has enough time to read the ball upon release, stride and cock, and get a good swing. The toss should be aimed at the strike zone of the hitter. Hit the ball with full extension just in front of a plate. The tosser can also simulate the different pitches (fastball, curveball, change-up) during a routine. *Fastball*: Thrown on a hard and direct line. *Curveball*: With an overhand circular motion. *Change-up*: With a fastball motion but with a slower speed upon release. By disguising the various tosses, the hitter can better improve game day reaction time.

LOCATION OF TOSSER: Rest on one knee at an angle in front of the hitter (some five to 10 feet away) to better simulate the trajectory of an actual game day pitch (kneel directly across from the hitter for the outside pitch). Always show the ball to the person before tossing, and cock the toss backwards before releasing it. This enables a batter to initiate his/her own swing before hitting the ball. The tosser can also move farther away than normal. This forces the hitter to follow the path of the ball longer (reading-the-ball phase) and react quicker.

PHILOSOPHY: Do this more than any other drill and before an actual game. Never rush a swing. Take time between tosses (i.e. no speed-swings, so swing correctly each time).

2. Knees

BATTER LOCATION: Take a normal stance with both knees on the ground (use a towel or glove for a cushion).

STYLE OF TOSS: Use the line drive toss aimed at a hitter's front elbow. Hit the ball in front of the plate.

LOCATION OF TOSSER: Rest on one knee at an angle in front of the hitter.

PHILOSOPHY: This drill works to quicken the hips. It also teaches the hitter to keep the front shoulder closed (Ike to Mike).

Soft toss on the knees. (Steve Berg)

3. One Knee

BATTER LOCATION: Take a normal stance. Put the back knee on the ground with a straight front leg (use a towel or glove for a cushion). Then switch knees after 10 swings. This stance works the outside pitch.

STYLE OF TOSS: Use the line drive toss aimed at the hitter's front elbow. Hit the ball in front of the plate and at the outside back corner for the opposite field pitch.

LOCATION OF TOSSER: Kneel directly across from the hitter for the outside pitch.

PHILOSOPHY: This drill also works to quicken the hips through proper balance, weight transfer from the back to front, and going with the pitch. Keep the weight back on every swing, keep the front shoulder closed, and eyes on the ball.

4. Step-Hit

BATTER LOCATION: Take a normal stance.

STYLE OF TOSS: This time the toss should be flipped (with an arc).

LOCATION OF TOSSER: Rest on one knee at an angle in front of the hitter. Tell him/her to "step" (stride), flip the ball, and have the hitter swing (make sure the weight and hands are back while the ball is in the air).

PHILOSOPHY: Use this drill for keeping the weight back, especially for waiting on breaking pitches. Most breaking pitches fool hitters, and weight is transferred forward before the ball has entered the strike zone. Instead of swinging with just the arms, this drill better utilizes the whole body and especially the hands. *Note*: Adapt this to virtually all hitting drills.

5. One-Handed

BATTER LOCATION: Take a normal stance. First, hit with the bottom hand (against or slightly above the knob). Second, hit with the top hand (high above the knob). Do one-handed swings while standing up, on one knee, and in close-range BP. Drive the elbow to the ground. One-handed swings work to better coordinate the different arms (since one is always more dominant than the other), and since one swings with two arms, work to improve the non-dominant one.

STYLE OF TOSS: Use the line drive toss aimed at the hitter's front elbow.

LOCATION OF TOSSER: Rest on one knee angled in front of the hitter.

PHILOSOPHY: Hitting down on the ball (correct mechanics) quickens both hands, keeps the front shoulder closed, and eyes on the ball. Work on contact, not necessarily bat speed.

6. From Behind

BATTER LOCATION: Take a normal stance, but focus on the tosser and ball coming from behind.

STYLE OF TOSS: The toss should be flipped.

Soft toss from behind. (Steve Berg)

One-handed soft toss. (Steve Berg)

LOCATION OF TOSSER: Rest on one knee directly behind the plate and hitter (some eight to 12 feet). Arc the ball, so it comes down into the strike zone (near the hitter's thighs) over home plate.

PHILOSOPHY: This is another weight-back and breaking-pitch drill. Follow the path of the ball (back eye) and use both eyes (head down) on contact. Work on waiting for the pitch. Swing for strikes.

7. From the Backside

BATTER LOCATION: Take a normal stance with both eyes on an imaginary pitcher.

STYLE OF TOSS: The toss should be flipped, so the batter can hit the ball somewhere near the middle of the thighs and in front of the plate (back corner for outside or breaking pitches).

LOCATION OF TOSSER: Rest on one knee directly behind the hitter's back. Arc the ball, so it comes down into the strike zone over home plate. The hitter can either watch the ball coming from behind, or the tosser can verbally notify the hitter.

PHILOSOPHY: This drill keys the hitter into waiting for the ball, quickly reacting to the seen pitch, and aggressively using the hands to drive it. It's great for practicing the late-breaking slider. (Though not designed to be thrown for strikes, the slider looks like a fastball and then darts across the plate.) Work on the senses and then reacting. Extend the hands to the opposite field.

8. From Above

BATTER LOCATION: Take a normal stance, and focus on an imaginary pitcher.

STYLE OF TOSS: As the ball is dropped from above, swing when it comes into the strike zone — somewhere above the front knee.

LOCATION OF TOSSER: Stand on the ground or on a barrel/chair across from the hitter. To avoid the bat, have the hitter extend his/her arms beforehand. Then stand a foot or two away from that point.

PHILOSOPHY: This works on quick reaction and hands (bat speed).

Soft toss from the backside. (Steve Berg)

Soft toss from above. (Steve Berg)

9. Bounce Drill

BATTER LOCATION: Take a normal stance.

STYLE OF TOSS: The toss (tennis ball) should be flipped.

LOCATION OF TOSSER: Rest on one knee angled in front of the hitter. Command the batter to hit the ball in the air ("lob") or after hitting the ground ("bounce").

PHILOSOPHY: Besides the step-hit drill, this is another great way to practice hitting curveballs, quick reaction, and waiting for the ball. The hitter must decide within a millisecond whether to hit the ball in the air or on the bounce. The bounce symbolizes the curveball hit with the weight and hands back. Quick reaction to the off-speed pitch can result in base hits to the opposite field.

10. No Stride

BATTER LOCATION: Take a normal stance except with a wide base.

STYLE OF TOSS: Use the line drive toss.

LOCATION OF TOSSER: Rest on one knee angled in front of the batter.

PHILOSOPHY: This drill works to quicken the hips through elimination of the stride. Try to rotate forcefully while swinging down to the ball. The hands and hips should move together.

Tee Work

Great hitters usually have a best friend. It's the batting tee. No one should assume it being just for kids or slumping hitters. Make the tee a part of every practice and pregame routine. It's the epitome of the basics since it promotes seeing the bat hit the ball with a downward swing.

Lower (low strike) and raise (high

A hitter's best friend. (Steve Berg)

strike) the tee, or leave it at belt level for a pitch down the middle. Batters should always line up the "sweet spot" with the ball before hitting. The tee also serves as a hitting partner. And tape the top of the tee to reduce wear and tear.

Swing as If in a Game

Kids should start by looking at the ball on top of the tee and progress to swinging as if in a game. Do the bat and body movements, rock back and forth, and get ready to hit. First focus on an imaginary pitcher, and then rotate the eyes to the ball. Don't generate bad habits by simply concentrating on the ball sitting there. Look at the bat-ball contact in front of the plate — not directly at the ground.

The tee can display the difficulty of hitting a moving round ball with a round bat. Ask your hitters to try to hit 10 line drives up the middle with the tee resting on home plate. Sounds simple, right? The ball is just lying there. No player will be able to hit all 10 on the first try. Keep working until they do, and remember that hitting is difficult (not just with the tee) and the only way to get ready for a game is through hard work.

Flat Bat

Though every good hitter swings down, the top portion of a bat is almost "flat" or level to the ground when the ball is hit on the "meat" or "sweet spot." This is a key to proper wrist alignment and arm extension on contact. If done correctly, one may not even feel the bat-ball impact. This is the essence of hitting.

Tape the Bat

Apply athletic tape over the "sweet spot" (for practice) to check for actual bat-ball contact. If a hitter is often jammed, have him/her move slightly off the plate ("free the hands") in subsequent at-bats. Also, pitching machine balls stain the bat. Check the consistency of these swings. Marks should be left near the "sweet spot." Clean the bat with rubbing alcohol after each practice. Tape over a wooden bat or fungo protects it from the weather and possible splintering.

Hand-Eye Coordination

Hitting requires hand-eye coordination. The eyes judge the ball coming, and the mind processes those messages into triggering the hands and body.

My L.L. coach noticed me missing pitch after pitch at one of our late afternoon practices. I thought it was too dark out. He called my parents to insist on getting my eyes checked. To my surprise I needed glasses. With the corrective lenses, my hitting stroke immediately turned around. I made the All-Star team, which went to the town's first-ever L.L. state championship. It's safe to say my future baseball career would have been put in serious jeopardy had my coach not suggested seeing an optometrist.

Ask the kids to have their eyes checked before each season. No other sport skill besides car racing relies on eyesight more than hitting since a wild pitch could cause a serious head injury. The ability to judge a ball's velocity and spin, then apply that knowledge to the swing, makes the practicing of hand-eye coordination techniques vital to a hitter's makeup. Lastly, a motivational tool: Hitters don't improve their hand-eye coordination by playing video games.

Thunderstick

The thin-handled Easton aluminum bat (one inch in diameter) should be used to bunt, in drills, and even close-

Add thunder to your swing. (Steve Berg)

range BP. Swinging the Thunderstick works the "sweet spot." It also forces the hitter to keep the head down, eyes on the ball, and front shoulder closed on contact. Using this bat isn't easy and takes time to fully master. Focus first on contact of any kind, and then solid contact on every swing. This bat allows the hitter to take actual swings at a real baseball.

Broomstick and Wiffle Balls

An old broomstick handle (just a little longer than the regular bat) serves the same purpose as the Thunderstick. Hit golf-ball sized wiffle balls or taped-up balls of newspaper. The more difficult the drill (thinner bat and smaller ball), the better the hand-eye coordination becomes. Make use of an assortment of bats and balls. Regular-sized wiffle balls (or even tennis balls hit from the foul line into the outfield) could be hit as an alternative to soft toss or BP before a game (i.e. lack of time or inclement weather).

Follow the Bouncing Ball

Hitters must judge the movement and dip of a breaking ball. For indoor swings or in the cellar, buy some boat rope, drill a hole through an Incrediball, slip the rope through the ball, tie a knot in the end of the rope, and fasten the top of the rope to a ceiling or basketball hoop. The ball should rest about belt level. Swing the rope, and all of a sudden the ball is moving in different directions. Attempt to hit to all fields and in different parts of home plate. It's difficult but a great challenge. *Note*: Have the kids play an outdoor competitive game between teammate(s) (similar to the bas-

ketball game of Pig or Horse) by attempting to hit the ball to different parts of the field. Use pop-ups, ground balls, fly balls, and line drives. If one hitter is successful in accomplishing a style of hit, a teammate has to equal the feat. If not, the next batter gets to try.

For outdoor swings, attach a clamp to the backstop pole with the same idea. This serves a valuable purpose as a BP/on-deck station.

Color-Coded Balls

Perform a hitting drill with the pitching machine using white and yellow Jugs balls. Try hitting the white one and bunting the yellow. Or hit-and-run the white, and hit to the right side for the yellow. But stress the importance of picking the ball up as early as possible.

This drill works two disciplines. First, hand-eye coordination through concentration (from release to contact). Second, actual grip of the ball at the pitcher's "L" (hard focus upon release). Deciphering grip is the ultimate challenge for the batter, but lay more stress on picking the ball up. Hitters shouldn't guess. Trust the hands and instincts to react quickly and efficiently.

Another drill can quicken reactions

Toss two balls. (Steve Berg)

and help to recognize the type of pitch and spin. Put two balls into regular soft toss. Flip a ball from each hand at the same time, and command the batter to hit one of the two balls. For example, "high" for the high pitch or "low" for the low pitch. *Note:* During a game, a hitter can decrease his/her strike zone by crouching on a high pitch. Down in the count (i.e. 0–2, 1–2), a pitcher invariably throws high to entice an offering.

Paddle-, Hand-, Racquet-, and Pickleball

Purchase paddleball rackets for all of the hitters. It's enjoyable and challenging. Encourage handball and racquetball competition. Not only are these fast-paced sports great at enhancing hand-eye coordination, but they're also a fantastic workout to build stamina and leg strength. Handball can be played against a gym wall as part of an indoor practice. Pickleball is also great. You play on a volleyball court, attempting to hit a wiffle ball over a small net with a wooden paddle. It's an unbelievably fun and exciting game which combines badminton, tennis, and ping-pong all in one.

Pepper

Many feel pepper is a game used simply to pass the time. However, it's an excellent drill for hand-eye coordination. A batter stands some 20 to 30 feet away from a group of fielders. One person tosses a strike to the batter, who attempts to hit a ground ball. Batters should choke up and take a modified swing. Toss and hit strikes. Keep four things in mind: (1) Eyes on the ball, (2) use proper mechanics, (3) hit down on the ball, and (4) maintain bat control.

Once the ground ball is mastered, then add some competition. First, hit grounders to any particular fielder. Second, hit to players in a line, going left to right or right to left. Third, call out the name of the person to hit to. Fourth, fielders who make an error have to move to the end of the line. After a swing-and-miss or line drive caught in the air, the person at the front of the line hits. The batter then goes to the end of the line and everyone shifts up a spot. A fielder can only go after balls hit to his/her area. All catches must be clean (no bobbles or traps). For that hitter who just seems to stay up forever, huddle up and have everyone fake a toss with someone actually throwing the ball. It'll get the batter every time. For younger players, the instructor should begin hitting. Teams can also practice their bunting techniques in this game.

Juggling, Two-Ball, and the Bouncing Ball

Juggling is the ultimate in hand-eye coordination. It takes a keen eye and hand to keep the balls in the air for an extended period, just as the hitter has to read the ball after release. Start by tossing one ball in the air with the dominant hand. Catch it with the other hand. Repeat this over and over. Now reverse the direction of the ball with the non-dominant hand. Repeat this over and over. Then put a ball in each hand, and toss the ball from the dominant hand towards the other hand. When this ball reaches the top of its arc, toss the ball from the other hand towards the dominant hand (below the arc of the first ball). Catch the balls, and repeat it over and over. Now reverse the direction of the balls, non-dominant hand first. Get a rhythm by saying, "1-2, 1-2." Juggling isn't easy but keep trying.

Play two-ball with a person, starting with two balls in one hand. Toss the two balls at the same time to someone else in the group. The balls must be flipped (not thrown on a line) within the vicinity of a person's spot in the circle. Don't make the arc too high. The receiver must try and catch both balls with their hands. Youngsters can use their chest. If either ball drops to the ground, this person must turn his/her hat to the side. For subsequent drops the hat should turn back, to the side, front, etc. After a full turn, do 10 push-ups. If someone catches both balls with one hand, that person has the option of reducing one turn of their own hat or adding a turn to the tosser. For a large group make the latter an elimination factor; plus, one is also penalized if any toss hits the ground first.

All hitters have probably tried to keep a ball in the air by bouncing it off the bat. Grip the bat towards the knob with one hand, and try to consistently bounce the ball off the "sweet spot." Concentration and coordination; it's also a great challenge. Then hold the bat with two hands and hit the ball back and forth with a partner or in a group. This works on bat control and bunting skills.

Obscure Drills

Big-league catcher Paul LoDuca improved his hand-eye coordination as a boy by hitting dried beans thrown to him by his mother. Edgar Martinez hit raindrops falling off his roof. As a child Mike Easler hit bottle caps out of his hand. And I played a game called T-ball, hitting a tennis ball with a juiced-up Wiffleball bat. Small objects are more difficult to hit, but these drills make the regular baseball seem larger than life.

See the Ball

Pitching is action, while hitting is reaction. Kids need to practice seeing the ball. Pair hitters up, about 30 to 40 feet apart, each with a glove. The tosser throws a baseball towards the "hitter," who catches the pitch in his/her glove while taking a "swing." First, work on seeing the ball into the glove with full extension upon contact. Second, work on catching the ball and swinging the arms through just as in the follow-through phase. Third, throw the ball harder and harder, and add in breaking pitches. The philosophy here is that you can only *catch* what you can *see*.

Play catch to practice seeing the ball. (Rex Baker)

Working the Outside Pitch

Every mature batter should be able to hit the inside pitch. However, the best hitters go to the opposite field. Inexperienced batters only want to hit the outside pitch during a hit-and-run play (discussed later on). A base hit to the opposite field with a moving base runner can create a first-and-third situation for the offense. The outside pitch is also the pitcher's "money pitch." Knowing hitters look to drive the inside pitch, a smart pitcher throws outside for two reasons: (1) The hitter isn't looking for a pitch there, and (2) difficulty in hitting a solid line drive. I know just from throwing BP that it's even difficult pitching to the outside corners. You're so trained in hitting and throwing inside pitches that it's almost become an unbreakable habit. Continually harp on being able to hit the outside pitch and also curveballs. A good offense is strong one through nine in the lineup and can hit anybody, anywhere, any time.

Kids need to think power when hitting the outside pitch. Don't just fight it off. Go with the pitch and use the whole body. If the back foot comes off the ground and one is able to drive the ball—good job. Generate speed and explosion the other way. Don't get accustomed to just fouling these pitches off. Go with it.

Inside-Out Swing

Understand the hit-and-run philosophy for a right-handed batter hitting to the opposite field. With a runner on the move from first base, a base hit to right field probably moves him/her to third base. Pulling a base hit to left field probably only allows him/her to get to second base due to the close proximity of the left fielder's throw to third.

An extra base can be achieved by hitting the outside pitch or using the "inside-out" swing for the inside pitch by keeping the hands compact near the body and shooting the hands directly towards the other way. This motion should appear as the letter "U" towards the opposite field. This swing also provides an advantage over traditional defensive replacement. Remember back to throwing the hands at the baseball.

Fielders instinctively play most hitters straight away and often to the pull side; even more so for left-handed batters. But infielders even play over a position for those dead-pull hitters (third baseman moves to shortstop, etc.). While the batter shouldn't change philosophy according to the defense (i.e. infield in on the grass), expect inside pitches in this situation, which gives the defense a better shot at getting a ground ball to them. Move kids slightly off the plate and have them attempt to line a pitch the opposite way. Use the whole field. Lastly, before every at-bat, the hitter should always take a mental note of defensive alignment before stepping into the batter's box. Fielders moving around in the diamond may tip off a particular pitch and/or location.

The outside pitch must be constantly worked on. That's why so few hitters are able to go the other way. Its difficulty makes succeeding on such an at-bat all the more rewarding and disappointing for the pitcher. The following are outside pitch drills:

1. Two-Poled Tee

Tees can be purchased with two poles. Place a ball on each with one closest to the batter lower than the other. One should be located in the middle of the plate with the other located outside. Instruct batters to first swing at the ball down the middle. Get in the same stance, and then hit the outside pitch. Notice that the stance doesn't have to change according to the pitch location. Go with the pitch. Drive the ball up the middle and then to the opposite field. Work on striding slightly the other way for the outside pitch. Same swing each time, but use the hands to go with each pitch.

Use the two tees for a fastball-curveball recognition drill. Have a partner yell "one" for fastball and "two" for curveball the moment the swing begins. React by pulling the fastball, or wait for the curveball and drive it the other way. Once this skill is mastered teach the inside-out swing.

If using the one-poled tee, align the hitter in a normal stance in the box. Give three commands: "Inside" (get back in the box and closer to the plate, get around the outside of the ball, and pull the pitch with the bat extended out front with the top hand ahead of the bottom), "middle" (maintain the initial stance and drive the ball up the middle, palm-up palm-down), or "outside" (move up in the box and away from the plate, and hit the inside half of the ball to the opposite field, this time with the bat head actually behind the tee on contact). After each command, the batter has a split second to react and swing.

In a live hitting session with pitches to the three areas, hitters can move back to work on pitches that break early. Move up to work on pitches that break late. Use this exercise off the pitching machine. While the pitch should be in the same spot each time, simply move around in the box as suggested above to work on each discipline. These are fantastic drills for quickening reaction time, going with a certain pitch, and hitting to all fields. It's also fun and challenging as the kids are hopping around in the box. Have the hitters chant to themselves: "Inside, middle, outside" and so on. Mix up the order. Confidence will rise, as will talent.

2. Back-Hip Swings

Have a tee serve as the plate with a ball on top. Now align the hitter's back hip with the pole. Take a compact swing (hands close to the body) while concentrating on hitting the outside pitch. The first few swings may feel awkward because one isn't making a full extension on compact. Don't panic.

The keys are: (1) Keep the weight back, (2) go with the pitch to the opposite field, (3) practice striding to the pitcher and/or then to the actual pitch location, and (4) realize that a strike can be thrown to the far back corner of the

Hit two pitches at once. (Steve Berg)

plate. So many hitters lean forward on a curveball when the hands and weight should still be back. Coach so kids can fight that tough deuce off by flicking their hands at the last possible moment. Fouling a nasty pitch off is the difference in surviving the greatest battle in sports: pitcher vs. hitter.

3. Bottom-Hand Swings

Perform various drills emphasizing the bottom hand. This hand leads the

Back-hip drill. (Steve Berg)

swing. To hit the outside pitch the hitter needs complete command and extension of the bottom hand.

4. Simulated Swings

Have the hitters get in a normal stance next to a plate. Without a bat, simulate hitting an outside pitch. Throw the hands at the ball. Work on the swing until it feels natural. I've even seen players simulate swings the day before (or early before the game) in the actual batter's box. This could be a relaxing and comforting feeling especially those youngsters playing in playoff or All-Star tournaments.

Working the Inside Pitch

Even though the inside pitch is a favorite for hitters, never take it for granted. Concentrate on keeping the head down and front shoulder closed. If one recognizes it early enough, a hitter with bat speed can even get the bat out front farther than normal to rip a ball down the line.

Fence Drill

Instruct kids to face the backstop or net, and stand an arm's length away. While swinging bring the hands across the body as closely as possible. This compact swing allows the hands to get to the ball (not extending beyond an area equivalent to a fist and a thumb) much more quickly as opposed to swinging around the ball.

This is a valuable two-strike tool when pitchers throw high and inside. Spoiling a pitch (or series of pitches) may force the pitcher into grooving one by mistake. Hitters should love two-

Compact swing. (Steve Berg)

strike counts, because they're swinging for anything close. There's nothing better than a two-strike base hit to totally tick a pitcher off.

Keep the Weight Back

Batters should look fastball and adjust to the curveball. It's a simple saying, but take it to heart. Batters should never guess. Relax, pick up the ball early, react to a strike, and swing hard. To hit the fastball (looking "dead red" or the No. 1) the batter needs to generate bat speed quickly and efficiently. To hit the curveball (looking for a "deuce" or the No. 2) the batter must adjust to the slower pitch by keeping the weight back and hands in close to the body. The curve forces many hitters into overstriding onto the front foot. Early transfer of the weight to the front side usually results in a swing dominated only by the arms. Keep the weight

back and hands in (stride) for better usage of the lower body.

Soda Can Drill

Rest a soda can behind the batter's back foot, so that it touches the heel. Now swing. Make sure the hitter can knock the can over. Proper hip action and use of the lower body are triggered by the back foot. Lift the heel, and explode it inward towards the plate.

Knocking the can over also keeps the weight back through the collapse of the rear leg (and don't roll the foot over). Also, check to see where that rear foot ends up after the swing by drawing a line

Kick the can. (Steve Berg)

in the dirt behind it. Stay balanced with a low center of gravity. One is more sturdy and powerful. Plus the strike zone is smaller. This is also why pitchers love throwing to catchers smaller in size who can get low to the ground. Low strikes usually equal infield ground balls which pitchers favor over deep flies.

Push-Over Drill

Stand behind the batter. After a swing, try to push the hitter towards the mound. In the stance push from a hitter's backside. Think of a football lineman or guard in basketball: balanced, in an athletic position, and ready to attack.

If he/she falls forward, the weight is probably on the front leg and too far front. If he/she stays stationary, the weight is properly back and utilized to drive the ball. This is also great for practicing curveballs. As a team-hitting drill, tell the kids to count to three out loud

Be balanced. (Steve Berg)

while staying balanced during and after the swing. By staying back, the batter can hit the ball in front of the plate. Slap hitters are overaggressive and make contact too far out front.

Pitching Machine

Batters need to keep the weight back on breaking pitches. Use the step-hit drill while hitting off the pitching machine. Most machines have a function to simulate the curveball (both left- and right-handed pitchers). Before dropping a ball down the chute, remember to show the ball to the hitter, or make the arm circle and then drop it in accordingly. You may still see the Iron Mike machine around (with the mechanical arm) as well as the Casey Jugs machines. Companies also make a machine with two chutes for both the fastball and curveball, so the hitter doesn't know which one is coming. Plus the new Titan Pitching machine throws curves, fastballs, sliders, sinkers, and knuckleballs at speeds 40 to 95 mph. Remember, pitching machines throw more strikes than actual pitchers. Plus, this way you can work with kids in the cage or on the side.

Diggin' in

Encourage kids to dig their rear foot into the batter's box. This forces them to keep the weight back and puts the rear foot in place. First, hitters won't be as prone to stride too far in front (shifting the weight too early), because the foot is in "cement." Second, the rear foot needs a push-off mechanism. Power hitters "dig in" as a base for the back foot (i.e. track sprinter coming out of the blocks). Use the legs, and drive into the pitch. For older players, metal spikes provide better stability and control plus prevention of slippages. And the aggressive hitter needs to show the pitcher that he/she means business. Dig in, and be ready for battle. And no matter how close that pitch comes, never give an inch.

Hitters can also make a little mound of dirt behind their rear foot before each at-bat. This is a launching pad for a powerful swing. Hockey goalies do a similar act with ice shavings around the goal posts, hoping that the piles slow up a puck sliding into these areas. Again, little things like these can be the difference between wins and losses.

As an afterthought, a hardened batter's box serves as an important element—just as the pitcher's mound. Take the time to rake and pound the dirt or clay. Fill in the holes, especially the deeper ones on the right side. Not only will hitters appreciate the better footing, but they'll feel better about the appearance of their home field. Plus, you don't want hitters being distracted by avoiding or stepping in large holes. Umpires also love to stand in a finely manicured batter's box.

Hitting Down on the Ball

The key to good fundamentals is driving down on the ball. There are many ways to do this:

Chair Drill

Place a waist-level chair (not wooden) resting against the backside of the batting tee. Have kids focus on an imaginary pitcher. Don't look at the chair, and take a normal swing. Concentrate on swinging down while keeping the hands and back elbow up. This is a

Have a good foundation. (Steve Berg)

Swing down. (Steve Berg)

conscious reminder not to uppercut. Also try this in regular BP (remember not to swing at low pitches).

Tight Hands

The hands need to be relaxed. Think back to the fence drill and one-handed swings. The batter's hands control the swing. React to a strike, and fire the hands to that location over home plate. Remember Carlton Fisk, who did all of those stretches and movements. Yes, he was a "human rain delay," but Pudge tried to relax and be fully ready for every pitch. Tell youngsters to feel "loosey-goosey" in the box. Don't be stressed. It's the pitcher who should be scared.

Quick Hips

Hip rotation (chest and bellybutton facing the pitcher) generates power, bat speed, and proper extension of the lower body in accordance with swinging down. Place the bat behind the hitter's back at waist level, and have them hook their arms around the bat. Simulate an arriving pitch. Now rotate and explode the hips. Also, put the hands on each hip and repeat the same routine. Using the bat, however, adds to stability and balance. Make sure rotation extends from Ike to Mike and the head is looking down at the ball. Hip twists are also great for an on-deck stretching routine.

Left: Russian twists. *Above:* Good rotation. (Steve Berg)

Helmets

Helmets should be worn whenever baseballs are being thrown and hit. Football players always practice with their helmets on, so ballplayers should do the same. Not only does the helmet provide protection from an errant toss, but it also relates to game day hitting.

Never assume complete safety when batting, even against pitching machines. Always prepare for the unexpected. You also want plenty of helmets, so on-deck hitters don't have to scramble to find one. Throw away any cracked ones. Purchase new helmets each season, because flashy new ones with the team decal add to a first-class mentality. Have each helmet professionally sanitized by a sporting goods company after the season. They will also do a pressure test to ensure that the helmet passes a compression safety standard. *Note*: All amateurs must wear the double ear-flap helmet. We now see helmets with the protective face cage. I don't encourage this, because of difficulties in vision. Kids need to play the game and not be so afraid of being hit by the ball. Hockey helmets have cages, but with the boards and ice being so hard these are necessary. Safety is a major concern to any sport, but the helmet has protected hitters for so many years that I don't see a need to add the cage.

Wear your lid. (Bruce Baker)

Block Everything Out

Hitters should focus their knowledge and concentration underneath the helmet. Nothing else should matter except what's going to happen at the plate. Pitchers mold the brim of the hat down around their eyes to better focus on the batter. The helmet should be a reminder to block out any fan interference. Put the helmet on, focus on the pitcher, and then the ball. Slap on some eye black, and your kids will be menacing figures. Also buy personal helmets. They'll fit perfectly and be more sanitary.

Balls

Modern technology has produced many sorts of baseballs coming in all shapes and sizes. For indoor or preseason practices, use rubber or Incrediballs. Equipment catalogs sell baseballs consisting of the same size and weight as regulation balls. They can be used for live indoor scrimmages, so you don't break any windows. Tennis and wiffle balls (regular/golf-ball size) are cheap, safe, and have countless uses. Hit towards a corner of the gym via close-range BP with wiffle balls and use game day situations (counts, imaginary base runners, and strategy). Pitching machines now shoot the smaller wiffle balls. This is a tremendous hand-eye coordination drill, and also useful for indoor/rainy day practices.

Here are some notes for an indoor scrimmage: (1) Use the portable mound from regulation distance, L-screen, and plenty of Incrediballs in a bucket behind the pitcher. (2) Use a catcher in full equipment, umpire, base coaches, and ground rules. (3) Employ set batting lineups (two teams or groups of four) and a full infield. (4) Use throw-down Hollywood bases. (5) Put in strategy and a catcher who throws to second base on steals (no sliding).

Purchase as many regulation baseballs as possible. Practices are so much better with plenty of balls to spread around. Buy cheaper balls for practice, and order plenty of game balls for the season (a rainy day can claim the lives of many new balls). Just like breaking out the new bats just before the season, kids will go nuts when you open a new box of gamers for pregame BP. The balls just jump off the bat so much better than the dirty old ones that have been in the bucket for months.

Search for lost balls at Little League and high school diamonds, and check in the players' bags. For some reason kids like to keep extra team balls for their own. Employ a count system: For every ball lost at a practice the team runs laps.

Stations

The following provides an overview for the hitting station. The goals include: (1) Better utilization of time and space, (2) more disciplines accomplished, (3) increased interest and enthusiasm through variety and movement, and (4) better focus because you can witness and even videotape the proceedings.

No matter how small or large your practice facility, station work is the difference between success and failure. Take the army mentality: Get more done in two hours than teams do in a week. Get in, work hard, and make progress each day.

Each station should have a separate focus and may come at a different part of the practice or season. Many teams don't have access to five batting tunnels or a pitching machine. Most need a more economical way to approach station work. But all teams have access to a baseball field, and many practice indoors during the winter or preseason. Stations can be accomplished indoors or outside by any group with some imagination and appropriate modifications.

All-Bat Drill

Start by explaining techniques of the stride, and then place the team in lines or a circle, so you can see every hitter. The following team hitting session is derived from the teachings of Harvey Krupnick, who coaches in Massachusetts. His video, *How to Teach and Learn the Art of Hitting* (1990), has sold nationally. Each phase should be done in sequence, starting with number one and concluding with one through five in succession.

1. **Movement**. In a comfortable stance, rock back and forth in the stance. Keep the weight back on a firm rear leg.

2. **Stride-and-cock**. With the weight and hands back, the front hip and shoulder should be cocked inward while striding to the pitcher.

3. **Check swing**. With the hands going to the pitch (the bat second), pivot the hips so the bat head is up (i.e. hit down on the ball). The bottom hand should be in front of the top. Remember, the path of the hands to the ball should be straight down.

4. **Contact**. Fully extend the arms with the hands parallel to one another, front leg straight, and back leg bent. The bat should be at the front edge of home plate and parallel to the ground.

5. **Follow Through**. After contact with the ball, turn the wrists over. The bottom hand leads the bat through the strike zone. Finish high. *Note*: In this

Check swing. (Rex Baker)

Swing together. (Steve Berg)

drill the swing is being broken down into separate parts. Think of climbing a ladder or doing a math equation. Start small and conclude with a game day swing. Once each phase is perfected and understood, then move on to more complex techniques.

Wrist Hitting

Another component includes Krupnick's wrist hitting. Hitters need strong and quick wrists. The following drills work on keeping the bat above the hands during the swing, quickness, and a level swing. For each drill start slowly until progressing to the point where the bat becomes a blur. This is also great as a warmup exercise.

Quick wrists. (Rex Baker)

1. **One hand.** Bend over with one arm behind the back, and the bat in the other hand located directly out front. Smoothly flick the bat back-and-forth about waist level to the left and right. The wrist should turn over fully (for good wrist action). Keep the arm as straight as possible. This works both wrists; especially the non-dominant hand. Then switch hands.

2. **Two Hands.** Do the same routine except with two hands (i.e. chopping wheat with a sickle). The bat should go as high as the hips. Work on the wrist turnover action.

3. **Figure eight.** Do the same as the two-handed drill, but form a figure eight with the swing. Work on a smooth motion. This trains the wrists to move in varying positions for pitches from all directions.

4. **Circle above the head.** Extend the arms out front, and circle the bat above the head (elbows away from the body). Keep the arms parallel and swing level. This works on full extension.

5. **Shoulder-to-shoulder.** Extend the arms out front, and whip the bat from the back to the front shoulder. This gives a hitter confidence in relation to bat speed. Swing hard and slowly bring the bat back. The plane of the swing should be shoulder-high. Focus on full extension of the arms.

6. **Loop-and-hammer.** Point the bat at an imaginary pitcher. Take a normal swing. This ensures that the hands go first and the bat second (above the hands). It's almost two swings in one. Try it in BP. A hitter must be quicker than normal, but again swing down on the ball.

Loop and hammer. (Rex Baker)

Location Drill

Perform a swinging drill, but call out the exact pitch and its location. For example, fastball (look to drive the ball up the middle or to the pull side), curveball (stride with the weight back and swing to the opposite field), low pitch (stay upright but extend the bat down to the ball), high pitch (get on top, swing down slightly, and extend fully), inside (use the compact swing), outside ("throw the hands" to the opposite field), or a ball out of the strike zone (stay back and look the ball into the mitt). The hitter can then work on individual strengths and weaknesses.

Ball Drill

This drill improves reaction time and ability to focus. Align the hitters with a pitcher facing them. First throw (use the stretch and full wind-up) in slow motion, and then after five to ten pitches throw regular speed. Hitters have to yell "ball" when each sees the pitch at the "L." Then alter the grips (fastball, curveball, change-up, and knuckleball). See if they can pick each of them up at least the fastball-curveball arm action. A "fat wrist" (pitcher's palm faces the hitter) depicts a fastball arm motion. A "thin wrist" (pitcher's palm faces to the side) depicts a curveball.

Good wrist action. (Bruce Baker)

To fully facilitate the mind at work and seeing the ball out of a pitcher's hand, have the kids close their eyes and visualize the pitch coming. Without vision, the hitter will have difficulty dealing with a change in the body's equilibrium and control over balance. To emphasize this point, close the eyes and attempt to stand on one leg with the arms above the head. It's not easy. Try to have them feel the pitch. Mental prep and execution is rarely practiced, but needed to perform at a high level.

Like all of the best skilled players, from golfers seeing the ball into the cup, quarterbacks seeing the open receiver from their back side, or karate masters executing a perfect maneuver, hitters must imagine a variety of pitches coming and then react with positive results. Confidence is a huge factor to success. Moreover, the more games a player attends or watches on TV, the better an understanding that individual has of the strike zone and pitch types. Even speaking with umpires one can learn a lot about what the pitcher is trying to accomplish. Modern slow-motion analysis on TV also provides excellent interpretation of the pitches and rotation.

Perform normal soft toss drills without vision. Get kids in a stance with their eyes closed. Have someone toss the ball. As it's in the air, tell the hitter to open their eyes. The batter must react quickly to the pitch and see the ball, hit the ball. This teaches patience and quickening the senses in order to react to the pitch coming in so fast. *Note*: The swinging and location drills can be done as a pregame batting routine. This reinforces a good hitting team's mentality and shows the game day pitcher that he/she is going to be in for a rough afternoon.

Preseason Practice: First Week

Before any hitting can take place, review the fundamentals of the stance and swing. Some players may feel insulted by reviewing "simple" terms, but never take anything for granted. Have physical tests for each phase (i.e. Axe Bat for grip and push-over test for a balanced stance). Focus on learning techniques and less on actual swinging.

Preseason Practice: Second, Third or Fourth Week

Actual stations and BP can now occur. Partner up and perform soft-toss drills on both knees, one knee, one-handed, standing, from behind, the side, and from above. Work on each discipline. The tee should be used often. Work the low, high, middle, inside and outside pitches. Begin to work on pitches other than fastballs. Only add in BP until the team has effectively progressed with the fundamentals and drills up to this point.

Swing a hockey stick (without the blade) before a drill or live BP (for better balance and a smooth swing). First swing a weighted or wooden bat, then the hockey stick to counterbalance that weight, and finish with the regular bat to offset that weight. By swinging the lighter hockey stick a hitter will feel more confident (in relation to bat speed) when they pick up a heavier bat.

A team can also utilize other stations including the batting cage (close range and regular distance) and pitching machine. With two machines, move hitters from a live bunting station to soft toss, then to slow-velocity BP in the cage. Get hitters concentrating on the pitch, spin and location. Soft toss can be

Do the drills. (Steve Berg)

performed against a gym wall or curtain divider (tennis or tape balls) or into hitting nets. Use different bats (i.e. Thunderstick and smaller/heavier lengths) and all sorts of balls for different disciplines and concentrations (i.e. wiffle balls, rubber, Incrediballs, Jugs, and the regulation baseball). This also adds variety to each practice.

Also, incorporate sprints, speed-swings, push-ups, sit-ups, and reverse dips (off a chair or bleacher) during "dead time." Make even-numbered groups (i.e. by position or ages). Strive for improvement at every practice. Look for kids who ask to hit first, pick up the equipment, hustle to and from each station, stay after practice, ask questions, and help their teammates. And no one should ever sit down at a practice for any reason (water breaks are OK).

Post a written schedule of events for practices and games. Review the events beforehand, so kids know what to expect. Look for a good two-hour practice, and only extend beyond that time frame if you're including scrimmages. Bring players in at different times (pitchers for the first hour and regulars the second

hour) to dedicate early-season practices to certain positions. Concentration is always better (for coach and player) at an organized practice. Knowing who will be hitting, when, and for how long makes for an effective training session. If possible type out a daily planner for each coach. Modify and adapt it after each season. Being prepared eliminates the stress of trying to accomplish all of one's goals.

Batting Cage

Work on fundamentals in the cage. If anything, work on line drives up the middle and to the opposite field. Challenge hitters to drive balls off the back parts of the cage (gap shots), off the L-screen (line drives), and attach targets/taped foul lines for a simulated hitting game. Start with soft-toss stations on both sides of the cage, and progress to station work.

The following should be attempted at some point of a BP session: (1) regular distance (hit against left- and right-handed pitchers/coaches who throw a variety of pitches); (2) close range (work on reaction time and bat speed); (3) Thunderstick (concentrate on making contact on every swing); (4) one-handed (forces one to use the entire body and going with the pitch); (5) Bratt's Bat (works on bat speed; use tennis balls to start); (6) hit to left, center, and right field in succession (work on using the whole field); and (7) step-hit (stay back on curveballs).

To utilize space, have close range double-barrel BP in the cage. Put a divider in the middle complete with two L-screens (hit in the opposite direction) with about 7-to-10 swings apiece.

Pre-Season Practice: Week Before Opening Day

Get ready for Game Day. Face live pitching (from the coach, teammates and actual left- and right-handed pitchers). Begin with fastballs and then against all pitches in the arsenal. Catchers can call out the pitch coming. This prepares a hitter for specific counts, seeing pitch location and spin, and how a particular catcher and pitcher are trying to get them out. Then simulate actual game competition. Remember, pitchers want to defeat the batters in practice no matter what their age. He/she wants to prove their own strengths and qualities to the coaching staff. But don't be afraid to dedicate some live hitting sessions to pitchers simply getting some work in; at the same time the hitter getting some rips at actual pitches.

Also, work on game strategy along with signals (i.e. hit-and-run, bunts, moving runners to third base, and sacrifice fly). Aim to perfect these situations. If you expect to execute in a game practice the same disciplines beforehand. Begin using game bats in all drills and stations (especially facing live pitchers).

For teams with the appropriate facility, bat hitters in a regular lineup. Get starters thinking and preparing for the season. And add in umpires (either have the catchers, coaches, or an actual umpire on hand), so players aren't complaining about strike/out calls.

Lastly, refrain from players throwing BP; more so for safety reasons but also to maintain the kids swinging on their own — not tossing BP. Ask parents to come in and throw on those hectic days as well as some former pitchers during the season.

Practice During the Season

When in-season, stress swinging the bat. Get game ready by adding breaking pitches during BP as well as strategy. Continue using the pitching machine; even for bunting. Everyone should be given the opportunity to swing every day in order to stay sharp (practice and especially Game Day BP). Use every opportunity to hit outdoors even if it means hitting Jugs balls on a rainy field. Teams can also rent out space at an indoor batting facility if your gym is being used. I've played full intrasquad scrimmages on our Astroturf field, and practiced in an empty parking lot on the weekends. There's no such thing as an off day!

Play scrimmages whenever possible. Nothing gets a team ready for a game more than actually playing. Plus, winners want to succeed in everything whether it's Checkers or a close ballgame. Use scrimmages (pitchers and coaches throw from the mound) and situations (players run from home plate to work on offense/defense). See what the new kids can do. Lastly, have fun and enjoy your baseball practices. Cherish the relationships, and take pride in your work. It'll pay off.

Afterthought

Modify these stations according to your facility. Have each player work with a different teammate each day. This promotes a family atmosphere and competition against more than one person. Peers learn and teach more from speaking and practicing with multiple players. Preach a positive and championship hitting mentality. If you mention negatives, come back with a positive approach to cure them. The players follow the lead of their coach. Work, teach, talk, and motivate them. When they're confident and successful, they make you look good. Want them to run through a wall for you. And never give up on anyone.

7

Strategy

Introduction

The following section is written for the game day advantage. At different times during a game, a call may come to protect or move a base runner up, or score someone from third base. These situations contribute to being the complete hitter. All techniques should be practiced until confidence is achieved in performing that skill in a competitive atmosphere.

Hit-and-Run

The hit-and-run is a valuable offensive weapon. It has two goals. First, the hitter swings at the pitch while a runner is breaking for the next base (even with runners on first and second). The runner should sprint hard, look in to the catcher (midpoint to the bag) to see what is happening at the plate, listen or pick up the ball on contact, and steal the base if contact isn't made. Pick up the third base coach if the ball gets into the outfield. The batter must swing at any pitch in order to protect the runner. Throw the bat at a poor pitch if need be.

Second, the hit-and-run confuses infielders on which base to cover for the steal attempt. In normal situations on a steal of second base with a right-handed hitter up, the second baseman covers the bag. With a left-handed hitter up, the shortstop covers. Providing the example given, a right-handed hitter successfully batting the ball through the now open right side should be able to move the runner to third base. Left-handed batters should aim to hit the ball to the left side. Runners here must read the play in front of them since the left fielder has a close throw to third.

If perfectly executed, the runner can sprint directly to third. Be aware that middle infielders are taught to fake the runner (as if fielding a grounder) into sliding into the bag. *Note*: In a normal situation with a runner on first and a left-handed batter up at the plate, note the open territory on the right side (second baseman moves to his/her right for double-play coverage). A hit-and-run may not be needed in this situation with the first baseman holding the runner on.

Technique

Instruct kids to bring their hands in towards the body (compact stance), raise the back elbow, and angle the bottom wrist slightly towards the opposite field (refer back to the chapter on grip). Use a slightly closed stance, choke up, move up in the batter's box, get off the plate slightly, and shorten the swing (i.e. slap the ball). Drive down and hit the inside portion of the ball. Some hitters even move their feet to the closed stance as the pitch is coming. Think contact and placement, not necessarily discipline and power. Note the difference between the hit-and-run (swing at anything), and moving a runner from second to third base (swing for strikes) with nobody out.

The hit-and-run puts pressure on the defense. Plus, it's an aggressive hitting philosophy. With bat control comes bat-ball contact. Especially when a pitcher is mowing down a team, the hit-and-run can put runners in a great scoring opportunity. Look for production on every single pitch, both at the plate and on the bases.

Short Compact Swing

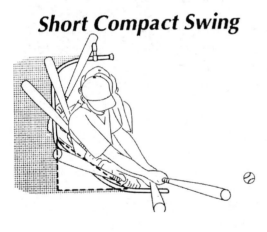

Keys

Look to hit-and-run on the first pitch or on a 2-1 count. (1) Pitchers tend to get ahead with first-pitch fastballs,. (2) If foul, the batter still has two strikes to work with (for the first pitch swing). (3) Statistically, 2-1 is a great count for a base hit.

Tell kids to try to bat the ball on the ground. Think about at least moving the runner up a base. Hit-and-runs score more runs, create more hits, and put more balls in play. Runners stay out of double-plays, batters strike out less, and the defense is always on alert. This play enhances confidence in making contact and bat control, and players develop a greater appreciation for game strategy. The hit-and-run is also great for those slumping hitters, and kids prone to taking first-pitch strikes. Examine a team's talent and makeup before calling this play early and often. A scrappy/speedy team may need and use the play more than a powerful/slow team.

Remember, a batter should never give away the hit-and-run by showing disgust after the play call (this also goes for a sacrifice bunt) or choking up higher than normal. Only slightly alter the grip and stance for the best possible weapon and disguise.

With aggressive base running, holes will open up in the infield. Once that ball gets into the outfield, things start to happen for the offense. Another play (not for the hit-and-run) is taking a borderline strike if a base runner gets a great jump (now in scoring position). Assess fielder positions before an at-bat, and possibly slap a ball through an open area. *Note*: Also watch for corner infielders who guard the lines in late innings of one-run games. Though protecting against doubles down the line, this increases the potential for a safe hit through the now bigger holes.

Other: Interference can be called on contact by either the hitter or catcher while the ball crosses the plate. The hitter can't fall across the plate on an outside pitch or the hit-and-run (runner stealing), and the catcher can't make contact with a hitter's swing (reaching out with the mitt). The hitter is also not permitted to step on home plate at any time (i.e. reaching for an outside pitch on a squeeze bunt play). Moreover, a catcher's balk may be called on an intentional walk if the catcher doesn't stay in his/her "box" until the pitch crosses the plate.

Drill

Practice the hit-and-run indoors or outside with the runner at first base stealing second. In a non-swinging activity, smack two bats together to simulate contact. At that point the breaking runner must pick up the third base coach. On contact, a runner will either slide into second (ground ball force play), go directly to third base (base hit to the outfield), or hold up (fly ball or pop-up). If the runner hears nothing (swing-and-miss or missed signal), he/she should slide into the bag. Infielders usually throw to first base on ground balls here. *Note*: If the runner touches a base on a fly ball out, that runner must retouch the bag before retreating back. Also, don't slow up on line drives in the infield. If caught the double play will occur anyway. If dropped or safe, the runner must be able to make it to the next base (i.e. force play).

When indoors have the kids hit from in front of a wall with a pitcher throwing behind the L-screen. Keep firing tennis balls to the batter in seven- to ten-swing increments. The kids should swing at everything. Fielders need to stand behind the pitcher, because balls will be flying everywhere. Use two on-deck hitters. Toss fielded balls to the side, and always focus on the batter. It's an exciting station.

Protect the Runner

Some hitters swing directly through the pitch (miss intentionally) to protect runners stealing a base. When a runner is stealing a base, catchers usually have a clear view of the action. By swinging through the pitch (complete cut), two things are accomplished. First, the catcher's vision is skewed and their concentration is altered from catching the ball as they wait for the completed swing. Second, infielders don't know if contact is going to be made or not.

This isn't a signal called from a coach. It's more batter instinct, and if done should be done early in the count. That's why it's good to steal on the first pitch. Players should swing at pitches in the vicinity of a "Little League Strike Zone" (i.e. anything close to this area), but avoid swinging for pitches in the dirt (save a strike), for example, because the catcher will have a tough time throwing from this position. Look to swing through those balls (high/outside or down the middle) that the throwing catcher would handle cleanly. Also take into account that it's easier for a right-handed catcher to throw with a right-handed batter at the plate. A fake bunt can also be used in this situation along with a fake steal, which may pop the catcher up in the crouch. Thus, a non-strike may be called. *Note*: In L.L. where leading isn't allowed, runners must wait for the pitch to cross the plate before stealing a base. Whether it's leads or no leads, a running game should be a goal for every team.

Moving the Runner to Third Base

Although it doesn't go into the scorebook as a sacrifice, moving a runner to third base with zero outs is the ultimate in team play. A ball to the right side moves a runner over 99 percent of the time (farther throw to the third base side). The offensive team then has two opportunities to get the run home. The right-handed hitter can refer back to the hit-and-run stance (move off the plate), but don't sacrifice power here. Drive a strike, with a full swing, to the right side. Don't jeopardize a potential base hit by lunging at the ball. Left-handed hitters have an advantage of pulling a pitch in this situation.

Contact Play

Teams use the contact play with a runner on third base and less than two outs. This may be a close game in late innings, or a team may have a fast runner on third. The batter's job is to get the runner in from third any possible way. The runner sprints home once the ball hits the ground (anywhere except back to the pitcher). Even with the infield in on the grass, this is a do-or-die situation for the runner. The batter should look to choke up, move up in the box, shorten the swing, swing down on the ball, and make contact. Swing for strikes. Have a touch signal for the hitter, and simply tell the runner that the contact play is on.

Sacrifice Fly

Avoid practicing the sacrifice fly. It preaches a fly ball swing which usually results in a fly out. The sac fly will happen during a game and it's a run for your team, but you'd rather have a double to the gap, one less out, and score more than a single run in an inning. However, the sac fly should be used by power hitters who possess a natural upward swing.

This play rewards the hitter with a RBI without it being an official at-bat. Other runners (even those on first) should look to tag up and advance if the outfielder throw is off-line or goes through to home plate. In a bases-loaded situation, runners on first or second, for example, can also fake a tag-up and induce an outfielder into an errant throw or missed cutoff.

To practice this type of swing, get farther back in the box, use a heavier bat with the bottom hand at the knob, collapse the back knee, and attempt to hit the bottom portion of the ball (look for an inside pitch up in the strike zone). Try the coil stance (cocking the front shoulder, knee, and hip inward) for more momentum into the pitch (see chapter on stances).

Billy Ball

Billy Martin, in my opinion, is the greatest manager of all time. Not only did he take four different teams to the playoffs (Twins, Tigers, Yankees, A's), but he did it with mediocre talent most of the time. His fiery philosophy was to attack, risk, improvise, rattle, unsettle and undo. He would bunt-and-run, hit-and-run, look to steal signs, and play for one run even early in the game. Martin's teams initiated the pressure. So should you.

Try a competitive game outside where the offense has to attempt something strategic for every plate appearance. This can include hit-and-runs, bunt-and-runs, steals, fake bunts and steals, slash play, sacrifice, squeeze and drag bunts, sacrifice flies, moving runners to third base, contact play, first-and-third rundown plays, you name it. While practicing offensive strategy, kids play more aggressively, start thinking about the philosophy of the team, and you just might be preparing some future coaches.

Extra-Base Hits

Greatness extends to a high batting average but also clutch hitting, especially with two outs and runners in scoring position. Extra-base hits also put teams in a tremendous situation to score runs. It's called hitting the gaps. Line drives or frozen ropes to the whole field may indeed reach the outfield wall. An extra-base hit may even score a runner from first base, put the hitter in scoring position, and eliminate the double-play possibility.

The double is quite common, while the triple is one of the rarest batting exploits. Speed manifests the three-bagger. But kids should never make the first or third out trying to stretch a double into a triple. The runner is already in scoring position when at second base.

On any base hit, runners should think double. Come barreling around first base with the intent of going for second, especially when outfielders overthrow cutoff people. Hit a double, and think triple. Hit a triple, and think home run. Never be satisfied. Put pressure on the fielders. Show a team's hustle in pregame and especially during on-field BP. And to prove what hustle can do, I once witnessed a ground ball base hit up the middle, the center fielder dogged the play, and the runner went into second base *standing up.*

Preach the philosophy that leadoff doubles better end up scoring. Moreover, big at-bats, which decide games, can come in early innings. Especially those bases-loaded, one-out scenarios, practice these situations during in-

trasquad scrimmages. Jumping out to an early three-run lead puts a team in great position for a win.

Hitting the Home Run

Home runs can be hit by anyone, no matter what their size. The problem comes when batters go up thinking and swinging for one. No one can predict a homer. Yes, Mickey Mantle went up wanting to hit a homer every time, but this advanced skill happens by accident.

A home run-hitting lineup can probably expect a lot of dingers—and a lot of strikeouts. But you want a team of athletes who don't simply go station to station or base to base. Home runs should be line drives.

Desire players with a high on-base percentage. Home runs are nice, especially the three-run job, but since many fields don't have fences, outfielders can play as deep as they want.

One tip is to look for a fastball down the middle after a manager, or pitching coach, goes to the mound for a conference. I knew this in 1992 after legendary University of Maine coach Dr. John Winkin went to the mound in the last inning of a tie game. With a runner on third base and one out, I ripped the next pitch to left field for the game-winning run. I wasn't thinking sac fly. Plus, the 3-0 count may also be a good time to "zone in" for that favorite pitch to drive.

As a home run is being hit, yell out, "Get on your horse." This signals the runner to sprint around the bases. Never watch a dinger, because one doesn't want to hit a ball off the fence and simply reach first. And don't show up the pitcher with a lazy trot, because the next pitch to a teammate might be in his/her ear. As my fellow coach Mike O'Brien likes to say, "Hitting is like poison ivy. Once you catch it everyone starts doing it." So get around the bases and into the dugout as quickly as possible. Then encourage the next batter to knock a single up the middle to keep the rally going. Get the lead and never relinquish it. Baseball can be a game of momentum, so keep swingin'.

In 2002 Worcester State's Eric Swedberg had hit his second home run of a game. As he sprinted around third base, the shortstop said to the third baseman: "He doesn't even enjoy his homers." I had quite a large smile on my face. Swedberg hit 15 that year and 46 in his career.

To reinforce power coming from the lower body, have kids use a wide stance. Imagine punching something straight up or crouched low. More power comes from that lowered, more balanced stance.

Hitting a home run is a pretty special moment. I still remember my coach presenting me the game ball for hitting my first Little League dinger. Two Worcester State players (Eric Swedberg and Matt Heenan) hit memorable walk-off three-run homers to win games. But I'll never forget senior Steve Coyle hitting a homer in his last regular-season game in 1999. The smile on his face as he ran around the bases lit up the whole field.

The Lucky 7 Home Run Tips

Don't preach the home run swing, but there are some techniques to use for anyone wanting to add some power to their stroke:

1. **Swing a heavier bat held at the knob.** Use one with a bigger barrel (wider "sweet spot"). The longer and heavier the bat, the more momentum

A power stance. (Bruce Baker)

and force is applied to the ball. Swing the Bratt's Bat to make the game bat feel lighter and also to strengthen the wrists and forearms. It's also a good idea to tape the wrists for added stability.

2. **Get farther back in the box** (more time to see the pitch and thus extend the arms). Move closer to the plate (for better extension in front of the plate on that inside pitch). Bring the hands farther away from the body and at the bottom of the "treasure chest" (to get around and under the ball). Use the open or coil stance (for better vision and more use of the lower body). Widen the feet (for better balance and lower center of gravity) and crouch (bend the knees).

3. **Before the pitch be as still as possible.** Be moving in the stance, but don't be jumping around in the box. Trust instincts and reactions. Once deciding to swing, forcefully go through with it.

4. **Collapse the back knee, lean into the pitch, and get under the ball.** Open the front foot slightly (away from the plate). Some hitters even land on the heel. Try to get lift to the ball.

5. **Stay semi-upright in the stance.** Power is lost if the front leg is bent. Though many sluggers release the top hand on contact, keep both hands on the bat. The two-handed swing starts the wrist turnover earlier and isolates more power at a given instant (when trying to pull a pitch).

6. **Think full extension on contact.** Rely more on getting to the ball quickly and less on "swinging through it." Finish high with the bat.

7. **Know the power zone and which pitches one can drive.** Left-handers seem to love the low inside fastball. Right-handers like the inside pitch up in the zone. Home run hitters do guess, but take the mentality that a hitter gets three swings to work with. So don't get cheated up there.

Strength and Power

The power hitter should work on starting the swing as quickly as possible with the most effective use of force, and accelerate to the greatest possible speed until contact is made. Even though only five-foot-seven and 175 pounds, I was able to hit a lot of home runs during my high school and college career. I never went up there thinking home run; almost every one of them was a line drive. Think stride-and-cock, weight back, driving into and through the ball, weight room work, aggressiveness, and the hardest swing possible. So the bigger the hitter, the farther the ball should travel. But it all takes discipline and hard work. Kids shouldn't be satisfied being just a singles hitter. Home runs are nice, but RBIs and scoring runs are even better.

Batting Average

Hitting for average means statistics. Baseball loves stats, especially since MLB has been keeping records of player accomplishments for over 100 years. The Elias Sports Bureau has the most complete and detailed baseball statistics. If stats weren't important, hitters wouldn't be heralded for their .300-plus averages, home run blasts, and RBI totals. Dare to be great. Focus on your kids being the best in the division, league and beyond.

Preach to the kids to try and reach base every time via a hit or hard contact. Don't just go up there looking for a base hit. One may draw a walk, have to put a bunt down, or even lace a double down the line. Don't think about batting averages or career totals. The only stat that matters is wins and losses.

Hitting is probably the most selfish act in sports. No one can help a hitter once in the batter's box. Plus, the pitcher controls the action. Don't show stats to the team until *after* the season. Have the kids focus on the team and success as a group. Have fun mostly. Later on reward the players for effort, desire, and overall performance. Play the game for the game, never just for the statistics.

8

Bat Speed

"When your hands are strong, all you have to do is get the hands to the ball. Once you generate bat speed, everything else takes care of itself."
— Gary Sheffield, 1992 NL Batting Champ

Introduction

Good hitters have bat speed. It doesn't come naturally, and it has to be worked on every day. By definition it's how quickly the hands can get to the ball. It's mind-boggling how the body can generate enough force beginning from a stationary position to hit a ball dipping, spinning, and moving in ways difficult to even catch — let alone get a base hit.

How can bat speed be used to hit a 90 mph Roger Clemens fastball? Heck, driving a car that fast is dangerous. Then apply that velocity to fouling good pitches off, getting jammed, and being fooled on breaking balls. The first step is using a bat that can generate the best possible velocity for the individual hitter. To hit Clemens, or anyone for that matter, one needs to have a quick bat, to meet the ball squarely, and to be in control throughout the swinging phase. So whether a big-leaguer or a 12-year-old, anyone can achieve bat speed. It made me into a great hitter.

Bat Velocity and Impact

There's a lot happening when one hits a baseball: bat head velocity and speed of the pitch, overall mass of the hitter, bat and ball, and all of these things coming together upon impact with the ball, hopefully on the "sweet spot." Obviously the faster the pitch, if everything is done correctly from the hitter's perspective, the farther the ball should go. The slower pitch (breaking balls) is designed to screw up a batter's timing.

Speed-Swings

The "easiest" way to get quicker is to simply swing the bat. Try to get the heavier wood bats (same lengths as your aluminums) to use in practice. Keep swinging until the kids get exhausted. The wrists, forearms, and hands will throb and burn. Relax and wait a few seconds between swings. Then do a few more sets.

Assess off-season dedication with a bat speed test at the first practice. See how many quality swings the hitters can do in three and a half minutes. Stress quality before quantity. Use batting gloves here as the hands may become severely blistered (apply pickle juice or vitamin E for faster healing). Build up calluses around the base of the fingers. Take care of the hands (i.e. encourage feet-first vs. head-first slides), because they do all of the damage at the plate.

Attack the Ball

Every time a kid picks up a bat, imagine it being their last swing ever. They should attack the ball with ferocity and aggression. Bats cost a lot of money (sometimes up to $200), so get your money's worth by swinging them hard. The ball is the enemy.

Line the team up and practice this "last swing" phenomenon. Swing as hard as possible and grunt. Then grunt louder and louder. Try to heard in the next town over. Then swing altogether without the grunt. You should hear a nice swoosh sound since every bat is being swung in harmony. Before you know it, the team is fired up. Boxers punch as hard as possible looking for a knockout. Pitchers throw hard trying to blow the ball past the hitter. Line drives can only occur with the same mentality. A game day tip: get up in the batter's box for those slower pitchers. Move up there and rip!

To fully view the intensity of a swing, set up a "demolition derby." Affix an automobile tire to a pole. Have the kids take aggressive practice swings into the tire. Bales of hay also suffice. Taped-up football tackling pads can also used for this (only use aluminum practice bats for this drill). Remember, hitting hard makes hitters happy!

How Many?

Basic steps to strengthen the wrists and forearms include swinging the bat, squeezing tennis balls, and dribbling a basketball. Start with rounds of 25 to 50 baseball bat swings with a 30- to 60-second break between each set. Swings should be done in consistent groups or sets, as in lifting weights. Increase the number each week. The bat should feel light in the hands. Do speed swings in front of the TV or before bed. Take three to five speed swings before a game at-bat. This prepares the hitter for the quickness needed to catch up with the ball.

Swing in the Pool

Kids can swing a wooden bat in the pool. Start with the hands underwater, and swing as hard as possible. It's more difficult than simply swinging a regular bat, and the water applies more resistance. Since the water serves as a buffer, movement is enhanced without threat of injury. After a time the bat will become waterlogged. Swing until feeling tired, relax and rest, and then repeat the same number of swings. After swinging in the pool, swing a regular bat out of the water shortly thereafter. This adds to better bat control, feel and confidence. Also, bringing a team to the pool breaks up a traditional practice.

Bat Wrap Drill

Have hitters face a tee with the bat head pointing at the ball (wrapped around the head). The top-hand wrist should be above the bottom. Now explode the bat back and down to the ball. It's not easy, but this facilitates a fluid and forceful swing (similar to the loop and hammer). Add in soft toss and close-range BP. The batter has to be that much quicker.

Bratt's Bat

Kids can swing the Bratt's Bat to increase bat speed and power. This bat is manufactured by the Bratt Corporation in Holden, Massachusetts, and Dick Bratt and his father have sold the weighted practice bat all over the country and to the majors. Use it to increase bat speed and as a warmup device.

The heavier bat, which comes in various lengths and weights, forces the hitter to work. The weight is distributed along the barrel, where it's most needed and more efficiently utilized. That's why hitters love the big-barreled bats with thin handles. With more area to smack the ball, the greater chance for a smash. The Bratt's Bat can weigh almost as twice as much as a regular bat, but should increase a hitter's batting average and power. Donuts make the bat feel top-heavy. The Bratt's Bat weight is more evenly distributed, which adds to better control. After swinging it, the arms feel

Swing a heavy bat. (Steve Berg)

stronger as in lifting weights. Then swing a regular bat; it feels lighter. The batter has more confidence to hit or foul off any pitch. It's an advantage for an aggressive style of play. Swing this bat with two hands to avoid straining the arm (i.e. top-hand-released swing).

In my first year as a college head coach in 1996, my shortstop at Worcester State (Jason Akana) hit .514 to lead the nation (all college divisions). Akana, who had never trained with the bat before, swung the Bratt's Bat virtually every day from September 1995–May 1996. This included speed swings, live BP/drills with tennis balls, and before game at-bats. Standing only five-foot-four, the senior leadoff hitter had 54 hits in 105 at-bats in 27 games. He hit .311 in 1995 — an improvement in 1996 of 203 points. Upon graduation, he played professionally with the Meridien, Mississippi, Breakmen of the Big South Independent League. The Worcester State team, also using the bat for the first time, hit .335 to place 31st in the NCAA, Division 3, (they hit .307 in 1995). This started a streak of eight straight years of placing among the nation's best team batting averages. My hitters have also led in individual categories, including slugging percentage and doubles.

Use the heavier Bratt's Bat for a power drill (full two-handed swings), and the smaller models for one-handed swings (soft toss with tennis balls), a live close-range BP quickness drill, and to improve the compact swings of each hitter (i.e. keeping the hands in close to the body). Use it for speed swings, during dead time, or as a warmup device.

The Bratt's Bat slows the swing down in order to analyze strengths and weaknesses. Is the kid swinging down on the ball? Is he/she falling backwards? Can the hitter stay balanced throughout? Work and talk to the kids about which Bratt's Bat is best for them.

The Donut

The donut-shaped weight slipped onto the end of a bat has been around forever. But it's lost pretty frequently, gets stuck in the middle at the wrong times during a game, and makes the bat feel top-heavy. Also, refrain from filling bats with sand. They're too heavy and create bad habits.

Some sort of weighted device can develop that added quickness. If golfers today are into weight lifting, conditioning and the like to get bigger, stronger, quicker, faster — just to drive the ball farther off the tee — shouldn't hitters of all ages continue to work on a quick swing?

9

Mental Preparation
and Confidence

"You've got to concentrate on each play, each hitter, each pitch. All this makes the game slower and much clearer. It breaks it down to its smallest part. If you take the game like that — one pitch, one hitter, one inning at a time, and then one game at a time — the next thing you know, you look up and you've won."
— Rick Dempsey, 1983 World Series MVP

Introduction

I take you back to my seventh grade industrial arts class. Part of my midterm was to rebuild a faucet from the parts located in front of us — blindfolded. At first I was terrified, but after some soul-searching decided that the only way to pass this exam was to concentrate on the task at hand. I visualized the manual and my learning about plumbing that year. My memory enabled me to connect the parts and then calmly re-check my work at each stage. After a while the faucet had been successfully built. I was pretty proud and relieved.

The same can be said about visualizing the pitch. Hitters should think about connecting the bat to the ball just I connected the washer to the nut. Remember: Relax, take a deep breath, be positive, think rationally and logically, and never give in.

Visualize Being the Best

Hitting is all about confidence. I was always a confident hitter, but my

Stay focused. (Steve Berg)

coaches throughout the years kept harping about being the best, outworking the opposition, being "The Man" up there at the plate — never giving at inch and believing anything was possible.

Visualization techniques include seeing the pitch before a game and especially before an at-bat. Hitters have to focus on the ball in the pitcher's hand and determine grip just before release. See that imaginary pitch and where it might break. First a fastball down the middle, then a looping curveball, and finally a slider painting the outside corner. Pick a pitcher to face. Put your kids at the ballpark with a full count and the bases loaded. Go through counts, situations and strategies. Get into that game day frame of mind. Hitting prep means better reaction during the game. Be ready at all times. With confidence in a pressure situation, success is always a possibility. And think about that last inning with your team behind by a run. Hitters that inning should be telling each other, "Get me up there. Get on base, and I'll drive you in. I want to hit with the game on the line." *Note*: Go for the win if you're the visitor and the tie if you're at home (game can end in the last at-bat).

Go the next step by having kids act out these moments where the game will be played the next day. Feel the dirt and smell the grass. Get used to the surroundings.

Some players get physically prepared for competition by eating a high-carbohydrate meal (i.e. spaghetti) the night before a game. All hitters should get mentally prepared as well. Lie in bed, close the eyes, and begin thinking about the contest. Think only positive thoughts: solid base hits and driving in the winning run. Have players to whom everyone looks for the big hit.

Since hitters fail so often, constantly reinforce the positive. Relaxation also strengthens the will to win. Combining concentration and relaxation helps to increase a hitter's attention span — vital for the at-bat lasting about two to five minutes.

Relax

Positive thoughts relax the hitter. Negative thoughts only lead to confusion, stress, and overanalyzing a situation. Football stresses aggression, because the game involves heavy contact. Not so in baseball. Calm players rise above the pressure. And never worry about who *might* be pitching; for that matter never be concerned even if a team's ace is hurling against you. Want to face the best. There's just as much pressure on the pitcher to throw strikes as there is on the hitter trying to hit them.

Other tips include listening to soft and comforting music such as sounds from the forest or ocean. The non-threatening remedies help the individual to visualize performance in a Utopia-like setting.

Muscular Relaxation

Relaxation is the opposite of movement. Have kids lie down in a quiet room and close their eyes. Contract each of the major muscle groups and inhale deeply. Hold the contraction for about three seconds. Then relax the muscles while exhaling. Repeat these routines until feeling comfortable: (1) face and neck: put the chin on the chest; (2) arms and hands: make tight fists and bend the arms; (3) trunk: tighten the stomach and bring the shoulder blades together; and

(4) legs and feet: bend the knees, ankles and toes.

Sometimes highly excitable players want to succeed more than anyone. That's fine. However, leave the cheering in the dugout. The batter's box must be a place of solitary confinement. Some players relax by playing cards, watching a game on TV, or listening to music on headphones. Hear the bat hitting the ball, and imagine where it travels. Put your kids in those future moments.

Sleep

Sleep is a fundamental need to living, and relaxation is the key to it. Try "power naps" before big games to get the body at ease. Do 15 to 20 minutes but no longer. Kids will wake up refreshed and focused. When we sleep our bodies are relaxed, which means the heart and breathing rates slow down and the blood pressure falls.

Concentration

Concentration, just as in hitting, takes time to master. Don't let the kids get frustrated or upset during interruptions. Relax and adjust to changing circumstances, but take the same approach to each at-bat. A hitter can perform the following exercises the night before a game:

(1) Recite the alphabet, and picture each letter. (2) Count from one to 100. Picture each number, and progress to 500. (3) Hold a baseball. Find a distinctive feature as the focus point, such as a letter or part of a seam. Concentrate on this feature for one minute. Progress slowly for five minutes. (4) Find a distinctive object in the room. Concentrate on that object for one minute while blocking everything out. Progress slowly for five minutes. (5) Close the eyes. Concentrate on inhaling and exhaling for one minute. Progress slowly for five minutes. (6) Concentrate on the second hand of a wristwatch for one minute. Progress slowly for five minutes.

Highlight Tapes

On bus rides or at a team dinner before a big game, watch a highlight videotape or listen to a motivational cassette tape. Watch *The Greatest Finishes in Sports* or relive memorable World Series. These moments bring out the champion in all of us. Choose movies to pick up the spirits. Thinking positive thoughts, and not dwelling on the pressure of a game, is the key here.

Former LSU baseball coach Skip Bertman showed highlight tapes in the locker room during an opponent's batting practice. Bertman, who won five NCAA titles, wanted his players to get into a positive frame of mind. He also posted motivational quotes in the locker room as well.

Show inspirational films like *Rocky*, *Miracle*, *Field of Dreams* and *The Natural*, or even those WWF wrestling extravaganzas that kids seem to love. Whatever works, use it. Just like playing pregame music that the players want to listen to, it's not about what the coach likes. Let the kids be kids.

Have a Game Plan

Never have a batter go to the plate with only one thing in mind, "I have to get a hit." A game plan applies for coaches and hitters alike. Being able to adjust to changing circumstances separates the thinker from the hacker. Hackers are too aggressive and make more outs. Thinkers draw walks, drag bunt, move runners over, hit-and-run, put the ball in play, and don't strike out as much.

Baseball is a thinking man's game. There's no time limit. Use strategy over strength and stamina. Try tactics to frustrate the pitcher and defense. On any given day, a team has the potential to win no matter how successful or talented. This can be said of very few sports. The only ingredient is an inner drive for success. So if you have a chance to win a game, do it. Remember: Sometimes you win, sometimes you lose, and sometimes it rains. Never worry or plan around the weather. Win today, and focus on tomorrow when that day arrives.

Dugout Preparation

When in the dugout, encourage the kids to key into the action. Have them talk with other hitters about the game so far. Think about future situations (i.e. two outs, man on third, possible drag bunt, etc.). Make adjustments from the last at-bat. Log this into the memory bank and apply it as the game moves along. Be prepared, relaxed, loose, and armed for success. Have the bat readily accessible whenever possible.

On-Deck Circle

Before stepping to the plate, there should also be two people getting loose. Let's call it the "on-on-deck circle." This gives hitters more time to get game ready. Be prepared early on, especially in a seven-inning game where a player may get only three at-bats. Take nothing for granted.

Get loose. (Steve Berg)

Prepare in the dugout three batters beyond the person at the plate — no matter how many outs. Find a helmet, adjust the batting gloves, and get the game bat. For example, in the first inning the number four batter should be ready in the dugout with numbers two and three warming up in the on-deck area.

Many things can occur in the on-deck circle. Hitters should look for a consistent approach each time. First, always stand in the circular spot or designated on-deck area. Warmup bats are located here, and the hitter isn't in the way of the bench coach giving signals to base runners, for example. Second, being closer to the plate provides a better look for pitching (velocity and movement) and catching clues (setting up the hitter). Third, one is out of the way of a potential foul ball. Fourth, give sliding directions to a scoring runner(s), and always get the bat out of the way so no one steps on it. Lastly, when your team is hitting, designate a player to retrieve pitched balls that go to the backstop. On-deck hitters shouldn't be chasing balls when they should be focusing on the game and getting ready to hit.

Note: Umpires can and do enforce batters standing in the on-deck circle (avoid interference with fielders), coaches standing in the base coaching boxes (halting coaches trying to steal the catcher signals), and players standing in the dugout (safety from foul balls, and not interfering with play of a potential errant throw into foul territory). Umps may also enforce keeping one foot in the batter's box. And no matter what an umpire says to a team, repeat the instructions out loud so everyone hears him and to reinforce the rules, especially for bench jockeying. Also, know and relay the ground rules to the entire team before the game, especially fields with tricky outfield fences and bushes/trees. Make sure all equipment is stored in the dugout or against the backstop, so fielders don't trip on anything. And read, know, and have the rulebook handy in the dugout for all games.

Stretch out. (Bruce Baker)

A Recipe for Stepping to the Plate

Hitters should take the same approach before an at-bat in the dugout and on-deck circle, first stepping in the batter's box, between pitches, and when swinging the bat. Just as families rely on special ingredients for a spaghetti sauce, the recipe travels from generation to generation. Never mess with success. Hitters can try the following:

- Find a bat and helmet, and adjust the batting gloves (if used).
- Drink a glass of water.
- Take a deep breath, and walk to the on-deck circle.
- Bend down and touch the toes. Do three trunk twists side-to-side.
- Do three arm circles with the bat in each hand.
- Take three to five quality swings with the Bratt's Bat.

- Time the swing against the pitcher by swinging the game bat.
- Bang dirt out of the cleats.
- Relax, stand/kneel, and watch the batter hitting.
- Take a deep breath, and walk to the plate.
- Check the positioning of fielders, signals, and dig in.
- Take another deep breath.
- Grip the bat, get plate coverage, and have movement (stance).
- Just before the pitch, take another deep breath, stride and swing.

Some Questions to Ask

- How will the pitcher throw to me in this at-bat?
- What are my strengths and weaknesses against this pitcher?
- What's the situation, and what's my job for this particular at-bat?

- What did he/she get me out on the last at-bat or previous game?
- What's the pitcher's favorite pitch early, during, and later in the count?
- How has the pitcher been throwing to other hitters in the lineup?
- What pitch should I look to drive?
- Anything about the ballpark (fence, dimensions), weather conditions (wind, rain, sun), or defense (weak, strong, positioning) that may effect this at-bat?
- How hard is he/she throwing, what are his/her favorite pitches, strike/ball ratio, and what can I or the base runners do to rattle him/her?

The Pit

Have hitters step into the batter's box. Take the mentality of being in a pit with a tiger. It's you and a savage animal, and it's time to do battle. It's you against the pitcher — the ultimate one on one competition. There's no one else to coach or motivate you. You're on center stage. Be the person of the hour. Your weapon is an aluminum or wooden bat. Dig that back foot in the dirt, and stare the pitcher down just like boxers do in the pre-fight meeting. Concentrate and focus. It's showtime, and the lights are shining. Stars are made here. The strong survive. The weak go home.

A lot happens in the pit. (Bruce Baker)

Vision

Pitchers can't wear jewelry (reflects off the sun and can be a distraction) outside the uniform or a white undershirt (same color as the baseball). Be aware of glare from car headlights or a fan's wristwatch. Have kids call time out, and ask the umpire to have these objects moved or removed.

Against common belief, and if you have quality lights, hitters can see the ball better at night because there is never any glare from the sun. Obviously big-leaguers play the majority of games under the lights to please the TV and the nine-to-five working audience during the week. I also like the night game mentality, especially for youth players; parents can see the games, and you're not rushing right out of school to get to the game on-time. Plus, the energy/focus level is usually heightened at night, and most of the time you're not playing in sweltering heat.

Eye black does reduce the sun glare a bit, and hitters are now getting smart by wearing sunglasses to the plate. At sunny late-afternoon games with those tricky shadows, have hitters try to drive that first good pitch that they see. This also goes for a hard-throwing closer coming in to save a game. They'll most often try to get ahead of the batters to avoid walking anybody in a tight contest. On rainy days make sure to wipe the brow of the helmet, so water doesn't drip over the eyes, and cover all of the equipment. Have a towel in the on-deck circle for every game.

Lastly, base umpires may stand in an unfavorable spot in the infield. Simply ask the home plate umpire to move him/her. The base umpire should stand behind the mound on either side depending on the pitcher's throwing shoulder (hard focus).

Techniques for Improvement

You need near perfect vision to be a good hitter. Whether it's glasses, sport goggles, contacts, or laser eye surgery, proper vision is vital.

Test for the dominant eye by holding a finger out front at arm's length. Focus on it until it becomes blurry and two fingers appear. Close one eye and then the other. One eye should focus better on the finger. That's the dominant eye. Note that the left eye is closest to bat-ball contact for a left-handed hitter (my own dominant eye), and the right eye for a right-handed hitter.

A lot of things are happening when one decides to swing at a pitch. The brain, body, and vision are all making split-second decisions and movements. Batters need to make adjustments in timing, judge speed, and use focus and concentration. That's why not moving the head, following the path of the ball with the eyes, and then using the hands to go with the pitch is how you're suppose to hit correctly. If the head moves the hitter gets an incorrect view instead of proper depth perception of the pitch. Keep the plane level; baseball events happen in a straight line. Hone the swing in practice, and make it the same in a game. Don't jump at pitches, fling the head out, or spin around in the box like an oil drill.

Create proper muscle memory for your team; train the body to swing correctly, use the body and mind together, and make this something one can repeat without even thinking about it. I remember reciting a short story in my high school English class. I just did it so many times that the words simply came out. But doing it in front of your classmates and for a grade, that's where relaxation, proper breathing, concentration, and a positive attitude can assist the student/athlete. And when I really needed to concentrate and work on specific things at the plate, sometimes I'd mumble to myself: "Stay back," "be quick," "stay closed," or "see the ball."

Hitters focus on the pitcher's head and then the ball just as it's coming out above the shoulder. Practice balls (which consist of colored portions) are sold today for hitters and pitchers to recognize the various pitches. For example, a slider is suppose to look like a spinning red circle. There's even a motion-picture batting cage on the market today called ProBatter to let the batters hit against a pitcher. There's a video screen and a ball actually coming at the hitter — just as that particular hurler would throw. It's pretty amazing.

Confidence

Confidence isn't something one is born with. It's earned through repeated experiences both in victory and defeat. Professional athletes, businessmen, and scholars all possess it. In reality, one can only be a good hitter with confidence. I remember back to Little League when our coach bought champagne in preparation for us winning the league championship series. We lost, but the precedent of expecting and knowing you're going to win was put in my head from early on and continues to this day.

I Know I Can Do It

Avoid using the following words: can't, won't, don't, wouldn't or couldn't.

Those words aren't found in a winner's dictionary. Anything is possible. No pitcher is unbeatable. No deficit is insurmountable. We were once down 10–0 after the first inning and won 13–12. From 1996 to 2005, my teams had won 36 games in our last at-bat. It's called "Baker Ball." We'll play anyone, anywhere, any time. We've swept nationally ranked teams, looked to play the defending College World Series champion, and played for a championship every season from 1998 to 2005. When you surround winners with winners, wins happen.

I witnessed two amazing comebacks in 2003. Grafton Hill Legion Post scored seven runs in the ninth inning to tie its state semifinal contest with Fall River, Massachusetts, at 10–10 — the tying blow coming on a three-run homer. Then it was Texas scoring six runs in the last inning of the L.L. World Series to tie its game with Massachusetts, who eventually won in extra innings.

Those who can't...never will. Remember the children's book, *The Little Engine That Could*. That little train was going to reach the top of the mountain no matter what. Negative thoughts never crept into its mind. A hitter can do anything he/she sets their mind to. One may fail, but a winner can be satisfied in putting forth a 100 percent effort at every practice and game. Harp on this adage. Don't just tell the kids to get a hit. Show them, work with them, motivate, instruct; be their coach and confidant.

Never Be Satisfied

Have your players strive to go four for four every game no matter what. A lot of batters get two hits in a game and take lazy swings in later at-bats. Why?

They're satisfied. And never be happy after getting a few hits in a team's loss. Winners have goals that focus on preparation and perfection. Preach that a hitter is only as good as the last game. Try to take the same approach for every game, whether it's intensity from the bench or a more quiet mentality. Don't be a light switch and only turn up the heat when it's a big game. Every game is a big game. Overcome those groundouts and fly balls by picking each other up — today and tomorrow.

Stay Positive

In a game so mentally draining and lasting so long, hitters of every age have to stay positive. Golfers and hitters probably go through more frustration and must practice more than any other athlete, basically because all diamonds/ courses are different and hitters face a different pitcher each game. A great saying during a down time is, "The only place for us/you to go is up." Turn negative situations into something positive. The glass should always be half-full, not half-empty.

Talk to every player at every practice and at every game. Daily greetings, even a simple hello, show that you care about them as players and people. Get in their heads on a positive angle. Talk hitting, school, improvements, whatever you see fit. Challenge them and explain how their roles help the team win. Shake hands during stretching, tell a joke, or put an arm around a struggling hitter. And ask questions and encourage non-baseball topics.

When dealing with the media, be careful what you say. Players only respect a coach who believes in them. Never verbally knock a team. Mention the team, generalities, give credit to the kids and assistant coaches, take it one game at a time, and always be positive. Find out what the players find effective and not effective for the team. Have an informal yet confidential form for them to fill out before the first practice. Even stay in contact with them during the off season. And when confronting a player, do it without causing a scene.

Fear No One

The Five Cs: Confidence, Cocky, Courage, Calm, Clutch

No matter what size, talent, game situation, or record, the best hitters fear no one. They want to face the best as a measuring stick. Youngsters first deal with fear when a ball either hits or just misses them in a game. It's like falling off a bike for the first time. Some kids even quit baseball for fear of being plunked. Others survive and strive for excellence. Some successful hitters are in "the zone" (a state of mind when the ball seems slower and larger than usual). Not only do hitters have to block out the fear of being hit by a wild pitch, but they also used the confidence of having a positive at-bat each time up.

Believe one can defeat the pitcher on any given day. Don't be timid if a hard thrower is hurling. Kids should demand to bat in those like-handed situations. Never be intimidated by another person. If knocked down, get right back up. Believe that a base hit is the only option. Swing to hit the ball instead of swinging not to miss. We're all human beings with strengths and weaknesses. Assume the hitting position and come up clutch.

There's a difference between being cocky and arrogant. Arrogant players tell everybody how good they are. Cocky/ confident players show it. Expect to hit a double, and don't take a home run trot around the bases like it was the first time ever. And those with a big mouth better be ready to back it up.

Reggie Jackson once said, "Fans don't boo nobodies." Winners visualize being the best and stepping up to the plate in pressure situations. That means staying calm. The key to overcoming stress is to relax, breathe, and focus on the pitcher and baseball. Kids play pickup games emulating the many great World Series home runs. They see themselves up in the bottom of the ninth with the basesloaded, two outs, and the team down by three runs. We don't feel pressure in the back yard, so why let it get to us on the field?

The more competition, the more accustomed to pressure the hitter becomes. Nerves are part of risky situations. Think confidently, and step up in clutch situations. Teams have rally hats and sometimes won't leave a particular seat on the bench during such moments. During a comeback or rally ask the bench, "Are you starting to get wet? Because the dam is breaking." Never be overconfident, because baseball is a humbling game. As Mike Schmidt said, "Any time you think you have the game conquered, the game will turn around and punch you right in the face."

Role of the Coach

It's dumbfounding to see coaches criticizing and ridiculing hitters at a game and especially during an at-bat. Hitting is mentally draining and slumps can occur very easily. Provide positive reinforcement, especially since the pitcher invariably wins more often. How many times does a team get more hits than outs? Almost never.

Be aware of verbal and nonverbal actions. Make sure kids walk to the plate with a purpose and carry themselves like winners. Know that kids do remember a lot, both positive and negative. Reward success and effort, but be aware that support is needed more during a slump or negative result. It's easy to criticize a bad play and praise a good one. Give confidence by applauding an aggressive swing instead of yelling for not swinging at a strike.

Teams should salute hits and outs. After an out jog back to the dugout. Forget a poor at-bat and focus on the defensive part of the game and subsequent at-bats. Try to "pick up" every hitter who comes back to the bench (handshake or pat on the back). This shows support of teammates, no equipment will be tossed, and the other team sees that you stick together. No one is perfect. And remember, you win and even lose as a team.

Refrain from too much information right before an at-bat. For example, a former coach of mine once said to me, "We may hit-and-run on the second pitch, so be awake." While I was focusing on the second pitch, the first one was the one I wanted to rip. Focus one pitch at a time. Yes, signals are important in a game, but players can see a play signaled from a coach without worrying about it beforehand.

Never speak about a pitcher's superiority or prior success (i.e. win-loss record or high velocity) before or during a game. Provide information to the team (i.e. pitches the kid throws, where he/she falls off the mounds, etc.), but don't scare them. That's why I hate statistics so much. The best pitcher in the league just may not have it one day. And that goes for inferior pitchers as well. Every pitcher is good when they're facing my team.

Work on focus and reaction and avoid overanalyzing the situation. Here are some confidence builders to use in the on-deck circle: "There's nobody better." "Hey, good hitter." "You're the best." "You have to have a lot of confidence against this pitcher." "The pitcher doesn't want to face you." "This kid is nothing." "All of the pressure is on the mound." "You're swinging the bat better than ever." "We need a fire extinguisher because you're smokin'." "You better call out the National Guard 'cause there's going to be an air raid." "Stay hot." "Have a hit." "No takes." "Step up." "Stay aggressive." "You go...we go." And the one I love most, "You're so hot the pitcher should get down and bow to you." Use these to motivate the individual, not to rile up the other team.

Different hitters need to be dealt with differently. Some may need more confidence than others. Some may be better off with nothing said to them at all. Be consistent in team rules and discipline, but take mental notes on which buttons to push for each player. But for all, emphasize the continuation of strengths and improvement on weaknesses.

Relax by Breathing

Every hitter should be able to take three to four deep breaths before an at-bat. When you breathe, you relax the muscles and mind. Hitters need to be relaxed (i.e. state of reading a good book). Being relaxed has to do with patience, pitch selection, focus, temperament and concentration. One tip is to avoid caffeine and sugar before games, because at some point one has to come down from that "high."

The mental aspect of hitting goes hand in hand with the physical. Since the swing must be accomplished in such a short period of time, it must almost be a non-conscious action. When thinking about swinging, the body just seems to do it. This applies to the person singing the National Anthem. One can't think about the words; they must flow out from habitual memorization. The same goes for hitting: Trained reflexes triggering a forceful swing. Simplify hitting to the following: See the ball and hit it.

Rewards

Use simple rewards for hitting technique, hard work and success. Implement postgame running relating to the execution of fundamentals. For example, not scoring a runner from third base with less than two outs results in one full sprint around the bases. Good teams practice and preach the basics over and over, and know that they do decide games. Go to a movie after a victory. And award a case of soda to those who hit a homer.

10

Common Mistakes

"Baseball is a lot like life. The line drives are caught, the squibbers go for base hits. It's an unfair game."

— Rod Kanehl, Former Mets Infielder

Introduction

At one time or another, every coach will see the mistakes listed in this chapter. Some kids have fundamental flaws caused by misinformation, and others have had poor swings due to what the pitched ball did on its flight to the plate. Read about the mistakes here, refer back to previous sections, and learn to correct these for your team. Noticing a flaw is the easy part of coaching. Coaches who win develop hitters, provide remedies for mistakes, and work with the individual until improvement has been achieved. Here are the most common mistakes and corrections for them.

Mistake: Gripping the Bat Too Tightly

Reasons and Signs: Some players feel they need a tight grip to hit the ball hard and/or so the bat doesn't fly out of their hands. Thus, the wrists and arms don't have enough freedom for a smooth and relaxed swing. The motion seems awkward and tense.

Corrections: Use the Axe Bat for grip and Direct Protect for hand alignment.

Have a hitter point his/her index fingers, or even shake out their arms as a way to relax.

Poor grip. (Rex Baker)

Mistake: Improper Stance

Reasons and Signs: Watch how a hitter preps before batting. There's a problem if he/she seems ready once they step into the box.

Corrections: Have a game plan and purpose. Don't have kids just jump in and hit. Have a swagger. Start by touching

106

the far edge of the plate for complete coverage. The feet should be pointing at the plate with the front foot near the middle. Stand on the balls of the feet, bend the knees, lean over slightly, have the back arm level or relaxed, front elbow pointed to the ground, chin on Ike, two eyes on the pitcher, and have bat movement. Draw a line in the dirt as a physical reminder for a proper stride to the pitcher. Check for balance, weight shift, and flexibility with the "push-over drill" (from in front and behind). Remember the "treasure chest." Make sure the hands are four to six inches away from the body, underneath the back shoulder, and in line with the breastbone. Get in the stance and look in the mirror.

Mistake: Bat Wrap

Reasons and Signs: Bat wrap is an unconscious bad habit for "jumpy" or tense hitters. This flaw slows bat speed. Hitters lose valuable milliseconds in bringing the bat head forward (going in front of the head) instead of going directly down to the ball. This usually occurs in the cocking phase of the swing.

Corrections: Simply take the time to see if the bat is directly behind a hitter's head. Have them point the bat back to the backstop as a conscious reminder. Limit cocking, and drive the hands to the ball. The hitter may rest the bat on the shoulder; this position relaxes the body and saves energy. When the pitcher is ready to throw, lift the bat off the shoulder to be in the ready or launching position. Also, hit in front of a mirror. Tie a string to the bat head, and attach it to the backstop. See where the hitter and bat are. Or invest in the Shortstroke Trainer (see chapter on switch hitting) for a compact swing.

Bad bat angle. (Rex Baker)

Mistake: Shifting the Weight Too Soon

Reasons and Signs: This batter shifts all of the weight to the front leg. It's a common mistake of being ahead of a breaking ball. The back foot is released forward and up from the ground.

Corrections: Kids should dig the back foot in the dirt. Also, put a soda can behind the rear foot. Knock it over on each practice swing. This triggers proper foot/hip action and makes sure the weight is back on contact. Use the step-hit drill. Also hold the batter's back arm. Some hitters are prone to shifting the upper body during the stride. Reinforce this concept by creating resistance. Also, use the shadow drill.

Shifting the weight too soon. (Rex Baker)

Keep the hands up. (Rex Baker)

Mistake: Hitch

Reasons and Signs: Critics say hitching destroys the smooth swing. However, a hitch may be used as a cocking action (trigger for an explosive swing).

Corrections: Only change a hitch for the player not hitting line drives. Some physically weaker kids need a hitch. For all others, work on keeping a compact and smooth swing. For the hitchers, make sure the hands don't drop.

Mistake: Dropping the Hands

Reasons and Signs: For hitters whose hands start near the back shoulder (top of the strike zone), it's a natural instinct to drop down to swing. The difference lies in throwing the hands on a direct

Long Looping Swing

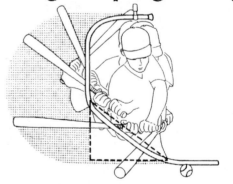

angle downward to the ball, not straight down and then across/up.

Corrections: Look to purchase the Gordie Gillespie Power Hitting Vest to cure this mistake. This patented Velcro vest attaches the torso to the front shoulder, which restricts the bottom hand from dipping. Use the vest with one or both hands on the bat. The Shortstroke Trainer also corrects the uppercut or looping swing. To correct casting or the long swing (too far down or around the ball), hold a rake handle under the back elbow for a correct bat path. After consciously concentrating on not hitting the rake, attempt to unconsciously concentrate on the swing and not the rake. Lastly, hold onto a fence/net with the top hand and swing with the bottom hand. This motion perpetuates a downward swing. Also, place a tee on home plate during soft toss or BP. The ball can only be hit by swinging down and over the tee.

Mistake: Dropping the Back Elbow

Reasons and Signs: This hitter swings up and hits pop-ups.

Corrections: Focus on swinging down. Think about balancing a glass of water on the back forearm. Make sure this arm is relaxed (i.e. flap the chicken wing). Then drive that front elbow to the ground. Also, see the review on dropping the hands.

Mistake: Pulling the Head and Front Shoulder Out

Reasons and Signs: Ike doesn't move to Mike (front shoulder in the stance to the back shoulder on the swing). This batter may be able to hit the inside pitch (closer to the hands), but rarely the outside. By pulling the front shoulder and head out, nothing is left to reach outside.

Corrections: Concentrate on the chin first resting on/near the front shoul-

No Mike. (Rex Baker)

der (Ike), stride, rotate the hips, bring the hands through the strike zone, and finish with the chin on the back shoulder (Mike). Do this without a bat (hands on the hips and then throw the hands at the ball). Vision is impaired when the eyes move within the sockets during quick jerks. So keep the head still.

Mistake: Stepping Too Early

Reasons and Signs: This is the overanxious batter too far out in front on contact. Some even step out of the box. Hits are pulled virtually every time with the outside pitch rarely utilized.

Corrections: Start farther back in the box. Work on a short stride. Read the ball upon release and step to the pitcher. Practice being patient and wait longer than usual. Stepping a bit later keeps the weight back. Improve on bat speed. During BP, throw primarily outside pitches. Consciously make the batter avoid pulling the ball, even taking inside pitches until getting an outside pitch to hit.

Mistake: Stepping in the Bucket

Reasons and Signs: Many youngsters "step in the bucket," insistent on pulling the ball while others are afraid of being hit. The front foot is thrown open and away from the plate/pitch. The hips, head, and front shoulder are improperly rotated out. Unless missed entirely, the batter can only pull the ball.

Corrections: Step to the pitcher.

Draw a box. (Rex Baker)

Draw a line in the dirt from the back foot, front foot, and to the pitcher. Note where the front foot lands on each swing. Also, place an actual footprint (shoe innersole) as a target for the front foot. For problematic feet, place hockey sticks or rope parallel with each foot (in front and behind). Then designate a special area for the front foot to land. Reinforce this drill later on without the physical barrier(s).

Mistake: Dead Back Foot

Reasons and Signs: The back foot is left planted in the stance. Weight may not even be transferred from the back side to the ball.

Corrections: The back foot should turn into the plate (remember the soda can drill) and elevate all in one motion. This action rotates the hips and promotes leg drive (low center of gravity). Without use of the lower body, this hitter swings only with the arms.

Mistake: Landing on the Heel

Reasons and Signs: Land on the balls of the feet and not on the heel (front

Step to the pitcher. (Rex Baker)

Dead Back Foot. Use the feet. (Rex Baker)

Use the balls of the feet. (Rex Baker)

foot). Some sluggers land on their heel to dip under the ball.

Corrections: Landing on the ball of the front foot promotes a downward swing. Kids should concentrate on "mashing the bug" (even keying on both feet) on contact. Go back to the weight shift drill and rocking back and forth in the stance. Also, watch for hitters who roll the front foot (away from the plate) and back foot over (into the plate). Balancing slightly on the back side of the front foot is fine.

Mistake: Opening the Front Foot

Reasons and Signs: This is another problem for power hitters who love to pull that inside pitch. The hips, front shoulder, and head all open up too far.

Corrections: Keep the front foot closed in the stance, stride and swing. And lean over the plate.

Mistake: Hitting the Ball Behind the Plate

Reasons and Signs: Watch for those hitters who are often behind or late on the pitch. Hits go to the opposite field — even on inside pitches.

Corrections: Use hand-eye coordination drills such as the dangling ball. Work on confidence in hitting the ball in front of the plate on the "sweet spot." Use the "slap the ball" drill, and even hit tennis balls wearing a wooden infield paddle on each hand. "Throw the hands" on each swing. There may also be a problem with vision. Work on soft and hard focus, use brand new baseballs in BP (easier to see), and get an eye exam. Lastly, never start with BP as a way to work on bat speed, trying to get out of a slump, or achieving full extension. Start with the tee, soft toss, close-range BP, and then top it off with live BP from regular distance.

Mistake: Poor Follow-Through

Reasons and Signs: The two-handed swing should finish with the bat behind a hitter. The top-hand-released swing should form a "V" with the bat and bottom-hand arm. Hitters with poor follow-through prematurely turn the wrists over and end the swing just after contact. You don't want slap hitters. You want kids to make contact, but concentrate on driving the ball. Some kids are even running to first base before they take a complete cut.

Corrections: End high with the bat (near the head), and "swing through the ball." Make a complete circle with the bat. This finish promotes bat speed, strength, and full extension. Realize that the ball has already been hit by the time the follow-through occurs. However, the swing must be forceful from start to finish or else bat speed will slowly begin to deteriorate. Think of shooting a basketball. Proper form needs to be maintained throughout the complete phase of any athletic skill. Lastly, swing and hold that finished stance for three seconds. Have the kids count out loud. Though many hitters fall into the plate (momentum takes over), each should be able to maintain balance of some kind after following through.

Hitting the Ball Behind the Plate. Get out front. (Rex Baker)

Poor Follow Through. End high. (Rex Baker)

Mistake: Indecision

Reasons and Signs: Indecision is a mental mistake. This hitter has few quality swings and looks at an abundance of good pitches. Watch out for the check swing, frustration after taking a strike, and weakly hit ground balls. Kids should never nod the head in agreement on a strike call — show zero emotion in the batter's box. And never take a pitch as a way to get ready to hit. One should be ready in the on-deck circle. The first pitch is usually a good one to hit. The only time a kid may want to take a pitch is the first curveball one sees in a game (i.e. to view the spin). Other than that, go up swingin'.

Corrections: An offensive mentality is to initiate the action. Don't let the pitcher dictate the game. Look to drive that first good strike, and avoid getting behind in the count. Take aggressive swings in practice and games. Grunt if need be. Take swings against a tire or bale of hay. Use a Bratt's Bat to make the regular bat feel lighter.

Stay positive. (Rex Baker)

Mistake: Lack of Confidence

Reasons and Signs: Lack of confidence shows up in a slump, losing streak, or against a difficult pitcher (i.e. like-handed confrontations). Watch for a kid who won't look you in the eye, walks to the plate with their head down, jumps into the batter's box without checking for signals or defensive positioning, doesn't seem interested, swings at the first pitch regardless of location, lacks discipline, or takes weak swings.

Corrections: Hitting is difficult and the most unfair skill in sports. Believe in your kids, and have them work the pitcher. Go back to the fundamentals, and avoid complicated drills or theories. Reward outs that are hard-hit. Use positive reinforcement. Encourage players to smile and hustle. Reinforce the adage: one pitch, one at-bat, and one game at a time. For Tee-Ball hitters, use those big plastic bats or even a tennis racket in soft toss (wide "sweet spot" for easier contact).

Conclusion

In the movie *Mr. Baseball*, Tom Selleck's character travels to Japan in an attempt to find his old swing and resurrect his career. His new coach takes Selleck off to hit soft toss with golf balls. The slugger crushes ball after ball to the far reaches of the driving range. With renewed confidence, the American goes on to a stellar season.

I've been on Little League, American Legion, college, and Cape Cod League teams where we've run early BP sessions (optional hitting in the cage) starting two to three hours before games. Then we run regular team BP on the field. Whether it's tee or soft toss work, close-range BP, or talking hitting, baseball needs to be worked on if you expect to succeed.

11

Switch Hitting

"Baseball is the only field of endeavor where a man can succeed three times out of ten and be considered a good performer."

— Ted Williams, Hall of Famer

Why Become a Switch Hitter?

All kids should experiment with switch hitting. If done correctly, this added component could be a most valuable asset. Children learning something naturally pick up habits and stay with them. Most never know why. I do everything right-handed: write, throw and eat. But I hit left-handed. It's just the way I picked up the bat as a kid. It would be interesting to see if newborns could be trained to throw with both hands and hit from both sides. But that's a study for another time.

Switch hitting has nothing to do with playing a position or even level of intelligence. The ability to switch hit is a skill — not an IQ level. Improvement comes with hard work and a proper mental approach. A skill must be worked on over and over until it becomes habit, similar to a basketball player dribbling with both hands and a soccer player kicking with both feet.

Right vs. Left

Society is dominated by right-handers. More Americans bat, write, golf, and shoot the basketball with the right hand than the left. We even run to the right side towards first base. The lefty population is simply outnumbered. It's just a freak of nature. So what we have is a game like baseball with the majority of players batting from the right side. Thus, those right-handed hitters should now be opening both of their eyes.

First, with more right-handed pitchers in the game, lefties have an advantage

The switch hitter. (Steve Berg)

of seeing pitches from a better angle — outside to in towards the plate instead of inside to out. It's much more difficult to react to a pitch coming from the inside portion of the body since many breaking pitches, for example, first appear to be coming at the head. That's why coaches sometimes pinch hit to get a better hitter-pitcher advantage (left-handed hitter vs. right-handed pitcher or right-handed hitter vs. left-handed pitcher).

Second, many left-handed batters throw right-handed. Their dominant right hand leads the swing. This hand generates more power than the top and can also better reach the outside pitch.

Third, a left-handed hitter is actually closer to first base. A hustling player with at least average speed should be able to generate two to three extra infield hits or drag bunts from that added step. Plus, with a runner on first base the left-handed batter has a much bigger hole on the right pull side since the first baseman has to hold the runner on, and the second baseman has to play over for a potential double play.

Fourth, look for left-handed batters and pitchers for these same reasons. And try to mix up the left-handed batters in the lineup; never play them back to back. This way pitchers can't get comfortable throwing to the same left-right batters in succession. Also, a left-handed pitcher usually gives a lineup a "different look." Most hitters aren't comfortable against southpaws, because so few players face lefties in practice.

Advantages of a Switch Hitter

The switch hitter has the initial advantage against any arm. They give opposing managers and players fits on pitch location, defensive strategy, and deciding whether or not to bring in a relief pitcher. A tired right-hander may be forced to stay in knowing a right-handed hitter bats next. The switch hitter may then be able to take advantage of a pitch left up in the strike zone.

Sidearm pitchers are a nightmare in like-handed batting scenarios. One moment that ball appears destined for the ear, and the next moment it drops over for a strike. But successful switch hitters rarely get pinch hit for and can play every day. They need to take the same approach on either side and against either arm. Add a steady defensive game, and the switch hitter can expect to see plenty of action throughout the season.

Ways to Go About Becoming a Switch Hitter

Rare talents, like pots of gold, include: left-handed pitchers, home run hitters, exceptional speed, and the elusive switch hitter. Switch hitters are essentially exceptional athletes, because they can perform acts few others can. It usually all starts in playing wiffleball or stickball as kids. The following all must be in sync from both sides of the plate: hand-eye coordination, plate coverage, comfortable stance, lead-arm extension, and consistency in hitting from both sides.

The only way to master a skill is to practice, practice, and practice some more. Remember, there are no true experts in this world, but hard workers get closer to that point than anyone else. Switch hitters must do double the work of the average player. Take the same number of swings from each side of the plate. The muscles and mind must be coordinated to work functionally in similar fashions from both sides.

First, a right-handed pitcher naturally builds up the right side of the body from thousands of throws. The individual must work the left side (stretching, rubber tubing exercises, or weight lifting) or else face an imbalance in strength.

Second, catchers and infielders naturally strengthen the hamstrings by crouching. Many position players have had hamstring problems, because running forward continually skews a balance between the hamstring and the now stronger quadriceps muscles.

Third, everyone has a dominant hand. One-handed swings are designed to strengthen both hands but mostly the non-dominant one. The bottom hand leads the swing. A switch hitter has the advantage in both scenarios. Attempt to build an equal distribution of quickness and strength on both sides of the body. This applies to speed swings, BP, soft toss, and even hitting prep.

The switch hitter should use a slightly open stance (vision) and use the same bat (unless there are problems in bat speed from the non-dominant side). Emphasize keeping the head down and "swinging through the ball." *Note*: The batter must stay either left- or right-handed after the first pitch against a particular pitcher unless a relief pitcher comes in during the middle of that at-bat. Note the arm of the starter before game day BP. But always hit from both sides during BP. So for the player who loves to hit, switch hitting reserves more total swings. Lastly, if one is going to be a switch hitter, do so for each plate appearance to gain the hitting advantage. Stay with the different stances unless a kid is slumping badly from a particular side. Keep working at it in practice, and stay confident with it in games.

For a drill, do speed swings while alternating the grip (left- and right-handed) on each swing while facing both directions. Left-right, left-right, and so on. Basically you swing one way, switch the grip, and then swing the other way. Try not to move the feet around too much.

Play a fun scrimmage where everyone has to play opposite-handed: hitting, throwing and catching. Even without a lot of gloves to throw left-handed, for example, simply catch with the left hand, take the glove off, and throw lefty.

Switch Hitting Device

Switch hitters should use the Shortstroke Trainer. Invented by Tim Hardison, president of Diamond City Baseball Inc. of North Carolina, this device simplifies the approach to hitting. The bat head is "loaded" or cocked behind the head and positioned for a short/compact swing down to the ball.

While switch hitters may have differing stances and difficulty hitting from their weaker side, the Shortstroke Trainer promotes a level swing, closed front shoulder, weight back, and an aggressive swing. Time is saved from the bat head (at the loaded position) to actual contact. The now quicker hitter can wait longer in recognizing the pitch and its rotation. Also, the hitter is less likely to be fooled by an off-speed pitch.

The unique track design prevents premature extension and restricts the bat head from dropping (long swing). Use the device for station work, at camps, or when hitting alone. Emphasize a proper stride. Too many youngsters lunge and look to pull the inside pitch for home runs. The trainer forces the eyes on the baseball with a short stride to the pitcher

Shortstroke trainer. (Tim Hardison)

while also working the entire field. The hands should never be in front of the rest of the body on contact.

The track (with five sizes) guides the bat to a ball resting on a tee. The height of the track and tee can be adjusted for the hitter and/or pitch or location. The trainer also comes with a permanent tee attachment — a pitching machine ball. Batters can continue to hit a real ball without chasing after it. It's a great device for switch hitters and for working on the compact swing. It corrects flaws such as bat wrap, the uppercut or looping swing, dropping the hands, and improper weight shift.

Switch hitters may also try Direct Protect (see chapter on grip). Since consistency is a key, this thumb device maintains proper grip in both stances and throughout the swing.

12

Pinch Hitting

"They'll keep you in there gener'ly, as long as you can hit. If you smack that ole apple, they'll send you out there if they've got to use glue to keep you from fallin' apart."
— Thomas Wolfe, author

Introduction

In Game 6 of the 1975 World Series, the Red Sox were on the verge of elimination. Down 6–3 in the eighth inning, the Reds appeared to have the series clinched. Bernie Carbo was summoned off the bench. He stepped to the plate with two runners on base and the task of bringing his team back to life. Carbo hit a bullet that landed in the center field bleachers to tie the game and sent the Boston faithful into a frenzy. The Sox were able to win the game on Carlton Fisk's homer in the 12th inning, but Fisk never would have had the chance to hit without Carbo's dramatic blast. Another Sox highlight occurred in 2003 when Trot Nixon launched a walk-off home run to center field in the 11th inning of Game 3 of the Division Series against the A's. Boston went on to win the series in five games.

There was also Game 6, final inning, of the 1985 World Series. With one out and the bases loaded, Dane Iorg of the Royals pinch hit with his team down 1–0. His broken-bat flare to right field scored two runs. The Royals won Game 6, and then Game 7 for an improbable comeback after being down three games to one. Credit Iorg for being the turning point in the Royals' first world championship.

Who Is the Pinch Hitter?

Each team starts nine position players for a game, but lineup cards should list the names of every roster player. Some names are included on the "starters" and "pitchers" list with the remaining names placed under "substitutes" at the bottom of the page. Even though the word "sub" has a negative connotation, players like Carbo and Iorg have gone down in baseball history for what they did as a substitute hitter. Pinch hitters perform the ultimate clutch task: Coming in cold off the bench with one shot to get a base hit.

The pinch hitter obviously is not an everyday starter, so skills lacked on the playing field must be sharpened off. But most players at some point in their careers are called upon to pinch hit. Each must know how to prepare for such an at-bat, what to expect, and how to perform under the added pressure. It's not an easy task. If pinch hitting was easy, it wouldn't mean as much when done correctly.

Three points to consider: (1) Every kid must play in every Little League game. Kids want to hit more than they want to play the field. So in a six-inning, 18-out game, make sure players are ready and willing to hit off the bench. (2) Pinch hitting is one way to get injured starters back into the groove. (3) Avoid using pinch hitters during tight ballgames in cold weather. Sitting for a long period of time in the cold makes getting loose for a single at bat difficult. Try to stay with the starters in these particular games.

Even more difficult than batting is pinch hitting, especially in a close contest. The pinch hitter is the one player the coach looks to when the game is on the line. At-bats come with the score tied. One sits all game, yet is asked to get the big hit. Sometimes the batter gets one swing. So why should a non-starter have to be so revered in a game dominated by starters?

Have the kids stay motivated and into the game. Know what the pitcher is throwing, and be mentally and physically prepared to hit, especially in the later innings. If kids want to get their name in the newspaper for a highlight hit, they have to be ready to play at all times. Prepare them by running sprints between innings, swinging a bat, stretching, talking to the starters, doing the scorebook, and even hitting in the batting cage while the game is going on.

Preparation

Perhaps the most dramatic of all pinch hitting exploits came in the 1988 World Series. Kirk Gibson's walk-off home run off Dennis Eckersley won Game 1, but did you know that he was hitting almost every inning in the runway between the dugout and locker room? He hit off a tee with the bat boy putting the balls back on between swings. Since a leg injury kept him out of the starting lineup, Gibson (MVP that season) was preparing for a possible late-inning at-bat. It was Gibson's only at-bat of the Series as the Dodgers beat the favored A's in five games.

Some coaches substitute to gain the opposite-hand advantage and replace weaker batters (numbers seven through nine) who may be coming up late in the game. Generally speaking, the better hitters (numbers one through six) appear at the top of the lineup to ensure more total at-bats each. Number nine may bat only twice in a six-inning game. If a kid is good enough to make a team, he/she should be good enough to play. Try to play everyone, so use the pinch hitter.

Here's the situation for a left-handed pinch hitter, for example. The game is tied in the seventh inning. Your team is batting. The hitter will probably get a shot against the starting right-hander, because he's allowed only two hits and one run. The coach, and the offense, needs a spark. The starters haven't been able to solve this pitcher. What should he/she do?

Have kid(s) do some hitting in the later innings when your team is out in the field. Work with another teammate, who may also get a chance to play, and do soft toss into a hitting net. Swing the Bratt's Bat, and hit in the cage. Live BP should be done to practice timing. Don't be too concerned with breaking balls or determining grip or spin. Get them in there and rip. While this is going on, have another player be the middle man to relay messages to and from the coaching staff. Never go off to the cages behind the outfield wall, for example, without making sure what the team needs first (in case of hitting the next inning). One isolated drill can be done against a nearby hill. Stand at the base of the hill and do soft toss. Swing level, so the balls roll back down.

If without off-field batting facilities, kids can simply swing a bat in or beside the dugout. Once in the on-deck circle, never rush. Do one's complete pre-hitting routine.

When do you tell kids about possibly pinch hitting? It all depends on the player. Try waiting until the half-inning before a possible appearance. Winners, on or off the bench, watch the flow of the game. You don't want a sub thinking too much about a situation, and as long as they're stretched and loose they'll have plenty of time to prepare. Never just send a kid up to the plate without knowing something about a possible at-bat. Always have a game plan for late-inning moves.

Preparedness wins games — not spontaneity. Never just toss the bats onto the field and expect to mash. Hitters, and soldiers for that matter, need to know what to expect from the enemy before walking into battle. Though a pinch hitter may fail — at least go down swinging. Just as in studying for an exam, the student will feel more relaxed and calm by looking over the material days in advance rather than cramming the night before. Advanced notification allows the pinch hitter time to stretch, relax, and concentrate on the situation at hand.

pitcher's 0-2 location, first pitch type to left- and right-handed hitters, and when the breaking ball has been typically thrown. Pinch hitters should look to drive that first good fastball thrown for a strike. Pitchers invariably go right after subs with the hard stuff— the mentality is that these players aren't starters for a reason, probably because of slow bat speed.

Think back to Francisco Cabrerra's Game 7 pennant-winning hit for the Braves over the Pirates in 1992. It was a 2–0 count, and everyone expected the pinch-hitting Cabrerra to take a strike with the tying and winning runs on base. However, Cabrerra looked "dead red" (fastball) and ripped a pitch to left field that scored two runs and put the Braves in the World Series.

The pinch hitter has only three strikes to work with. A first-pitch strike could be the best pitch of that entire at-bat. While some pitch hitters feel intimidated in a first-time appearance, take solace in the fact that the pitcher and fielders know nothing about the batter either. Heck, there's more pressure on the pitcher (or relief pitcher for that matter), because they're the one suppose to throw strikes and get outs.

The bench player can witness the pitches, velocity, movement, and location from the dugout. Treat the bench as the playing field — not the bleachers. However, understand that watching and actually hitting are two totally different views.

What to Think About

Take mental and physical notes during games. The pinch hitter doesn't have the luxury of processing clues after each previous at-bat, but can talk with the other hitters to find out about a

Be Aggressive

The definition of a pinch hitter is one who *hits*. Simple enough. Never look for a walk, especially in a blowout game. Display one's skills by getting as many swings as possible. Attempt to work the pitcher by fouling off pitches, going to a long count, and if the pitch is there, drive the ball. Take time in between pitches. Also, coaches love aggressive hitters (especially younger players trying to break into the starting lineup).

Mentality

The pinch hitter must have nerves of ice. Tune out the surrounding crowd and noise. Take a deep breath of air. Concentrate and focus. Take the mentality that each pitch is the last one ever. Since pinch hitters usually bat in the late innings, the game will probably be on the line. So be disciplined in games and practices. Swinging at non-strikes in practice will carry over to the game, and that goes for swinging for good strikes as well. Pinch hitters see fewer game day pitches, so it's a tough task. But relish the moment. Be the hero. And that goes even for pinch hitting in lopsided games.

Confidence

Kids need to work hard at hitting and believe in defeating the pitcher. Deserve the opportunity to bat in late innings. Visualize clutch performance under pressure. See the pileup after a game-winning base hit. A confident hitter is a winning hitter. This performer is remembered by teammates, opponents, and fans for what they accomplish, not for what they didn't do. Have some swagger on the way to the batter's box, even a wiggle in the stance. Walk, think, and swing with confidence.

Coach's Role

You're the person most responsible for the team. Talent wins games, but make that talent work together. Make sure pinch hitters are ready and eager. Give them a pep talk beforehand.

Designate roles for everyone before the start of the season. Be honest, and remind them that their spots could change due to injury, a particular opponent, or performance of a teammate. Ease a player's feeling of neglect from not being a starter. Sitting the bench isn't much fun, especially in baseball. That's why I like the DH and want to see the re-entry rule (where starters can be replaced and then go back in) put into play in high school and college. But emphasize the need for a bench player who can be counted on late in the game. Communicate with the starters and more importantly the non-starters.

Treat players equally and never play favorites. If you tell a kid he's going to hit in the last inning, you need to follow through. Be consistent, truthful, assess talent, take calculated risks, and be trusted. Have players willing to do anything in order to win. On the flip side, the starter should realize that a team wins and loses together. After being lifted, show a sign of support to the substitute.

Before the actual at-bat, inform pinch hitters of the game situation. This could be as simple as the number of outs or a review of the signals, or as complicated as reviewing the pitch selection of an opposing pitcher. Attempt to give confidence rather than explaining hitting mechanics. Never get a player too high or too low, but make the batter feel invincible.

Note: A pinch hitter is officially into the game when announced on the PA system or written on the umpire's scorecard. With this in mind, the defensive team can bring in another pitcher to gain the like-handed advantage.

Here are some of my favorite pinch hitting successes during my coaching career at Worcester State. You may be able to use some of these examples for your own team. Though we lost both times, we emptied the bench in the ninth inning when behind in championship games: first in the 2001 ECAC Tournament New England title game and again in the 2003 MASCAC conference title game. In both instances the bench guys scrapped for three runs and put a lot of quick pressure on the opposition in games they thought were already won. Getting bench players into any playoff game provides huge dividends in experience for future seasons.

Jason Miller's two-RBI game-winning double beat conference rival Fitchburg State College in 2003. Jason became a starter through the remainder of the season and into our run to the conference championship game. Though good enough to start for us that season, Jason was used primarily as a defensive replacement in late innings. He kept his mouth shut all year, his name was finally called, and he rose to the occasion. Earlier that season our backup catcher, Pat Welch, had the game-winning single in a close game against Worcester Polytechnic Institute.

Steve Dicker was sent in to pinch hit in the ninth inning of a conference playoff game in 2003. With a chance to tie the game with two outs and runners on first and second base, I called him down for a talk. I said, "Well, we have a chance to tie the game with a single and possibly win the game with an extra-base hit. What do you think?" He answered, "I want to win the game." Just what I wanted to hear. However, Steve was hit by the pitch and our next batter flied out to the fence to end the 4–3 game.

Jason Grenier, who broke his hand late in the 2001 season, had his cast re-moved early, but I figured his career had come to a close. He could barely grip the bat. But in the dugout the week of his return, he constantly put thoughts in my head. "I'm good to go," he'd say. "I have an AB. Whenever you need a hit, I'm right here. If you need someone to win the game, just give me a shot." I tried not to acknowledge him, because we were trying to win ballgames, but I was smiling every time he said something to me. Finally, his chance came. In his first at-bat, Grenier singled. Later that week he hit a home run and ended up being our starting DH as we advanced to the championship game of the ECAC New England Baseball Tournament.

And because of lineup changes in a blowout game, we were forced to pinch hit a pitcher who hadn't had an at-bat all season. I told LJ Grasso not to be afraid to "lean into one." Grasso did in fact get grazed by the pitch, which scored a run with the bases loaded. This was one of the key plays of our 13–12 win after being down 10–0 after the top of the first inning.

Conclusion

My first college plate appearance came as a pinch hitter in 1989 against Big East power Providence College. My team was down by four runs with two outs and the bases loaded. A grand slam would tie the game. A base hit or walk would continue the inning. After working the count full, the right-handed closer reared back and fired to the plate. Strike three swinging. Talk about a warm welcome to Division 1 baseball. Well, by the time I was a senior I was a Conference All-Star, set two school batting records, and played in the New England College All-Star Game at Fenway Park.

Pitcher and Strike Zone

"Trying to hit him is like trying to eat Jell-O with chopsticks."
— Bobby Murcer on knuckleballer Phil Niekro

Introduction

The legal strike zone starts from the letters of the uniform and descends to the knees. Swinging for pitches in the strike zone dramatically increases one's batting average, potential for a line drive, and chances for reaching base safely.

Note the contrasts of a home plate umpire's strike zone. Some call the high strike and some the low. Others have a broad zone and others squeeze. On a cold day, some may call a lot of strikes to keep the game moving. Others may be former ballplayers and want to see pitchers who throw consistent strikes. And understand that an umpire's strike zone may widen during a blowout game or pending darkness. The variables are many.

Watching the first half-inning gives the home team an advantage. It's up to the away team to decipher an umpire's strike zone as this inning progresses. Have a game plan before the first at-bat, and encourage kids to talk with their own pitcher and catcher.

Hit strikes.

Know the umps.

Swing for Strikes

To get an idea of how wide home plate really is, lay seven baseballs across the middle of it. The plate is actually 17 inches wide, and the baseball is three inches wide. That means a pitcher can operate with 23 inches of area on either side in which to throw a strike. If a batter swings for balls out of this area, a good pitcher can throw borderline non-strikes knowing this kid may swing for bad balls. Walks hurt, as does swinging for pitches out of the strike zone.

In 2003 during an American Legion game, our team was being no-hit into the fifth inning. But we were drawing walks. By the end of the game we had 12 total walks, tied the game on an infield error, and later won it with a two-out double in the last inning. We took a strike for the last two innings, which paid huge dividends in winning a close game against a good team.

Pitchers remember at-bats, and so should the batter. One who swings at a bad pitch isn't maximizing their own ability, gives the advantage to the pitcher even though he/she tossed a poor pitch, puts extra information into the pitcher's head about future at-bats, dampens the potential for a big inning (in case of contact), and may frustrate oneself for later

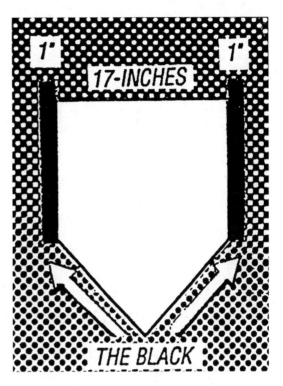

Plate is 17 inches wide.

on in that at-bat. Note that a pitcher will probably continue to "climb the ladder" against hitters who swing for pitches up in the zone. And in regard to strategy, watch for poor defensive catchers who have difficulty blocking balls in the dirt. If a pitcher isn't confident in throwing low breaking balls, for example, the hitter may end up seeing more fastballs to his/her liking.

Know the Grip and Pitch

Know thy opponent. Have kids watch a pitcher's wind-up and/or stretch. Some pitchers give different looks on almost every pitch: sidearm, over the top, moving to different spots on the rubber, head bobs, you name it. Pitchers try to make batters feel uncomfortable with an overall goal of upsetting timing.

Plate is seven balls wide. (Rex Baker)

Good pitchers hide the ball in their delivery, throw inside, work quickly, and set up batters with a variety of pitch selections. Analyze the time between pitches early and late in the game, pitches to left- and right-handed batters, first pitches of the inning and to specific batters in the lineup (especially the first time around the order), pitches thrown with two strikes, and even the pitcher's fielding position after release.

Look for visual clues as well. A pitcher may fiddle with the ball just before throwing. This might be an indication of an off-speed pitch due to the tricky grip. Be aware of tip-offs. Proper pitching technique calls for the ball to be hidden behind the body and only first shown at the "L." Inexperienced pitchers bring the ball away from the body instead of behind it. And while older players try to steal catcher's signs from second base, from a coaching box, or the hitter looking back into the catcher, just get up there and hit. If the defense sees someone trying to steal signs, and then pass that information off to someone else, a batter just might get a pitch in the ear.

Sidearm pitchers in like-handed situations are difficult to hit due to the pitch angle and natural movement to the ball. Moreover, submarine, left-handed, and knuckleball pitchers are all top commodities for the simple reason of difficulty in picking up the ball. However, the angle and viewpoint are more desirable against opposite-handed sidearm pitchers. Imagine eight baseballs (one after another without any added movement) arriving from a sidearmer and an over-the-top pitcher. A hitter could theoretically make contact with all eight from the sidearmer, but only two to three from the overhander.

Throwing overhand adds a downward plane to the ball. When facing the sidearmer, do make a note of the change in release point.

Also watch for pitcher's shaking off the catcher. Though catchers call the pitches (unless a coach calls them from the dugout), some pitchers either wait for another sign or shake off the one given. Look for patterns after a shake-off. A hard-throwing pitcher usually wants the fastball while a crafty pitcher, whose breaking pitches have been working well, may want the curveball. Young pitchers also want to show off all of their pitches. So a variety of fastballs may then be offset with a breaking pitch. Pitchers are human and want to be the center of attention. Sometimes they get caught up in the moment and throw a pitch that isn't in the best interest of getting the hitter out.

The basic catcher hand signals for pitches are: 1=fastball, 2=curveball, and 3=change-up. Pitchers can offset a base runner attempting to steal his pitches by rubbing the chest with his/her glove up or down, which signals a pitch up or down a number in the signaling sequence. Catchers also go through a number of finger calls, and the pitcher knows it's either the first, second, third, or sometimes fourth signal. Change the sequence up during the game if need be. But don't worry too much about the other team's pitch calls or even offensive signals for that matter. Focus on what you're doing — not what they're doing. It's called "stay with us." And keep it simple during the game for better results.

Bat Angle on Pitches

The bat angle on contact depends on the pitch. First consider the situation and location of the fielders. Then the batter can focus on going with the pitch whenever possible. Remember that the ball leaves the bat at the angle at which it meets the ball.

For middle-of-the-plate pitches, kids should swing down with a semi-level bat that on contact is even with the front of the plate. For the inside pitch, get the bat out in front of the plate and around the outer edge of the baseball. This pitch,

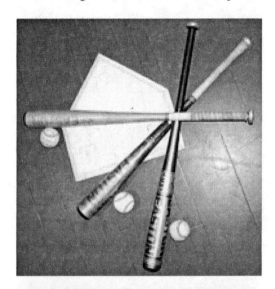

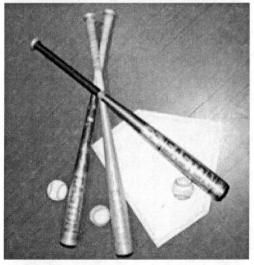

Different bat angles for different pitches. (Neal Portnoy)

even a non-strike but a mistake left up in the zone, must be recognized early to drive down the pull side of the field. For the outside pitch, the bat head may actually be located at the opposite lower corner of the plate. Attempt to hit the inside portion of the baseball. Patient hitters can wait as long as possible and "throw the hands" at the outside pitch and drive it to the opposite field. One can also release the top hand on contact.

Introduction: The Pitches

All kids should pitch at early ages as a way to better understand how pitchers try to get hitters out. Same goes for the catcher. Get as much information as possible, because hitting is difficult. Hitters and pitchers need controlled and correct mechanics. Kids should master three pitches, for example: both fastballs, change-up, and/or curveball. Little League pitchers shouldn't throw the curveball much at all, because of the strain applied to the growing arm, plus kids at this age usually throw the pitch incorrectly and not for strikes. Instead use the two-seam fastball (moves more than the four-seamer) and the change-up (gets the hitter out front).

Grip can be picked up by the batter just before release ("L"), movement while reading the ball (after release), and velocity (just before contact, or listening to the ball hitting the mitt). Though pro scouts focus on velocity with the "Here it is, try and hit it" mentality, all pitchers attempt to have movement on their pitches. Movement or "tail" (more dip or spin) is attained through different grips, arm angles, finger placement and pressure points on the ball, and varying arm speeds. Pitchers need to throw a lot both in the stretch and wind-up to figure out which pitches work best and move the most. But the concern is always to locate good strikes by using the whole plate (high, low, in, out — never down the middle) and get hitters out. And as Worcester State pitching coach Neal Portnoy says, "You don't have to throw a strike to get one." This means swings at pitches out of the strike zone.

Batters focus on mistakes left up in the zone (belt area) that have as little movement as possible. Traditional starting pitchers throw over the top. Difficulty then comes from the relievers (left or right) who may throw sidearm or slower/faster. Pitchers who hesitate in their motion prove effective, because it's not what hitters are used to. Also, pitchers love the high mounds so they can drive downward. This way the ball is coming in at a much different angle compared to a lower mound, which gives the hitter a more similar plane in regard to reading the ball.

The following sections are a general review of the pitches. Coaches at the many levels may have different philosophies on the grips and when to throw each pitch according to the count. This isn't etched in stone, but we just want the hitters to know what they're facing on a given day.

Fastball

Mechanics: The fastball is the most common pitch in baseball. It's the easiest for the pitcher to throw and for the batter to see. Since a fastball has a straight trajectory to the plate, the goal is to add movement to the pitch. The four-seam fastball is gripped across the wide four seams (looks like the letter "C"). Place the finger pads on the seam with the thumb under the ball. The two-seam fastball is gripped inside the narrow seam. Grip the top of the ball with

the index and middle fingers. The thumb is placed underneath. The four-seam is released with the fingers behind the ball. The two-seam has a side spin with the thumb coming underneath slightly.

Pitcher Philosophy: Velocity is the key. A good fastball appears to rise only because gravity is less likely to influence the speed. This pitch arrives end over

Fastball "C" grip. (Neal Portnoy)

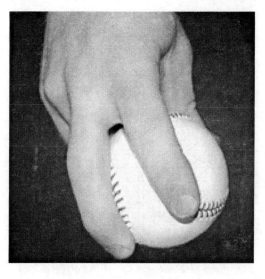

2-seam grip. (Neal Portnoy)

end. Control is needed to spot and locate the pitch (in and out/or up and down).

Hitter Philosophy: Aim to hit the middle/top of the ball. Look for the fastball and adjust to the curveball (body has more time to react). Move back in the batter's box, and use a lighter bat when facing hard throwers.

Other Varieties: The sinker. Turn the ball for more movement. Put the fingers closer together with a tighter thumb and wrist. Sinkerball pitchers force more ground balls.

Split-Finger Fastball/Forkball

Mechanics: The splitter or forkball has a similar grip to the fastball except it has less spin and breaks down and later. Rest the fingers on the outside portions of each seam. The closer the fingers the sharper the break (splitter); wider the fingers the slower the velocity (forkball). The thumb rests under the ball and to the side for better support. Put the ball back in the hand as far as possible. With similar velocity as the fastball, this pitch spins and dips more.

Pitcher Philosophy: This is a great "change of pace" pitch for a hard thrower. The splitter has the form of a breaking pitch without the arm strain. There is some question whether it decreases the velocity of the fastball arm action.

Hitter Philosophy: Be aware of pitchers who throw either pitch. Hitters can look foolish on biting splitters. Look for a late break down in the strike zone. Be patient. An effective splitter may appear impossible to hit. However, a hanger (little to no break) can be driven long distances.

Change-up

Mechanics: The change-up has an increase of movement but a decrease in velocity. It's our number one pitch at Worcester State, and we throw it at any time. This pitch can have many grips and spins. Grip the ball just as the four-seam fastball except with three fingers across the seams. The thumb and pinky are next to each other on the bottom of the ball for support. The ball is choked in the deepest part of the hand. Lift the

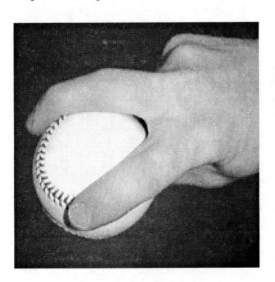

Splitter. (Neal Portnoy)

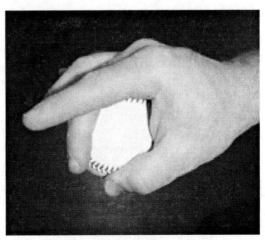

Change-up. (Neal Portnoy)

fingers upon release. The hand rotates away from the body for a side spin. The wrist doesn't snap. The arm comes straight down. This pitch puts less strain on the arm compared to other pitches. Some pitchers drag the back foot along the dirt (for decreased speed) as a way to slow the body down.

Pitcher Philosophy: This is a slower pitch usually thrown after several fastballs, especially after a batter pulled a ball foul (i.e. sets up the fastball). Throw the change-up in a fastball situation (i.e. 3–2 count). Little Leaguers who want a breaking pitch should throw the change-up instead of the curve.

Hitter Philosophy: Every hitter should be able to recognize the fastball. The difficulty comes in reading the change-up which appears the same. Keep the hands back and wait for the ball. For a right-handed batter facing a right-handed pitcher, expect the ball to go down and in; down and away to a left-handed batter.

Other Varieties: Circle change. The pitcher grips the ball with the three fingers, but makes a circle with the thumb and index finger. It works best with long fingers.

Curveball

Mechanics: The curve is one of the two breaking pitches. It appears to start high (out of the strike zone) and then drops while crossing the plate. Studies prove that this pitch doesn't actually curve but spins a great deal. Whatever the case, most starting pitchers throw a curveball to offset their fastball. The curve can be individualized due to hand/finger size and grip strength. It's gripped on the four seams. The middle finger is on the seam and rotated over

the first finger. There's space between the hand and ball. The curve is thrown with a loose wrist and the forearm muscles. The wrist is snapped inward. The thumb comes up and over (snap of the fingers). It's held longer in the hand, and the ball must be released out in front of the body. The release point must be consistent to be effective.

Pitcher Philosophy: This pitch gets hitters out in front due to the change in speeds. The key is wrist snap.

Hitter Philosophy: Aim low to hit the curve. Since it breaks low over the plate, keep the weight and hands back. Think base hit to the opposite field (not home run) when recognizing the curve in a like-handed situation. However, a hanging curveball hardly breaks at all (floats into the hitting zone), and can be driven long distances. The curveball should go down and away from a right-handed pitcher to a right-handed batter; down and in to a left-handed batter. Expect the curve to break over for a strike (this also applies to umpires and catchers, so keep the front shoulder closed, body over the plate, and watch a non-strike into the mitt). Never swing at the first curveball from a pitcher. This may

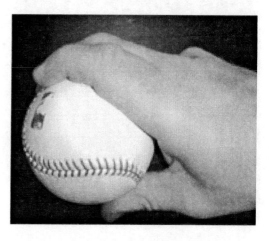

Curveball/slider. (Neal Portnoy)

occur in the second at-bat, but first assess the velocity, rotation, and location of an off-speed pitch before expecting to make solid contact. And rarely would a starter throw a first-pitch curve in the first at-bat of a game. Moreover, rarely can a pitcher throw three curveballs for strikes in a single at-bat. Look for that fastball, and adjust with the weight/hands back for the curveball.

Watch for Clues: The pitcher fiddling with a grip or a slowing of the motion during the delivery. Expect a curve after a first-pitch fastball called a strike, or pulling a line drive foul (a change-up may also be thrown). Because very few young hitters grow up facing good curveball pitchers (some Little Leagues even ban the pitch), hitters have difficulty in reacting to one. Try hitting off the pitching machine on curveball mode.

Slider

Mechanics: The second of the breaking pitches (also known as a cut-fastball), the slider darts fast with the spin of a fastball. The movement is sideways, later, and much sharper than the curveball. The slider is a cross between the fastball and curve. Use the four-seam grip, off-center to the right. The top fingers are between 12 and one o'clock with the thumb at seven o'clock. Apply a firmer grip, put it deeper in the hand, and the first finger is the pressure point. Upon release, turn the wrist in slightly and lift the middle finger. The hand isn't turned as much as the curve.

Pitcher Philosophy: The slider is easier to control than the curve. It can be thrown at different speeds and degrees of break. A slider should come in approximately five mph slower than the fastball.

Hitter Philosophy: This pitch looks just like a fastball with almost the same velocity. A good slider can be more difficult to hit than the curve. It should drop three to five inches with a late break over the plate. For a right-handed batter facing a right-handed pitcher, the ball goes down and away; down and in for a left-handed batter.

Knuckleball

Mechanics: The knuckleball dips, darts, spins and moves. It dances in all directions. The first three fingers and thumb dominate the grip. It can be gripped with the knuckles folded over (first two fingers on the seam) or with the fingernails (first three fingers on the seam). The thumb rests on the bottom of the ball (off-center), and the remaining

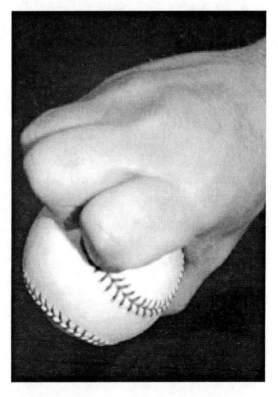

Hitters hate knuckleballs. (Neal Portnoy)

fingers on the outer half. It's thrown slowly with little or no spin and pushed to the plate with a stiff wrist.

Pitcher Philosophy: Due to aerodynamics, this pitch should float and not spin to the plate. The knuckler is great for pitchers who don't throw hard and even converted position players. Windy conditions add more movement to the ball. Little strain is put on the throwing arm. It's also fun to throw. A catcher should use a larger mitt and concentrate on blocking the ball. Knuckleballers maintain narrow/long fingernails for a better grip.

Hitter Philosophy: Most knuckleballers also throw a fastball and even the knuckle-curve (one knuckle on the ball with a curveball motion). Expect the knuckler to dart once it reaches the plate. Be patient. Move up in the box and closer to the plate to combat the breaking of the pitch. Swing only for strikes and attempt to draw walks. Because hitters think that knuckleballers invariably give up a lot of home runs, many aren't disciplined enough to wait on the ball. One can take a strike in the first at-bat to check out what the knuckleball is doing, and emphasize the head being down on contact even after the swing (since there is little threat of a blazing pitch).

Palmball

Mechanics: The palmball drops down. The ball is held deep in the hand. With the pressure being applied by the thumb and ring finger, place the first two fingers across the seams. The fingers and placement of the ball can be altered for the pitcher. It's basically thrown with the palm or hand covering the ball when released. On release the hand is behind the ball rather than on top.

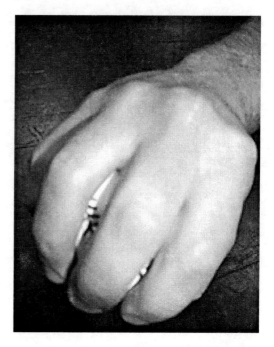

Palmball. (Neal Portnoy)

Pitcher Philosophy: Pitchers use this as a "change of pace" pitch. It has the form of a change-up with the effect of a forkball.

Hitter Philosophy: Look for the ball to drop sharply. Be patient, and move up in the box.

Other: If a batter notices any uncommon or severe movement to a pitch, simply ask the umpire to check the ball. Cuts/slices/scuffs off the grass/fence may add more movement to the ball. Also, if playing in diminishing sunlight ask the umpire to throw in a new baseball. The home team should only throw in new balls when they're hitting. *Note*: Pitchers like game balls with high seams that cut/move better in the wind.

Charting Pitchers and Hitters

Teams usually keep track of the number of total pitches (the scorebook is used for offensive statistics). The pitching chart is used to cite which pitch was thrown, when in the count, how many, and what happened when it was hit. The total pitch count provides an indication of a pitcher's makeup and endurance level (varies per individual). Knowing this, you can better plan the role of a relief pitcher in late innings. A tired pitcher takes extra time between pitches by slouching over, walking around the mound, and looking long at the catcher for signals. The tiring power pitcher may leave the ball up in the hitting zone. By using a stopwatch to clock a pitcher's time in between pitches, you can assess the effectiveness and conditioning of both starting pitchers.

Also chart the hitters. Include the team, date, field, weather conditions, pitcher's name, age/class, arm, and type of pitches he/she throws. Indicate the count on balls hit, pitches hit or missed, and the field location of hits and outs. General notes also include foul tips, bunts of any kind, sacrifice situations, and strategy. Teams can make charts for their own and/or opposing hitters with respect to defensive positioning. Draw a solid line to the field where a line drive was hit, jagged line for a ground ball, or a half-circle for a fly ball, blooper, or soft liner. Star those special at-bats, and look for patterns that assist the individual. Include the pitch type, count, and like- or opposite-handed situations. View progress each game or week, and pay special attention to using the whole field, line drives versus fly balls, hits with runners in scoring position, putting the ball in play with two strikes, working the pitcher, leadoff hitters (each inning) getting on base, drawing walks, extra-base hits, and pitch type to numbers one through nine in the lineup. Attempt to know more about the pitchers than they know about your team.

Strikes and Outs

Baseball is based upon strikes and outs. Hits and runs only prolong the game. That's why there is no time limit. Making the most out of each pitch and three outs each inning gives a team the best possible shot at winning. For example, a first-pitch out hurts. If the next batter does the same, there are now two outs on just two pitches. In a six- or seven-inning game, this deteriorates a major portion of the offensive attack. Depending on the situation, attempt to put the ball in play, take non-strikes, spoil the "pitcher's pitch" (favorite/best pitch of a hurler), minimize outs, bat around the lineup, draw walks, and frustrate the defense.

If a team does make two quick outs, the third batter should take extra time. Let the umpire call a batter to the plate. Hitters, not the pitcher, should control the flow of the game. I once let my captain swing away after two quick outs in a close conference game. He blasted a home run which led to a blowout victory. Moreover, here are some other tidbits to take a pitcher out of his/her groove: Extra warmup swings or stretches, walk slowly to the plate, visit the third base coach, fix the dirt in the box, take a practice swing between pitches, or step out during the at-bat. Pitchers want to work quickly (keeps the defense more alert plus umpires love it), so make them think and sweat a bit longer in the hot sun, for example. Simply ask the umpire for time, so one can get set in the box.

Emphasize the importance of the pitch and out. Baseball is unpredictable. Swinging at a poor pitch sways the advantage from the batter immediately to the pitcher. Never think a game is over until the final out. Good teams win the close ballgames. Believe in a rally when behind, and never just sit on a lead. If one makes a mistake at the plate or in the field, take a deep breath, and focus on the next play. Don't dwell on the negative. Learn from what just happened.

Watch the Pitch Into the Mitt

Have hitters watch every pitch into the catcher's mitt. This action improves vision, the actual swing, and even the hitter's strike zone.

First, the front shoulder stays closed. This is important for curveballs especially in those difficult like-handed situations. Staying closed keeps the weight back and hands in towards the body. Wait on the ball instead of bending back-

Watch the ball into the mitt. (Neal Portnoy)

wards. Stay upright in the stance and expect the curveball to drop over for a strike.

Second, watching the pitch forces the eyes on the ball. See the ball hit the bat. The best curveballs break over the plate after the commitment of the hands and weight. This takes the "head down after contact" phase to the next level by assisting in the reading of various pitches.

Third, when needing base runners, look to lean into borderline curveballs. Getting hit in the back, thigh, or front arm adds to on-base percentage. The umpire may call a hitter back for not making an attempt to get out of the way, but at least the curveball hurts less than the fastball.

Fourth, the hitter sees where the ball lands. This provides an indication of the umpire's strike zone. Umpires respect this hitter more, because a kid can see where the ball is caught.

Fifth, never argue with an umpire. Umpires don't decide the outcome of a game — players do. Contesting a strike only makes the hitter and team look bad. Plus, arguing balls and strikes can constitute an automatic ejection. Never argue from the dugout; go out and speak one on one to an ump. Avoid the tag of sore loser. Plus, some umpires may hold a grudge later in the game or season. A simple glare after a strike call, as if to say, "How dare you call a strike on me," goes much farther than a verbal outburst. Moreover, the thinking here is that a hitter is suppose to swing at strikes— not take them. Umpires are human, so invariably they may have make-up calls over the course of a game. A hitter may earn a future call in his/her favor by not saying a word, sprinting back to the dugout after an out, and showing sportsmanship.

On a check swing, a batter can ask the umpire whether the bat head crossed the front of the plate or whether the pitch was a called strike. Questions are fine in this situation. Face-to-face confrontations only lead to trouble. Avoid asking umpires for the count; stay in the game at all times. Remember that balls are signaled with the left hand; strikes the right.

Some other tips to get on the good side of umpires when your team is batting include bringing water out to them between innings, rubbing the game balls up before a home game, chasing foul balls on both sides of the field, staying in the vicinity of the batter's box, sprinting out walks, hits, home runs and on/off the field, staying inside the dugout to cheer, and always address them as sir and never "Blue." Get in good with the umpires for home games by providing them with a Gatorade snack, and sunflower seeds. They'll love it.

Pick Up Clues from Pitchers and Catchers

Learn pitching grip, movement, and location from your own pitchers. Have the hitters play catch with them to see how, when, and where a pitch breaks. Ask catchers how they call a game. Listen to the color commentary of baseball announcers. Go to minor league games and watch how catchers set up hitters and which pitches they call in certain situations. Watch your own competition by sitting right behind the backstop. And probably the best way to assess a pitcher is to talk to the umpires who call their games.

Put your batters in the pitcher's shoes. How would you get your kids out? What are their strengths and weaknesses? What pitches can a kid drive, and what is someone's "out" pitch? For hitters who also pitch, spend some time analyzing this point. One can also stand in

Know how catchers call pitches. (Steve Berg)

the batter's box facing your own pitchers during practice (don't swing though). On game day the pitcher should prepare in the bullpen by also facing a batter on both sides of the plate.

Try listening to the catcher's shin pads. In a situation where the pitcher has the advantage (i.e. 0–2 or 1–2), a catcher sometimes sets up for a "waste pitch" whether inside or outside the strike zone. Hearing the crackle of the pads or buckles may give an indication as to where the pitch is headed. A batter should never look directly at the catcher giving signs. Finally, inexperienced catchers may creep too far forward in the box. If really needing a base runner in a close ballgame, notice this and move kids back in the box. Hitting the mitt results in catcher's inference, and the batter is awarded first base.

Zone in

When up in the count, kids should "zone in" and swing for a pitch in the hitting zone or "wheel house." Imagine a little box where a favorite pitch would be. Take the pitch if it's not located in this area. Avoid taking too many strikes, especially against pitchers throwing an abundance of them and umpires with a broad strike zone (this becomes addicting to the rest of the team just as ripping good pitches). This favorite pitch is different for everyone.

Zoning up also means keying in on the pitcher. Kids should never dig in the box without keeping an eye on the pitcher who might quick-pitch. Simply ask for time from the umpire to get set in the box. Also be aware of pitchers who delay. Hitting is a series of nerves and anticipation. While on the rubber, pitchers sometimes stall as if having difficulty reading the signs. Call time out, but make sure the umpire grants time before stepping out. Pitchers like to work quickly. Alter that rhythm by staying calm, cool and collective. Say to the hitters: "You control the game — not the pitcher."

Like-Handed Hitting Situations

Enjoyment comes in hitting against opposite-handed pitchers: right-handed batters off left-handed pitchers and left-handed batters off right-handed pitchers. For the most part, the ball leaving a pitcher's hand appears to come from the outer part of the plate instead of the inner half. I remember taking three curveballs against a lefty from the University of Miami. Each one looked like it was headed for my skull. I ended up drawing a walk, but it was an at-bat that really made me respect the pitching capabilities of a big-time chucker.

In like-handed situations kids should crowd the plate and bend over more than usual, especially lefty vs. lefty. This forces the pitcher to alter his/her mentality and location, thus throwing to the outside corner, which in turn will be to the hitter's advantage in regard to the "sweet spot." Moreover, crowd the dish in a bases-loaded situation and/or against a new relief pitcher. This action puts the walk/HBP into the pitcher's mind more than anything.

All hitters need to train the body to expect the break of the ball. Time the pitcher's release-to-impact: fastball (quicker) and breaking pitch (slower). Because very few coaches throw curveballs in BP (let alone good ones) and even fewer have left-handed pitchers, utilize the pitching machine for bunting and live hitting. It throws left- and right-handed curveballs from various speeds. Also, drop a regular leather baseball into the chute. The ball darts all over the place, so hitters can really work on their hand-eye coordination via movement of a pitch.

Left-handed pitchers are a necessity for their natural movement on the baseball and to offset the higher number of right-handed pitchers on a particular staff. Every quality staff needs both sets of arms, just as the offense needs left- and right-handed batters to give the defense a different look. The more you see of something the more accustomed you are to it. Thus, facing a left-handed pitcher for the first time puts an uneasy feeling into the minds of a lot of young batters. So practice both varieties.

A modern trend for pitchers is the three-quarters arm angle upon release, and even throwing sidearm against like-handed hitters in a two-strike count. Hitters focus (hard) just above the throwing shoulder. An altered arm angle during an at-bat skews a batter's rhythm and approach. Smart pitchers also move to one side of the rubber according to the particular hitter; right side for the right-handed batter and left side for the left-handed batter.

To work on the back-door curveball (coming from the backside in) or even the slider (movement side to side), move the L-screen to the backside area of the hitter; thus the BP pitcher is throwing from an angle. The hitter should lean over the plate and work on picking up the pitch starting from the backside and moving inward. Look to drive the ball the other way.

The Count

The count changes on each pitch. Thus, strategy may alter but the hitter's demeanor should stay the same. Gear up for every pitcher.

Simplify tactics in every count. Pitchers throw according to the strike zone and sometimes to a particular batting stance. If a large hitter has trouble getting his hands through the strike zone, this player may see plenty of inside fastballs. A pitcher is at a huge disadvantage if they're afraid of pitching inside. Here are some tips for various counts:

0–0 Count

Before preaching a philosophy on 0–0 counts, make a proper assessment of your team's hitters (i.e. disciplined, ag-gressive or powerful). In every at-bat the youth hitter usually sees at least one pitch "with their name on it." A taken strike on the first pitch may be that one. Stress getting hits on first-pitch strikes. Work the pitcher with a mentality of swinging for strikes. React to pitches instead of guessing. Since baseball is a game of breaks and taking advantage of opponent mistakes, taking strikes provides no advantage at all for the offense.

For example, in frustration my assistant coach throws his hat in disgust if a hitter takes a perfect strike. It's not showing a hitter up, but a reminder to be aggressive at all times.

Start judging the pitcher during warmups. Think only about zoning in (versus taking a pitch) against a severely wild pitcher to view velocity and location. And when arriving at the ballpark, always find out which pitcher (right- or left-handed) is starting a game and hopefully have some statistics and a scouting report on such a hurler. Look for the walk-to-strikeout ratio, runs versus earned runs, innings pitched, and total hits given up. And if a left-hander is pitching it's always good to see pitches from a lefty in pregame BP.

Because youth pitchers want to get ahead of the batter, the fastball is the pitch of favor because it's the easiest to control. Throwing a first-pitch curveball isn't in the best interest of the defense. Walking batters more often than not ends up in runs for the offense. Pitchers need to get outs to stay in the game, and every starting pitcher wants to throw a complete game. By throwing strikes they allow the defense to make plays. *Note:* Have your kids look to drive a first-pitch strike after a long home run, after an opposing coach goes to the mound for a conference, or after a lot of action just occurred on the base paths. Pitchers who give up a big run(s) sometimes become frustrated. Thinking they need to get ahead of the next batter may groove a pitch down the middle. Look to continue the big inning with a frozen rope!

0–1 Count

Though the pitcher appears to have the advantage on 0–1, this count may occur during the first at-bat (foul ball or taking a borderline strike). The hitter still has two more strikes to work with. The pitcher may challenge a hitter again. No hitter should ever look at two consecutive strikes. In this case the pitcher may see the following: (1) A timid hitter unable to pull the trigger, (2) difficulty in reading the ball, or (3) a batter looking for a walk. So be aggressive. This is still a good count for a base hit. Hitting a close pitch at least provides the opportunity to reach base safely.

0–2 Count

The only thing to change when down 0–2 is the concentration level. It's actually a great hitting count, because one is swinging at anything close. Especially at the L.L. levels, preach putting the ball in play during 0–2 counts; even have simple rewards like packs of baseball cards for contact with two strikes. Kids may want to move up in the box, choke up, and crowd the plate.

Left-handed batters concentrate more when facing left-handed pitchers, for example. The same can be said about being down two strikes. Even though the end seems near, never give in. Give confidence by saying, "Don't let 'em call you out [meaning the umpire]. You have one left [a strike]. It only takes one [one pitch to get a hit]."

With no runners on base, a pitcher may throw an off-speed pitch in the dirt hoping to entice a swing (no threat of the passed ball at the Little League level, though older players can advance on a called/swing third strike missed by the catcher). With a runner(s) on base, a pitcher may throw a fastball high inside or outside. Most pitchers in this sequence aim outside, thus eliminating a potential hit-by-pitch. They also rear back with the fastball, because some hitters are hoping to just make contact, thus shortening their swing. That's why hitters don't want to change their stance or approach too much. Always think offensive vs. a defensive swing. Watch how pitchers throw to other batters in the lineup when the count is 0–2. Teams usually have a similar approach for this situation.

Kids need to concentrate, protect the strike zone, have confidence in making contact, slap the ball through the infield, and work the pitcher. Refer back to the "Little League Strike Zone" where anything near the "letters to the knees" is going to get whacked. A base hit and/or drawing a walk after being down 0–2 totally frustrates the pitcher and assists the next batter. That's why we say, "Take it one pitch, one at-bat at a time." I've even heard of the two-strike hit-and-run for hitters who are prone to taking pitches or strike out a lot. This play puts pressure on the defense (potential steal thus opening up holes in the infield), and gives the offense a weapon in an unfavorable count.

Two-Strike Stance

I used this stance in Little League, and it's a standard at the Doyle Baseball

Camps in Florida. Use it when a kid has extreme difficulty in making contact on the two-strike pitch. More than anything it gets youngsters swinging the bat.

This stance includes a wider than normal base (no stride), and the lead foot placed at the front portion of the batter's box. Without concern for the stride (a common fault of young hitters), the mind and body can relax and concentrate solely on making contact. Weight shift, balls of the feet, etc. are all compacted into one swing. Limit any cocking, and bring the hands slightly

Protect the plate. (Neal Portnoy)

forward (towards the pitcher). This lessens bat speed, but adds to reaction time for that borderline pitch. The arms are the main weapons. Angle the bat back (closer to level) to get to the path of the baseball sooner. By guarding the strike zone with two strikes, a frustrated or weak hitter can put the ball in play and possibly beat out an infield hit.

Experiment with this method before using it with kids in a game. Situations calling for a shorter and more compact swing include: (1) Moving a runner to third base with zero outs, (2) hit-and-run, or (3) contact play with a runner on third base (fewer than two outs). Remember, the stance should be used on all two-strike counts (0–2, 1–2, 2–2 and even 3–2). Once confidence and aggressiveness are regained in relation to contact, the hitter can resume with their previous batting stance.

Think Contact

No matter what the count, great hitters have confidence in making contact on every swing, fair or foul. The fear of swinging and missing should never enter one's mind. We practice this mentality at times during the preseason. Any called strike on a fastball or a swing and miss results in that hitter getting booted out of the batting cage. Because kids love to hit BP, going to the end of the line isn't what the doctor ordered. The same goes for facing a big-time pitcher. Always believe in success. I remember back in Little League when my coach brought in one of his former players who was then a star high school pitcher. I was 11 years old; the pitcher 16. He threw us BP. At first I was a bit timid, but our coach continually stressed confidence, no fear, and go up hackin'. Well, we won our division that year, and I made All-Stars as a 12-year-old. I do the same today by bringing in Eddie Riley, a former Triple A pitcher, to throw BP. Our kids really get geared up for these encounters. So no matter who we're facing on game day, we're going to hit him hard. For example, late in the 2000 season we faced the top pitching staff (by team ERA) in a pivotal away conference doubleheader. We scored 39 runs in 14 innings.

1–0 Count

Apply theories from the first-pitch strike, and move on from there. The hitter may want to "zone" the next pitch. No matter what, the batter has the advantage at 1–0. Expect a fastball, because a pitcher certainly doesn't want to go 2–0.

1–1 Count

Hitters should get a pitch to drive. Swing for strikes. This count is similar to 0–0, though the pitcher is one pitch closer to a strikeout. Expect a "pitcher's pitch" and be ready for something outside or possibly a breaking ball.

1–2 Count

Adopt the same philosophy as on 0–2. Stay alive by protecting the plate. Even with a count in their favor, pitchers want to get outs on *their* pitch. The previous pitch may have been high and outside ("waste pitch") but again, expect something off-speed and/or out of the strike zone.

2–0 Count

Be careful on 2–0. Don't jeopardize a favorable count by trying to hit a home run. "Zone in" on one's perfect pitch, or take the borderline strike. The hitter still has the advantage on 2–1. Go up swinging. With zero strikes there is no fear of striking out. Look for a fastball to drive up the middle.

2–1 Count

A high percentage of base hits occur on 2–1. A hitter has seen three pitches, so he/she probably has a good idea about the pitcher's velocity, trends for location, and spin/movement. The pitcher must throw a strike or be in jeopardy of going to 3–1 (one pitch closer to a walk). The batter can afford to take a borderline strike and still be even at 2–2. However, the pitcher may have a slight advantage knowing he/she can "waste" this pitch. Be very aggressive and focus on strikes. Never get cheated.

2–2 Count

The concentration level should be upped once again. Protect the strike zone, and expect the pitcher's best pitch (for that inning or game). Look for a pitch on the corners of the plate (black margins one inch in width)—most vulnerable hitting area. Note that a mistake over the middle is the easiest pitch to hit. That's why catchers almost never set up right behind home plate.

3–0 Count

This isn't the count when batters get the most base hits. Swinging poorly on the "green light" (no take sign) often results in flyouts. Hitters view 3–0 as the perfect pitch. But against a good pitcher, 3–0 doesn't always mean a four-seam fastball.

A contact hitter's mentality on 0–2 is to put the ball in play, and they may alter their stance in some way. On 3–0, a good hitter hopes for a fastball, maintains the regular stance, and has the count totally in his/her favor. Good hitters can swing away on 3–0 or even 2–0. That respect is earned through performance. Obviously the hitter gets better pitches to hit when up in the count. Assess discipline and hitting ability before allowing kids to swing 3–0.

On a 3–0 take sign (not swinging), hitters should look to gain an advantage. Avoid leaving the bat on one's shoulder; give the appearance of swinging. For example, after an assortment of outside pitches, crowd the plate to create an op-tical allusion that the far edge of the plate is farther away than it actually is. Also, after inside pitches step away from the plate. With another inside pitch, the umpire sees a hitter farther away from the strike zone. If the previous inside pitches weren't strikes, another one (in the opinion of the umpire) probably isn't one either. A batter can also crowd the plate or move forward/backward in the box. Pitchers with control problems have a distaste for hitters crowding the plate, and one may draw an inside fastball, thus drawing the walk. Moving around confuses a catcher trying to set up for a strike. Lastly, Little Leaguers like to wiggle the bat around (fake bunt) to cloud the pitcher's vision and focus.

Another goal, when up 3–0, obviously is to draw a walk. Since a pitcher has to throw three straight strikes for an out, swinging drastically reduces those odds. Only call for a 3–0 swing with a lead. But I've done it a few times in a deficit situation with an above-average hitter at the plate who can drive the ball. With runners on base against a pitcher who has shut us down, a double and/or home run can get us right back into the game. Never wait around for something to happen; take risks. Lastly, after drawing a walk only go to first base after the umpire makes the call. Never look for a walk in a three-ball count. And some umpires may call a borderline strike thinking the batter is "showing them up" by running to first without the call first being made. Although for that rare time a hitter is about to take a called third strike (i.e. on a devastating curveball), try and jog to first base as a way of "selling the call" to the umpire.

3–0 stance. (Steve Berg)

Classic 3–0 Hits

That one pitch per at-bat "with your name on it" can come any time. A consistent approach prepares the hitter for it on every pitch. In April of 1993, Harvard University's David Morgan was batting against Princeton University. The right-handed batter was given the "green light" on 3–0. Morgan zoned his pitch and laced an opposite-field run-scoring single. Though a power hitter, Morgan didn't swing for a home run. He drove an outside fastball, which produced a run batted in. This type of discipline made Morgan a .400 hitter and the Ivy League's Player of the Year. Later that spring he signed a professional contract with the Toronto Blue Jays.

In the 2003 World Series, Hideki Matsui launched a three-run homer on a first-inning 3–0 pitch to get the Yankees jump started to a Game 2 victory. In a 2003 State Legion playoff game, hulky six-foot-six, 310-pound Nate Nelson of Worcester, Massachusetts, tattooed a 3–0 offering deep over the center field fence. His Grafton Hill Post was down 1–0 at the time. The third base coach allowed Nelson to swing away to get his team back into the game. It proved pivotal as Nelson's team eventually won 4–3 and later won the state title. And Jeff LaHair hit a 3–0 offering for a home run in the bottom of the 9th inning to win the 2005 MASCAC Title. The win put Worcester State in the NCAA Tournament.

3–1 Count

A great hitting count, 3–1 should be treated something like 3–0. Remember to "zone in" and draw one's little box. In a pressure situation, give the take sign on 3–1 against pitchers having control

problems. Try it with the bases loaded and two outs. If it goes to a full count, you now have the advantage of the runners going on the pitch. Also expect a fastball in this situation, because the pitcher doesn't want to walk/hit anyone.

Obviously there's no such thing as a guaranteed hit. Teams who take non-strikes and hit strikes will get base hits, draw walks, tire starting pitchers, have quality at-bats, and knock pitchers out of the game. The starter should always be more effective than the reliever; that's why they're out there in the first place. A pitcher heading to the showers is a great thing for an offense. So make every pitch count. Hitters must be disciplined for the best results in a four-at-bat game. Take the 3–1 pitch not in the little box. If a strike is called, then it's 3–2 and then anything can happen.

3–2 Count

Hitters should love 3–2. Either a base hit or a walk. Be satisfied in working the pitcher this long. Use this information for subsequent at-bats. Concentrate on swinging for strikes anywhere near the strike zone. With the chips on the table, it's step-up time. The pitcher wants to throw their hardest (the fastball is the easiest to control), and the hitter wants to swing their hardest. No pitcher wants to walk someone on 3–2. And if by chance the pitcher drops off a nasty breaking ball and it's called strike three: Tip the cap and run back to the dugout.

Work the Pitcher

Hitters must see every pitch as soon as possible. The more pitches seen, the better the hitter will react later in the game. Moreover, an athletic offense can do more things at the plate and on defense. But like a poker hand, work with the cards you're dealt. Work to a team's strengths and possibly to the conditions of your home field. Take everything into account.

Lastly, as a veteran college coach who's also coached Senior Babe Ruth, American Legion, and even in the Cape Cod League, I can't emphasize enough that walks equal runs. Our Worcester State players continually draw walks, which has led to averaging almost eight runs a game in 2002–05. And leadoff

See, read, and hit the ball. (Bruce Baker)

walks, just as the leadoff out, give a team an amazing advantage in the inning. From 1998 to 2003 we've won 23 or more games each year (33 in 2002) to rank us among the nation's best in regard to winning percentage.

Listen and Learn from the Catchers

In the movie *Bull Durham*, Eddie Calvin "Nuke" LaLoosh (Tim Robbins) kept shaking off the signs from his catcher Crash Davis (Kevin Costner). That's a no-no in baseball. Even though catchers will probably not tell the hitter what's coming, as Davis did, realize that the catcher has the best view of anyone. Hitter tendencies show up, such as drop of the hands, ability to hit the outside pitch, bat speed, aggressive swings up in the count, ability to wait on breaking balls, and weight transfer. Catchers are the generals. The point here is not to think too much. Pitchers should throw what the catcher calls, and the hitter should swing at strikes. Don't analyze or guess. Let actions and abilities take over. With hard work and confidence, success will come.

The pitcher should rely on and trust an educated catcher for the majority of pitch calling and location. Jason Varitek is one of the best. Hold true to the fact that pitchers pitch and catchers catch. Don't try to do someone else's job. And the hitter should practice what to expect in the different counts. Again, play intrasquad scrimmages whenever possible, because competition breeds confidence.

In-Between Pitches

Hitters need to take the same approach to every at-bat. This starts in the dugout and concludes once the swing is complete. Work on habitual repetition (same swing every time) as often as possible. Take a practice swing between pitches as a subtle reminder of proper mechanics, especially after a poor swing. This also keeps the hitter loose, especially in those cold-weather settings. *Note*: Positive foul-ball swings include pitches fouled straight back and foul tips into the catcher's glove. Typically a coach will say, "You're right on it," or "You just missed it." Plus, shine the spikes, because for a foul ball off the foot there may be proof to show the umpire. And for a foul ball in the box that dribbles into fair territory, act like it hit the foot (i.e. limp or fall down). One is probably going to be out anyway, so try a little quick-thinking trickery.

Conclusion

Never have kids watch a called third strike, especially on straight fastballs. If they do, they shouldn't even come back to the dugout. Besides a lack of hustle, it's the worst thing in baseball. Hitters must be aggressive with two strikes and swing at close pitches.

Even at the beginning levels, where pitchers have trouble throwing strikes, sometimes a batter just has to swing at borderline pitches in order to get enough swings. In 2002 our returning All-American Eric Swedberg almost never got a good pitch to hit, because teams pitched around him. At first Swedberg got frustrated, but our coaches continually stressed discipline and "your time will come." Because we protected him in the lineup (hitters before and after him), teams soon had to challenge him. The results were incredible: Swedberg was named a first-team All-American, picked Conference Player of the Year for the third season in a row, and led Worcester State to the NCAA Tournament for the first time since 1983.

14

Bunting

"I don't understand how anyone hits a baseball. You play golf and the damn thing is sitting there, and all you have to do is hit it and that's hard enough."

— Ray Miller

Introduction

In the Red Sox' 1988 pennant race, new manager Joe Morgan pinch hit Spike Owen for slugger Jim Rice. Rice showed his displeasure at the switch by challenging Morgan in the dugout. But the manager sent Owen in, because he was the team's best available bunter on the bench. Owen laid down a perfect sacrifice bunt, which advanced the runner to second base. The Red Sox won the game and later that season the Eastern Division title.

Besides touching bases, bunting is the most underrated skill in baseball. So few teams use the bunt, but its advantages are numerous: to move runners up a base, get on base, get a runner home from third, and for taking a strike. Bunting isn't easy and should be practiced like any other skill. Unlike a typical at-bat, the bunt adds pressure to both the offense (to move a runner up) and defense (to get an out) because it should be successful every time.

The keys are bat angle, pitch selection, and placement. A friend of mine used to bunt 50 to 100 balls off the pitching machine at every practice while he was a scholarship player at Presbyterian College (S.C.).

Pivot and Square

Kids shouldn't square around with both feet pointing to the pitcher. This method leads to being hit by the pitch,

Pivot stance. (Neal Portnoy)

difficulty in bunting the low pitch, and giving the bunt away. In many cases, these bunts are popped up in the air for outs. Instead, batters should follow these 12 basic steps:

1. **Pivot the feet.** With the front foot, step slightly to the opposite field. This gives the batter maximum flexibility, balance, and the best body angle to bunt the ball on the ground. It's also useful in disguising the slash bunt (later in chapter). The back heel should be off the ground about two to three inches with the front balanced on the ball of the foot. The pivot should be smooth, fluid, and in one motion.

2. **Feet placement.** The front foot should land at the front of home plate and the back near the end of the batter's box. Thus, the bunter can properly place fastballs and breaking balls before the dip. Moving up in the box gives the bunter an advantage against foul balls. The closer to the pitch, the easier it is to put the ball in fair territory.

3. **Bend the knees.** This enables the bunter to go down and bunt the low pitches. Never extend upward on a high pitch.

4. **Slide the top hand up to the middle of the bat.** This disguises the bunt to corner infielders. Those who slide both hands up the middle show the bunt too early and reduce their balance, flexibility, and bat control.

5. **Hands should be in the middle of the chest.** The top hand should be higher in relation to the bottom hand.

6. **Grip the barrel of the bat with the thumb and index finger of the top hand.** Place it on the barrel of the "gun" and give a "thumbs up" sign. Protect the index finger (curl inward) from being hit by the ball. The bottom hand should be

Give the "thumbs up" sign. (Neal Portnoy)

near the knob. Be relaxed when holding the bat for a bunt.

7. **Chest should be pointed at the pitcher.** This keeps the eyes and head focused on the ball.

8. **Square/pivot when the pitcher breaks the ball from the glove.**

9. **Angle the bat up at 45 degrees.** This promotes a downward plane just as in the swing. The bat should be extended to about the front of the plate. Plus, the bat should be about eye level and even with the "letters." This is also the top of the strike zone, so the eyes, bat, and ball should all be on the same plane. Thus, any pitch above the bat won't be a strike.

10. **Focus on the pitcher, then on the ball when it hits the bat** (same focus points as in hitting).

11. **Extend the arms on contact.**

12. **Bunt the ball on the ground.** Don't push the ball. Let the ball hit the bat. The momentum of the pitch moves the ball its needed distance. Also, deaden the ball by "kissing it." Slightly detract the bat backwards just before contact.

Mechanics and Bunt Placement

The ideal bunt should be placed some 25 to 30 feet from the plate. It should land near either side of the foul line and never shoot back to the pitcher.

Since youth teams rarely practice bunt coverage, placing the ball correctly promotes a successful sacrifice and possible infield hit. Focus on the base lines, and don't worry about balls going into foul territory (unless bunted on two strikes, which coaches should hardly ever do).

Consider bunt placement according to where a pitcher falls off the mound after the pitch (left-hander to the right side and right-hander to the left side). Right-handed hitters, by nature of the bat angle and body position, have an easier time bunting the ball to the right side, and left-handed hitters to the left side. But hitters should practice bunting to both sides of the infield. Here's how to do both.

Left Side

This bunt (towards the third base side) is most desirable with a runner on second base. Proper placement to the third baseman removes this fielder from the play.

In a late close-game situation, the corner infielders (third and first) may charge moments before the actual pitch, looking for a play at second or third base depending on where the runner(s) are located. A third baseman is taught to go back to third on balls hit in the vicinity of the pitcher and first baseman. Base runners should get a good secondary lead after the pitch is thrown and an aggressive sprint to the bag once the bunt is down. Know when a tag or force play is in order. But as long as the bunter puts the ball softly on the ground and away from the pitcher and catcher, the sacrifice should work fine.

Right Side

This bunt (towards the first base side) is most desirable with a runner on first. First basemen usually charge on most sacrifice situations, knowing the second baseman covers first base. Traditionally speaking, first basemen take longer to get rid of the ball (larger glove) and have a weaker arm than the other infielders.

Bunting to a specific side depends on the situation. Look for visual clues from the infielders (i.e. corner positions charging too early shows fielder coverage for each base). In a bunt situation, pitchers are taught to step off on the first pitch. Inexperienced bunters square around too early, showing the play to the defense.

Sacrifice Bunt

Philosophy: The batter must give up their at-bat for the benefit of the team in order to move a runner(s) to the next base (i.e. from first to second or second to third).

Where it should be placed: Bunt strikes on the ground and away from the pitcher/catcher. Smart defensive teams, even with prior knowledge of the bunt play, still accept the sure out at first base. Only when a team has an aggressive catcher, who calls for where the ball should be thrown, can a team successfully get the lead runner.

When to use it: To play for one run, with the leadoff hitter reaching base, awards the defense one of the three outs, yet the offense has two opportunities to score a runner with a base hit to the outfield. Number two in the lineup typically is the team's best bunter (advancing the speedy leadoff hitter). Thus, the better hitters (numbers three through five) now have a chance for the RBI.

When to square around: Square when the pitcher breaks the ball from the glove (separates his/her hands). The bunter has plenty of time to pivot properly and bunt the ball. *Note*: Consider the type of pitch thrown in a sure sacrifice situation. Pitchers may throw high on the first pitch to entice the batter and thus force a pop-up. Knowing this fact, a batter may square around and take the pitch if it's not a strike. Then order "swing away" on the next pitch, with the defense thinking sac bunt, which invariably is a fastball down the middle.

Squeeze Bunt

Philosophy: The squeeze is used to get a runner home from third base. It's a do-or-die opportunity for the bunter to pick up a run batted in (successful sacrifice and squeeze bunts don't count as official at-bats). Throw the bat at the ball if the pitch is out of the strike zone. Always protect that runner sprinting home.

Where it should be placed: Bunt the ball on the ground. Even if bunted back to the pitcher, the runner should score each time.

When to use it: When a team desperately needs a run, call for the squeeze with none or even one out. The squeeze usually happens late in games. Squeeze with batters down in the lineup (numbers seven through nine), because the play may be a good weapon for getting the runner home. Weaker hitters typically have less power but more bat control. Call the "double squeeze" with runners on second and third base. The runner coming from second (in essence stealing third) should round third and head for home when the infielder throws to first base.

When to square around (high school and up): Square at the pitcher's "L" (just before release). The runner breaks from third when the pitcher's front foot hits the ground. A late break is better than an early one, because a squeeze anywhere on the ground scores the runner 99 out of 100 times. A pitcher who sees an early break is taught to throw the ball out of the strike zone; outside for a left-handed hitter and inside for the right-handed hitter (throw/ball is closer to the oncoming runner). And in any bunt situation, never step on the plate. *Note*: The safety squeeze can also be used. The runner should break for home only after the ball is bunted on the ground. Try this after scoring three runs in an inning. It's a crushing blow to the psyche of the defense (knowing they're behind in runs equaling a grand slam), and adds another run to an already existing lead.

Bunt everything. (Neal Portnoy)

Drag Bunt

Philosophy: The drag is a weapon every team should utilize, especially for a left-handed hitter (shorter distance to first base). Drag for a base hit. Moving a runner up to the next base (i.e. sac situation) may also be a goal for that gifted bunter.

Where it should be placed: The drag differs for each hitter, but focus on strikes. If a pitcher is wild, take the pitch on non-strikes (bring the bat back quickly). Left-handed batters should push the ball past the pitcher on the right side or lay it down the third base line. Right-handed hitters should push the ball to the right side of the infield or down the third base line.

When to use it: Drag bunts confuse fielders on where to play hitters. Drag when the infield is back (usually with two outs), or after a lot of action (i.e. multiple hits or play at the plate). Many times fielders are still reliving those previous plays, and the thought of the bunt

Lay it down anytime. (Neal Portnoy)

is the farthest thing from their minds. Even players in a hot stretch should look for the drag. After a series of line drives, corner infielders usually play back. Don't be afraid to drag even after a non-strike bunt try (third baseman moves in). Try it again and/or push a bunt down the first base line instead. Confident hitters even drag with two strikes. Infielders never look for the bunt here and move back accordingly. A player keen on dragging may also want to limp to the plate as a way of faking a leg injury. Also, look to drag on the first pitch right after a rain delay. An easy verbal signal for the drag can be, "Great time for it."

When to square around: Left-handed batters bunting down the third base line should move up in the box and only pivot the upper body. While facing left-handers, bunters should move back in the box (don't step over the chalk), use the crossover step to pull the ball either past the pitcher or down the first base line, and square just a bit later by delaying, lift the back leg and bring it across the front (back leg must still be in the box on contact). Angle the bat to hit on top of the ball. Make sure the bat is in front of the plate. Right-handed hitters should hop quickly in the stance (stay low and wide) with the body angled towards first base. This gets the body in a sprint position. When pivoting, slide the top hand up to the middle of the bat and push the ball down the first base line. To bunt to either side of the field, aim the bat in the desired direction. Once contact is made, hustle to first base.

Slash Bunt

Philosophy: This is an offensive weapon that teams and players rarely use. The slash is a fake bunt followed by a full swing down at the ball. It offsets defensive strategy and opens up the field of play. Along with bat control use the slash as a gamebreaker.

Where it should be placed: The best slashes are hit on the ground towards the corner infielders (decreased chance to field properly). On balls going through the third or first basemen, there is more opportunity for an extra-base hit and for other runners to score.

When to use it: Use the slash with runners on base with the looming of a sacrifice bunt. Slashers may wait one or two pitches into an at-bat. Fake bunt on the first pitch to force infielders into charging hard on the next one. Slash at pitches in the Little League strike zone (letters to knees), because a team may get only one opportunity to slash per game.

When to square around: Square around early or when the pitcher comes to a set position (open the front foot as in sacrificing). When the pitcher breaks the hands, choke up, step back in to the plate, and bring the bat back into the hitting position. Shorten the swing by chopping down on the ball. Also, to disguise the play the bunter may square early and hold the bat with both hands on the knob. The hitter can then move the hands up for a bunt, slash play, or to swing through.

Bunt and Run

Philosophy: This is another version of the hit-and-run play. With a runner(s) breaking, this play is designed to advance the runner(s) up one or even two bases. Watch for inattentive infielders here.

Where it should be placed: Bunt anything close to a strike. With a runner on first, bunt the ball to the left side. This takes the third baseman out of the play. The runner should attempt to steal, pick up the third base coach while rounding second base, and head to third when the third baseman (position is now vacant) releases the ball to first base. The defense is concerned with the out at first and not the runner already on base.

When to use it: The base runner must have above-average speed. When in need of runners (against a tough pitcher), the bunt-and-run is an aggressive play designed to spark a team and "wake up the bat rack." Use this play via the drag or in a sacrifice situation.

When to square around: Square when the pitcher breaks the hands (sacrifice) or later in the sequence (drag). Proper placement is key.

Fake Bunt

Philosophy: Use the fake bunt when stealing bases, for defensive clues, and in taking a pitch.

When to use it: Get a premature reading on how a team defends the bunt. Also, use the fake bunt when stealing a base (catcher comes out of the crouch position sensing a throw thus helping the hitter's strike zone). Fake bunting with an early square may also be useful on 3–0 with a take sign. This distorts the pitcher's vision during the delivery and the catcher trying to focus on the ball. With the intention of hitting, the fake bunt moves corner infielders up on the grass and increases the chances of a base hit, thus reducing their reaction time and fielding area. Try the fake bunt with a runner stealing third base. Once the third baseman commits, no one will be there to cover the bag. Also use it in a first-and-third situation with fewer than

Fake a bunt. (Neal Portnoy)

two outs. Fake a squeeze bunt and pull the bat back, have one runner steal second and the runner at third run about five steps down the line and then head quickly back to the bag. With all of this action, the runner going to second can almost walk down there without anyone noticing.

When to square around: Square around when the pitcher breaks the hands, but bring the bat back swiftly into the catcher's eyes just before the pitch crosses the plate. The catcher may just miss the pitch entirely.

Bunting Successes

Here are a few bunting highlights over my career. We literally advanced to the Massachusetts State L.L. Championship in 1982 by using the bunt. We beat a pitcher in the sectionals from Taunton, Massachusetts, who boasted of a 51–0 career pitching record with bunt after bunt. We then won our state semifinal 1–0 after an infielder threw a ball down the right field line after fielding one of our sacrifice bunts.

In a 1983 state sectional All-Star game, I missed the first two pitches for a sacrifice bunt attempt. My coach, John Stearns, called time for a conference. "You WILL get this bunt down," he blared. I was more scared of him than of failing. But I got the bunt down, we scored the run, and we ended up winning 1–0.

Our American Legion team pulled off two "double squeeze" bunts during the 1996 season (scored two runs each time). A UMass-Dartmouth player led off a game against us in 1996 with a successful two-strike drag bunt. And for a freshman who was striking out almost every at-bat (he stayed in the lineup because of his fine defense), he was instructed to sacrifice or drag bunt *every* at-bat. At least this gave him/the team a chance for some productive offense.

Brandeis University and coach Pete Varney pulled off a two-strike squeeze in the bottom of the ninth inning of the 1999 NCAA regionals against the University of Southern Maine. The play worked, and Brandeis later advanced to its first-ever College World Series. Jason Richards, a first team All-New England selection, once had four hits in a game against conference rival Salem State. This included three home runs and a drag bunt.

In 2001 we successfully pulled off a squeeze bunt with my cleanup hitter and on a few occasions have called for back-to-back squeezes. In 2002 we beat Bates College with a walk-off squeeze bunt (a pinch hitter no less) in the last inning. In 2003 we scored the go-ahead run in our conference semifinal tournament game after a successful sacrifice bunt. The catcher's throw hit our runner in the back and sailed into the outfield. We took the lead on this play in the eighth inning and advanced to the MASCAC final for the second straight year. In 2004 my catcher put down an 0–2 squeeze bunt which scored two runs. And in a summer Legion game, while we waited for the umpires to show up, the opposing short-stop (a freshman who started at Holy Cross College that spring) practiced his bunting skills against the backstop.

Bunting Drills

First, place two helmets 10 to 20 inches from the foul lines and 25 to 30 feet out from the plate. Practice bunting to each side of the infield. Left side, right side, and then repeat the drill. Then split the team into two groups. Pitchers can throw, and extra players can field. After successful rounds by each group, have the fielders play the bunts as if in a game.

Second, bunt off a live pitcher or the pitching machine (straight fastballs). The batter has one strike to work with (take non-strikes). Set up helmets as guides for proper placement. Take a tally of successful bunts throughout presea-son. Positive results should increase each time, while also giving confidence to the players bunting and you calling the play in a game.

Third, have equal groups of bun-ters, base runners, and pitchers/catchers at the four bases. Each area serves as a different bunting station: home plate (squeeze), first base (sacrifice), second (drag), and third (fake; throw towards a fence so the balls go away from everyone else). Each person has a job. Hitters are practicing the different bunts while mov-ing from station to station (work on the quick first step out of the box), pitchers

are throwing to different parts of the plate, and runners are working on their leads and breaks for each discipline.

Fourth, bunting should be done as part of every game day BP (sacrifice to the left and right sides, drag and squeeze). Once the fastball's mastered, then bunt off the pitching machine (higher velocity, curveballs, quicker sta-tions) and against pitchers throwing everything in their repertoire. *Note*: When bunting off the pitching machine, keep putting the balls down the chute. The hitter can stay in the bunting stance and just keeping bunting one after an-other. This provides more chances, plus more people get to bunt.

Coaching the Bunt

Practice (each style) and reinforce the qualities of the bunt every day. Each hit-ter should be able to lay one down at any time. Watch for proper technique in a mirror and on videotape; key on the pivot and square, getting on top of the ball, and full extension of the arms on contact. In a situation where the bunt must be exe-cuted, especially the one-chance squeeze play, hitters must be drilled on how the bunt contributes to a winning team. Thus, make competitive drills to simu-late these pressure situations.

Have separate signs for each bunt. Use a verbal signal for the squeeze with an indication of acknowledgement from the batter and runner (i.e. tap of cleats with the bat or adjustment of the hel-met). And if a kid fouls a pitch off in a sacrifice situation or you see poor tech-nique, don't be afraid to call him/her down for a conference. Sometimes a lit-tle encouragement goes a long way.

There are more and more mistakes with teams trying to sacrifice bunt.

Either it's frustration over not being able to swing away, or a lack of practicing this fine art, which has been around for over 100 years. Some bunts are popped up in the air and turned into double plays. It all comes down to coaching and what the philosophy of the team is going to be. Be good at all the fundamentals. Bunting means bat control, and in those tight playoff games, moving runners along can be the difference between winning and losing.

Baker Bunting Bat

Slice the top of a wooden bat down the middle (hitting surface only). The bat is now flat on one side. This tool better enables the bunter to place a ball accordingly (square bat and round ball). Confidence will skyrocket as teams first get to work on practicing the bunts.

Then reinforce the bunting bat with a regulation bat.

In 2003 our opponent in an American Legion game went to the plate with a wooden bat in order to better handle the sac bunt. It was perfect, the runners advanced, and the team later won the game that inning.

Sprint to First Base

Always run hard to first base. The bunter's job isn't done until that out is recorded. Some fielders, especially pitchers, are casual and take extra time in throwing. A sprint may result in a rushed or poor throw. Sacrifice bunts can end up as base hits. Running hard also applies to double-play ground balls. So always sprint. It's how the game is suppose to be played.

15

Inside Pitch and Getting Hit

"Fear is the fundamental factor in hitting."
— Leonard Koppett, author

Introduction

In the movie *The Mighty Ducks*, a youth hockey team had a goalie who was afraid of the puck. Whenever an opposing player shot, the kid ran and hid. The team was the laughingstock of the league. But a new coach came in and actually taped the kid to the goal posts. Players then unloaded shot after shot, with pucks hitting him all over the body. The pucks didn't hurt, because he wore the proper equipment. Once the goalie was able to deal with the fear of being hurt, the Ducks went on to glory.

Hitters may not have the luxury of goalie pads and chest protectors, but who wants to walk around like an un-oiled tin man? Baseball players catch with a glove and hit with a bat and helmet. The head is the main concern for protection, so a helmet guards against injury. Sure, there are times when a pitcher throws inside and the batter is either knocked down or even hit by a pitch. The pain goes away, and 99 percent of the time a batter can walk it off and continue playing.

Kids may be afraid of the pitched ball. But competitors want to hit and accept a HBP (hit by pitch) as part of the game. The more at-bats and inside pitches a batter sees, the more accustomed one becomes to these once terrifying occurrences. Kids need to show no fear by crowding the plate. And just think about this: Who's more afraid? The batter getting plunked, or the pitcher trying to stop a missile up the middle?

The Pain Factor

A baseball is hard, and pitchers throw it as hard as physically possible. Batters know that being hit by a baseball hurts. Understand that pitchers must work the whole plate to be successful, and that means throwing inside. Pitchers never want a hitter to feel comfortable at the plate. Sometimes hitters get plunked. It's part of the game.

But by seeing brawls on TV now (typically caused by knockdown pitches), kids don't develop as much tolerance for getting hit. Little Leaguers are sometimes afraid to pitch inside because of the aluminum bat. They don't want to hit the batter, and pitching inside may leave a pitch up which the batter can drive for a home run. But pitching inside and maintaining the inner half of the plate is a must for a pitcher. If not, what invariably happens is that pitchers are forced to pitch outside, hitters looking for pitches there, and thus an advantage accrues to the offense. Unless pitchers brush hitters off the plate, batters will continually feel comfortable crowding it.

However, when players are hit they don't just walk it off any more. Kids love to stare the pitcher down, and teams begin to take their frustrations out in negative ways. Relax, keep the mouths shut, and play the game. Remember that HBPs result in base runners who can then steal second and come around to score on a base hit.

Watch the Ball Into the Glove

Some hitters don't look the ball into the mitt. A strike is called, and they turn to complain to the umpire. What kind of argument do they have? Hitters can decide themselves by watching the ball the entire way. This action keeps the front shoulder closed. Repetition of this skill carries over to hitting by keeping the head and eyes on the ball. Don't bail out on inside pitches or those curveballs, or give up on a pitch outside the strike zone. Youngsters tend to fall backwards regardless of location. And some are simply trained to step out just as a pitch they don't like crosses the plate. Stay in the box and watch the ball the whole way. A batter may just pick up a clue.

Body Alignment

Many things should happen on a potential hit-by-pitch. First, the batter's front shoulder should be brought in towards the plate. The back, legs, or

Body Alignment. **Incorrect.** (Neal Portnoy)

Correct. (Neal Portnoy)

buttocks (most muscular parts) are less vulnerable to pain than the face or chest. Second, keep the bat out of the way when turning. Bats left out in front may be glanced by the pitched ball. *Rules to know*: The batter must make an attempt to avoid an inside pitch, one can't intentionally dive into the ball, and the jersey must be tucked in at all times (i.e. so as not to get intentionally grazed by the ball).

For a player to "buy" a strike on an inside pitch (not hittable from the batter's standpoint), form a "V" with the arms and lower body and fall into the plate, like jackknifing out of the way. Umpires may view this action as testament for a non-strike. Younger hitters "step in the bucket" (away from the plate) when afraid of the "beanball" or "chin music." Reinforce proper striding technique to counteract this problem.

Some of my college players have been called back by the umpire after getting hit by a pitch. Because we crowd the plate and hang in there on those tough curveballs, many times the umpire believes that we're trying to intentionally get hit. Getting hit hurts, so is it really worth getting drilled for one base? In a 2002 game in Florida, an opposing team was hit *eight* times by our starting pitcher and twice more was called back by the umpire for leaning into the pitch. We kept our starter in the game, because the score was close. But I had to tip my hat to those kids who wouldn't budge an inch — and our guy was throwing hard that night.

Hit-By-Pitch Drills

Instruct and demonstrate the proper technique on how to get hit by a pitch. Then perform the following drills.

(1) Throw pitches at or near the hitter's head, though the goal is not to be hit. Try bouncing balls into the plate. Make it fun by having the kids jump all over the place. Even if a batter is hit, make it an element of the game. (2) Now intentionally throw at and hit batters with tennis or wiffle balls. Kids can get accustomed to the HBP in this pain-free environment. Wear helmets during these drills, and remind them to "take the pain."

Try to get this mentality across: If grazed by a pitch, have the kids stay up and hit. Disguise the play to the umpire by not reacting. Obviously the score and inning dictate this point, but preach that hitting is the greatest moment in sports. It's still a ball (non-strike), but a hitter wants to get as many rips as possible. We once had a kid grazed by a pitch in a fall game. Because our player didn't run to first, the other team's bench started screaming that the pitch hit him. They gave away first base to our hitter — a negative for their defense.

Digging In

Whenever knocked down by an inside pitch, kids should stare the pitcher down and "dig in" on the next pitch. Just glance at him/her. Don't look for a fight. Just give the impression that the pitcher better watch out for a line drive. Digging in also shows the pitcher that any other close pitches won't be tolerated.

Play the game aggressively. Why be afraid of a pitch that *may* hit someone? Over four years and 500 collegiate at-bats, I was probably hit only three times. Never be intimidated. Be fearless and confident. Don't shy away from the hard thrower no matter what. Go up there swinging, and if one is indeed hit, don't rub it, and sprint to first base. And as heard yelled by players on those close inside pitches, don't be afraid to "wear it." Lastly, "hot hitters" can expect to be pitched inside.

Proper Equipment

Baseball is one of the safest of all contact sports. It requires toughness and guts to slam into outfield fences, collide with catchers, break up double plays, and even leap into dugouts chasing foul pop-ups. Though mandatory use of the helmet didn't come until 1971, some of today's players protect themselves with double ear-flap helmets, shin pads, forearm pads, jaw flaps, face cages, padded batting gloves, and protective wristbands. Since baseball relies so heavily on a sound body and mind, such equipment could be a good investment to those hitters prone to getting plunked and/or fouling balls off their lower body.

Many sluggers tape their wrists as protection from the vibrations caused by swinging a heavy bat so hard so many times. For a legitimate wrist injury, tape both wrists and cover the tape with wrist bands. Pitchers who view a hitter with taped wrists (possible injury) will probably throw inside to inhibit extension of the hands.

HBP Stories

Have pride in batters who can make it to base without a hit. This applies to walks, defensive errors, hustling to stay out of double plays, and getting HBPs. Worcester State's Keith Bianchini (1998–2001) was always the first player to hit in the batting cage. He initiated every BP session by leaning into the first pitch no matter where it went. "It gets me ready to hit," he used to say. Our second baseman at Harvard University, Bo Bernhard, tried to get hit in seemingly every game. An average hitter but above-average fielder, he was willing to get on base no matter what it took.

My captain, Jason Piskator (2001), was hit in the face by a high inside fastball, lost a tooth, and then tried to pass the injury off to someone else in the dugout when the opposing team's trainer came to check him out. Jason Grenier was also hit by Piskator in the cage during a live batting competition. His remedy to reduce the swelling was to tape his wrist as tightly as possible.

After undergoing surgery for a broken nose, former East Side Legion player Joe Albano bought a shield for his helmet just so he could continue playing in an Over-30 Summer League. A 2003 Massachusetts L.L. State Sectional game was won with a hit batsman with the bases loaded in extra innings. The deciding play in the L.L. World Series championship game was a HBP by Japan with the bases loaded. At the time the score was 0–0 and there were two outs. In 2005 my captain Zac Attaway was one of the NCAA leaders in HBPs.

16

Making a Lineup

"Managing is like holding a dove in your hand. Squeeze too hard and you kill it; not hard enough, and it flies away."
— Tommy Lasorda, manager of World Series and Olympic champs

Introduction

A lineup should have nine players who can *all* hit the baseball. There can be no weak links or sure outs if a team expects to win. Stress that number nine is just as important as number three. And there's always room for improvement since no one hits 1.000.

Score the First Run

Obviously, to win, a team must score more runs than the opposition. The first run is a key especially in games lasting six and seven innings. Get out of the gate first.

Pitchers, especially on the away team, love to have a lead going out to the mound. Moreover, starters would much rather pitch from the wind-up rather than the stretch (no concern for pick-offs or the sacrifice bunt). Teams who score first have more adrenaline knowing the other team has to come back to beat them. And from watching hundreds of games, teams have a tendency to stop being aggressive when they're down by a few runs (i.e. stealing bases, fake bunting or stealing, or taking extra bases). Catch-

ers, realizing this fact, can then focus more on framing and blocking when they know teams have stopped running.

Steal Runs

Working the count, swinging for strikes, putting the ball in play, using strategy, and playing aggressive baseball all add up to this first run. "Steal runs" by catching the defense off-guard. Use the hit-and-run, drag and slash bunts, bunt-and-run, fake steal, hit behind runners, delay steal (off the catcher's throw back to the pitcher), and take the extra base on errors and wild pitches. Put pressure on the defense, and create scoring opportunities. I've been so aggressive in tight ballgames that we've scored crucial runs on an infield fly rule pop-up that was dropped and on a shallow sacrifice fly to the left fielder, which could have been caught by the shortstop. So employ a running lineup. Refer to the adage, "Speed kills."

Know the Lineup

When a hitter walks to the plate, he/she should remember what occurred before the at-bat and who's coming up next. Teams do pitch around hot hitters to face someone else, or to have the like-handed advantage. A team may have runners on with first base unoccupied. The defensive team may intentionally walk the batter to set up the double play or the force play at more than one base. On the intentional walk, be ready to attack the ball.

Think about subsequent hitters with the RBI looming. For example, on 2-0/3-0 in a normal "take sign" situation, the hitter may attempt to drive the ball knowing a weak slap hitter is on deck. The team may need the big RBI in that particular situation.

On-Base Percentage

Be concerned with on-base percentage (reaching base via a hit, walk, defensive error, hit-by-pitch, or fielder's choice). Hitters who reach base are obviously more valuable than those who don't. The "table setters" get on base for the big bats to drive them home. Emphasize the importance of hustle, especially on comebackers to the mound. Once every season a pitcher will throw a lazy toss to first base.

The following example shows the importance of reaching base safely: at-bats (50), hits (14), walks (10), reached on error (3), and hit-by-pitch (2). The batting average is .280, but the on-base percentage is a stellar .468. In this example, total at-bats (62) and official at-bats (50) differ whether computing batting average or on-base percentage.

Stress that a leadoff hitter comes to the plate every inning. Make sure the bats, helmets, etc. are organized and ready to go when players come in from the field. The first batter in an inning is a huge key for the offense and defense. Being prepared and focused for these initial plate appearances sets the tone for the game and season.

Team Slumps

Coaches and players like a set batting order. However, keep them from being complacent. Indeed, I thoroughly enjoyed hearing my name called each day as the number five batter. However, kids of any age may start to feel comfortable if they're playing every single day. Try to use the same hitters one through five. Numbers six through nine can be interchanged at will as a way to reward success and even to see more fastballs down in the order.

If in a hot hitting streak, stay with the same lineup. Don't change what's working. However, switch the lineup around a bit during a slump. Don't push the panic button by totally revamping the starting lineup. But you can put the best hitters to date at the top of the order (without regard to power, speed, or batting average). The goal here is to generate at least a couple big innings of offense. It may be a drastic measure, but it's worth a try in dire circumstances. Lastly, when nothing seems to be working ask the players to make out the lineup. I've done this twice in American Legion play (with good hitting teams), and we won both games. Just goes to show you that it's the players who win games—not the coaches.

Value the Out

Continually preach, "Never go 1-2-3." Winning teams score with two outs, especially with no one on base. In 1987 my team scored four runs in the last inning of a big high school game, all with two outs and no one on. Scoring two-out runs frustrates pitchers, fielders, and opposing coaches. Make quality use of every out. Wait to use the sacrifice bunt until the late innings when a game can be decided by one play. Good hitters want to hit, so let them swing away in the early innings. Generating a big inning early in a game can totally demoralize a lot of teams. Use every weapon to get runners on, over and in. Here's an example:

Typical 1-2-3 Inning: first batter (ground out); second batter (strikeout); and third batter (fly out).

Non-Traditional Inning: first batter (walk followed by a stolen base with the second batter protecting the runner by swinging through the first pitch); second batter (sacrifice bunt moving the runner to third base); and third batter (infield ground out to score the runner).

In the second scenario, the same number of hitters came to the plate without getting a base hit (nothing even out of the infield) yet scored a run and still had an out to work with. Manufacture runs. Proper execution in scoring situations breeds confidence. Coming back from deficits is a winning characteristic. Get the most out of every hitter.

My West Boylston Legion team defeated the eventual New England regional champion (Milford) in a close 2–1 affair in 2001. We hit an early home run and later scored the game winner on a walk, sacrifice bunt, fielder's choice, and a steal of home. We had two hits in the game. The following section provides ideas for each spot in the batting order.

Number One

Characteristics: Leadoff is a team's fastest player and a good contact hitter.

Many switch hitters bat first. Get on base to steal bases and score runs. Number one should put the ball on the ground whenever possible to beat out infield hits plus have a high on-base percentage. Understand that every inning has a leadoff hitter. The goal each time is to get on base any way possible and work the pitcher. A leadoff base runner puts pressure on the pitcher (working from the stretch), third baseman (moving in for a possible sacrifice bunt and has less reaction time), first baseman (holding a runner on cuts down on his/her coverage area), and middle infielders (moving to their double-play position leads to more open infield space).

Tips: Number one, or the spark at the top of the order, provides pitching tips and clues to the rest of the team. Zone a pitch, work the pitcher, and see as many pitches as possible. Expect a first-pitch fastball and many or all of the pitcher's pitches. Possibly fake a bunt to see defensive coverage. Use a quick bat, choke up, and crowd the plate. Bat the best run producers at the top of the lineup; even the best overall hitter at leadoff.

Number Two

Characteristics: Number two should be the best bunter, another good contact hitter, and possess above average speed. Bunting the leadoff batter to second base, for example, can put a runner in scoring position in the first inning. Use the hit-and-run play since many number two batters are good opposite-field hitters.

Tips: Use the drag bunt to get on base and/or advance a runner. Stay out of the double play by hustling down the line. Try a switch hitter in this spot.

Number Three

Characteristics: Number three should be the best overall hitter, one who hits for average, power, and has decent speed. If the first two batters of the inning get out, at least the best hitter comes to the plate. Number three should also draw many walks and not strike out a great deal.

Tips: Number three should look for his/her zone pitch. Many pitchers throw this batter junk (breaking balls and pitches low in the strike zone). Teams may even pitch around numbers three-four-five—not intentional walks but borderline pitches. Be disciplined. Take the walk if it occurs. And never just expect fastballs early in the count. Pitchers really gear up for confrontations against the better hitters.

Number Four

Characteristics: Number four should be a leader in the "power department" (runs batted in, sacrifice flies, and possibly home runs).

Tips: Number four should get back in the box and closer to the plate. Use a heavier or longer bat. Look fastball and adjust curveball. Some sluggers have difficulty hitting off-speed pitches, but try to get at least three good swings each at-bat. Focus on driving pitches left up in the strike zone. Swing hard and never get cheated. Use the most of those three strikes. "Clean-up" bats behind many excellent hitters, so don't disappoint. Someone has to get them home. Number four should be clutch. Work on a strong upper and lower body as opposed to base running speed. Catchers seem to appear in the four-slot a lot, probably because of their knowledge of the strike zone and umpire tendencies, powerful legs, and invariably slow foot speed.

Number Five

Characteristics: "Mr. RBI." Number five is the person who drives in runs. Runners are in scoring position here more than for any other hitter. Number five may bat .280, but he/she should get those big hits when the team needs them most. He/she may not be the biggest or strongest player on the club, but a most valuable hitter.

Tips: Take a similar approach as to number four. Focus on driving the ball, especially in a RBI situation. Have a game plan for each at-bat and relish the two-out base hit. A reliable number five could be the difference between winning and losing. Make proper adjustments with runners in scoring position. For the sacrifice fly wait a bit longer, collapse the back knee, drop the hands slightly, and get under the ball. Do whatever it takes to get runners home.

Number Six

Characteristics: Number six could be "Mr. RBI #2." Good hitting teams have difficulty finding spots for everyone. Some of the best number six batters have "unfortunately" come on powerful offensive lineups.

Tips: Many pitchers relax after facing numbers one through five. A mistake may be thrown without regard to hitting ability. Drive that good fastball early in the count. Number six has been a mystery spot for my teams over the years. I do like having a left-handed batter here if my lineup has a bunch of right-handers (so the pitcher sees a different variety). I may flip-flop my numbers six and seven depending on who's been hot lately. But don't hide poor hitters near the top of the lineup. Bat your best for sane reasons and to score runs as often as possible.

Number Seven

Characteristics: Put a player here who can move runners along. Sometimes a player is a perfect mold for a certain number in the lineup. That could be number seven.

Tips: Utilize the drag bunt with average speed, or the home run if a larger player. Make things happen. Stress the importance of numbers seven-eight-nine contributing to the offensive onslaught. If the last three batters don't do anything in a seven-inning ballgame, you could be in trouble.

Number Eight

Characteristics: Number eight is the second "weakest" hitter.

Tips: First read up on the tips for number nine. Working the pitcher, if numbers seven-eight-nine get on base, gives a team an enormous advantage. Just as having multiple hitters standing in the on-deck circle, never give a pitching staff relief of any kind. Number eight should be a good bunter with above average speed, possibly a first-year player who will be a star down the road. Seventy percent of the outs occur after numbers seven-eight-nine bat. Reaching base with hitters down in the order provides a team more total at-bats and RBI possibilities.

Number Nine

Characteristics: Number nine is the "double leadoff." Traditionally the poor-hitting shortstop or center fielder, number nine is the weakest hitter with some speed. Reaching base allows the top of the lineup more base-running strategies. This batter may have slow bat speed, but plays for defensive purposes. Scrap for infield hits, drag/slash bunt, and put the ball in play with two strikes. Number nine must be a good bunter as teams may even sacrifice with one out. Also, this spot allows a hitter the most time to see the game before batting (i.e. pitching tendencies).

Tips: This batter should swing aggressively and look for fastballs. Take the mentality of "all or nothing" since number nine may bat only two or three times in a seven-inning game. Make the most of opportunities. Look for the squeeze bunt in this spot. A once good hitter may be dropped to number nine to relieve some pressure and to get back to a sweet stroke.

Designated Hitter

Characteristics: The DH is the best hitter with the weakest defensive skills (fielding, throwing and/or speed). To the downfall of pitchers, the arrival of the DH has added another hitter to the batting order. Teams with good-hitting pitchers (regular position starter) don't use the DH and play a nine-person lineup. The DH should be counted on just as heavily as every other hitter. DHs usually bat somewhere between numbers four-five-six, because you want a good hitter up there to drive in runs. The DH doesn't have to necessarily be a power hitter. Look for offensive production in all shapes and forms.

Tips: Since the DH is considered a starter, this person must be in the game at all times. Chart the pitcher to see tendencies on other hitters. Have a bat readily available. Too many DHs sit around, so stay loose every inning by stretching, running, swinging a bat, or warming up an outfielder. The DH should take infield/outfield before a game, because you never know when the DH may need to go into the fielding lineup when a position change occurs. The DH should sit next to the coaches during the game to discuss strategy. Platoon DHs game by game to get more people involved, wait for someone to get hot, or look to gain the opposite-handed advantage versus a particular pitcher. Remember that the pitcher takes the DH's spot in the batting order in a pinch-hitting situation.

If they're capable encourage starting pitchers to hit for themselves (they can come out of the game and remain as the DH). However, if your philosophy is pitching over offense, and you have people to DH, think about the starters focusing solely on pitching. Also, recite this out loud: "Designated HITTER." This player must produce. Lastly, try injured (leg) players in the DH spot. If a kid is cleared by the doctor and has a good pregame BP, play your starters. Competitors want to compete.

Conclusion

Make a draft of the lineup card before writing out the game day copy. Get suggestions from your staff when naming the starters. Always list the starting pitcher (even when not hitting). List substitutes on the bottom. Use full names, uniform numbers and positions, and include your overall/conference record. Write legibly since many teams use this form when calling in scores. Give copies of the lineup (and an updated roster) to the scorebook person, other team, and press box if need be. The hard copy goes to the home plate umpire. Keep a copy of the lineup in your back pocket along with both teams' rosters and space for notes to review later on. Especially when shuffling up a batting order, it's your job to keep a mental note, making sure everyone bats in the correct order. That's why it's good to have a PA person work your home games.

When making a change do the following: Add the replacement to all lineup cards, notify the umpire, official scorekeeper or press box, opposing club, and each member of the team. Do this in a team huddle, so there's absolutely no confusion. Note in the scorebook which inning a substitute plays (for hitters make a vertical line in the person's box, and for pitchers use a horizontal line to depict the first batter he/she faced). A dugout wall should have the game day assignment chart, both lineup cards, and notes for that game's pitching rotation. Make sure the game program is readily accessible along with any statistics on the opposing club.

Announce the starting lineup before infield/outfield or about an hour prior to game time, never the night before a game (only goes for the starting pitcher). This way every player works hard in pregame. Lastly, check all game contracts. This includes home game umpire assignments, length of BP for road games, and official start time.

17

Batting Practice

"I don't want to sound egotistical, but every time I stepped to the plate with a bat in my hands, I couldn't help but feel sorry for the pitcher."
— Rogers Hornsby, six consecutive NL batting titles

Introduction

Two things in baseball, when done incorrectly, drive me bonkers. That's Little Leaguers throwing an improper curveball with their arm and not their wrist, and a poorly run BP. Batting practice is a necessary evil. It should be done before every game, but not at every practice. Unorganized BP can take 45 to 60 minutes with each person receiving maybe 10 to 15 swings. Use that time instead for drills emphasizing the fundamentals. Hitters benefit more with 50 to 75 swings each. Thus, encourage players to get the majority of their swings before/after games. Live BP must be done correctly and as often as possible. Team practices don't provide enough time to become truly great hitters. It's all about what the individual does on their own.

Other problems with BP include: Hitters swinging for the fences and not line drives up the middle and to the opposite field; erratic pitchers with hitters who swing at bad pitches; slow throwers; and the rest of the team lounging in the outfield. Have a game plan for every BP equipped with soft toss and tee work, a team-swinging drill, 25 quality swings

and use of the Bratt's Bat, fungoes to the infielders, people designated to retrieve foul balls, and a bucket person.

Drills make the hitter, not how he/she performs in BP. In pregame BP hitters should work on their timing, and in the cage work on specific disciplines, for example. BP can be an enjoyable experience, especially hitting with new baseballs. But with the chips on the table, hitting five home runs in BP doesn't earn anyone the batting title. Lastly, using the pitching machine ensures a quicker and more accurate BP. Also, one can arrange the ATEC soft toss machine to automatically feed itself (20 to 25 balls) for those wishing to hit alone on the field or in a cage.

Pregame BP

Take BP seriously. It has a direct relationship to performance on the field that day. Have a purpose, and hit from home plate if at all possible. Pitches should be consistent fastballs down the middle and slightly outside at belt level. Focus on a hitter's timing and confidence. Avoid kids swinging and missing during BP. Throw a curveball and/or change-up as well, but show/tell the hitter it's coming. Use rounds of eight each (don't count foul balls unless a kid swings and misses). *Note*: Don't use catchers in BP, because their work is more beneficial in the bullpen and during the game.

BP Lineup

Every team has their own way to run a BP session. Here's what we do at Worcester State:

- Even groups of four: (1) catchers and outfielders, (2) second and first basemen, (3) shortstops and third basemen, and (4) rest of the outfielders.
- Each person in the group is responsible for the following: fourth: foul balls; third and second: stretching, warm up, soft toss or tee work; first: hitting off the BP pitcher and then running the bases (wear a helmet and use game bats). Rotate once a hitter is done. Each person should be able to stretch/warm up, do drills, hit live, and run the bases. Make sure to call groups in early, so they can start their hitting session on time.

BP Hitter

BP is separated into two parts: (1) bunting and strategy, and (2) live swings with game day base running. The batter does each part before moving to the next phase. Making good on the first attempt in regard to strategy (i.e. sacrifice bunt or hit-and-run) gets the hitter in the game day frame of mind. Second chances are rare in baseball, so concentrate on executing properly.

Part 1—Bunts and Strategy: sacrifice bunts to the left and right side, drag bunts to the left and right side, squeeze bunt, two hit-and-run swings to the opposite field, and a ground ball to the right side (swing at a strike to move a runner to third). Then take a slow jog around the bases.

Part 2—Live Swings and Game Day Base running: seven to 10 swings (depends on time constraints—teams usually get more swings at home games). Pitchers should throw strikes down the middle and outside. Let the hitter get set before each swing. Swing for strikes. After the last swing (try to end with a line drive), simulate a base hit by rounding first base. Go to second on a hit-and-run. Go to third on a ground ball to the right side, and score on a squeeze bunt. Simulate each base-running discipline, or work live off the batter at the plate. Coaches should be hitting ground balls to the infielders; shortstops and third basemen during groups one and two, and to the second and first basemen during groups three and four. Also, decide beforehand if foul balls and swings and misses count towards the total.

BP Runner

After hitting the last pitch, kids should work on their first quick step out of the box and sprint hard to first base. Remember to round the bag hard and think double.

On the hit-and-run, steal off the pitcher (L.L.: wait for the ball to cross home plate). Look into the catcher to find the ball when halfway to second base. Round the bag and stay at second base.

Go to third base on a simulated ball hit to the right side. Get a good secondary lead (hard steps off the bag) after the pitch and sprint to third. Once at third base, practice the squeeze bunt. Remember to be in foul territory, and break for the plate when the pitcher's front foot hits the ground. Run behind the hitter (safety reasons), and then complete any remaining routines of the hitting station.

Lightning Round

Once the last batter of the day has finished, have all/some of the hitting groups come into home plate for a lightning round (pick up the balls later). This all depends on time. Number one hits, followed by two-three-four, and so on. Each person has one opportunity to hit a line drive in fair territory. If successful, the hitter continues to bat until failing. It could be one swing or a few. Foul balls, swings and misses, weak grounders, and called strikes are all outs. After outs, the next player in the group hits. Hit in numerical order, and hustle in to the batter's box. And when BP is over, pick up the balls, sprint off the field, and make sure you have all of your equipment.

MLB BP

Watch a big-league batting practice. Hitters concentrate on line drives up the middle and to the opposite field. Pitchers (including the coaches, or pitchers on rehabilitation or a midweek tune-up) pump strikes from about 40 feet away (front of the mound). Lobbing the ball doesn't simulate game conditions.

Many hitters start their swings *before* the ball is released. The stride is taken with the weight and hands still back in the proper location. In a normal situation, a hitter focuses at the "L" and then strides after the ball is released. Pro hitters work on their timing. With the

expectation of a ball thrown to an exact spot (accuracy is a big key), the batter can quicken his focus point and swing before facing, for example, a pitcher who throws 90 mph.

Tony Gwynn was known to start a BP session by fouling balls off to the left and right sides. He slowed his swing down and worked on seeing the ball for each spot. This reinforced the contact theory and fighting off tough pitches, especially with two strikes. Some MLB teams, like the Red Sox, employ up to six BP pitchers (both left- and right-handed). We even sent a Harvard left-hander down to Fenway Park in 1993, so Mike Greenwell could work on hitting southpaws. And some clubs have scoured the Independent Leagues (not affiliated with MLB) for pitchers to throw knuckleballs to their lineup.

Also throw breaking pitches. My college team faces a healthy diet of "Baker Breakers." Hitting game day pitches comes only through practicing them first. Tell/show the hitter which pitch is coming to better adjust to the movement and spin.

Work on Different Pitches

To work on the curveball during BP, mix a lob into the regular routine. The hitter must wait on the unexpected off-speed pitch and attempt to drive it to the opposite field. Also, move the L-screen to the back side of a hitter to simulate the slider and/or like-handed situations. Read the pitch from the inner half of the plate across to the outer. Focus on leaning over, and keep the front shoulder closed. Teams should try facing the arm (left or right) of the pitcher they'll be opposing in the game. Use the pitching machine (curveballs) if need be.

Economical Strategies

If strapped for time outdoors, take double-barrel BP (hitter at each side of the backstop). Pitchers should be protected by a screen or barrier. If possible, left-handed hitters should hit from the first base side and right-handers from the third base side. On rainy days where the batting cage is the only option, break the netting into two areas. Use the large infield screens as the middle backstop and two L-screens to protect the two pitchers. Batters should hit in opposite directions, so line drives don't sneak into the other cage.

For regular close-range BP, set up the L-screen next to the backstop with the batter at home plate (facing the backstop). The backstop catches everything. Emphasize hitting down, so balls don't

Hit towards the backstop. (Rex Baker)

go flying over the top. *Other*: Try the short-toss flip drill from behind a hitting screen. Have the batter sit or kneel a close distance away and throw an underhanded flip to a batter. Work different areas of the plate. So instead of soft toss, now the hitter can actually simulate a pitch arriving directly from the mound. Plus, it takes away a lot of the arm strain from pitching the regular distance.

Lastly, for any BP the team can affix a simple tarp behind the plate to serve as a target for balls and strikes. Either place the tarp on the backstop or hang it on a screen behind home plate. This target serves two purposes: An area for pitchers to throw to, and hitters to learn and get a better appreciation of the strike zone. There will now be no excuses or complaints from a hitter on a strike call. Also use 1-1 and 3-2 counts during BP or intrasquad scrimmages to practice game situations and aggressiveness and to quicken the activity along. Use competitive games with hitting and fielding points (i.e. ground balls/line drives hit in fair territory along with defensive points/deductions). Remember, hitters need to swing the bat. No one should be up there looking for a walk.

Infield Work

Hit grounders to every infielder. Start with third basemen and shortstops (first half of BP) and conclude with the second and first basemen. Hit to the shortstops and first basemen from the fungo circle near the third base line. Hit to the second and third basemen from first. Besides the typical grounder, infielders may also want to practice their throws to first base, double-play pivot, backhands, pop-ups, and slow rollers.

Try to eliminate one-hoppers. Toss

the ball high and hit the top portion of the ball. Always wait for the BP batter to hit the ball, let infield pop-ups drop in, and watch for the batter running to first base. And a final note, players shouldn't be afraid to get the uniform dirty in pregame, sprint around the bases, take aggressive swings, and work on weaknesses. Plus, you never know who's watching.

Screens and Rugs

Some teams can't afford screens and rugs. However, both luxuries ensure for a more organized and safer BP session. All screens and nets should be handled by the home team, which hits before the visitors (some teams hit at their own facility before traveling, but check to see if you can use the cage at an away field). This pertains also to tarps and even raking the diamond. The portable backstop (aka turtle or shell) is wheeled around the plate area to shag errant foul balls. Place the L-screen (rug for the pitcher to stand on) at the front of the mound. Use an old paint bucket, milk crate, or shopping cart as the ball collector. Screens should be located at first base (protects the first baseman taking throws from infielders) and in center field (protects the ball-bucket person). A soft-toss net is great to have in the on-deck area. Rugs or rubber mats can be placed on both sides of the plate for the hitters to stand on. This protects the dirt from cleat marks, so you don't have to work on the batter's box again before the game.

BP Reminders

Every team should practice a typical BP routine. Look for a 30-minute limit. Avoid rushing, but make sure everyone is working hard. Remember, a lot is going on before a game: stretching and throwing, BP and infield/outfield for both teams, the lining, raking and watering the field and mounds, ground rules, National Anthem, and then play ball! Have a written schedule of the pregame format posted in both dugouts.

The BP pitcher should be loose before the first batter comes to the plate. Make sure this person is conscious of getting behind the screen. Everyone should be dressed in full uniform, wearing cleats and hats, and the team T-shirt or game uniform. Outfielders should play their positions and work on getting accustomed to the field, grass, sun, and wind conditions. Make sure the BP pitcher always has enough baseballs. Everyone should help pick up the balls.

Game Day Hitting/ Pitching Clues

Watch the opposing team hit. Pick up clues. Jot down hitter tendencies. Check for bunting success rate, hit-and-runs, etc. How many left-handed bats are in the lineup? Is the wind blowing out when facing a powerful hitting team? Are they swinging for the fences? And watch the opposing pitcher warm up to find out his/her pitches:

Fastball: flick of the glove forward.
Curveball: twist of the glove open and then down.
Slider: flick of the glove away from the body to the side.
Change-up: arm and glove come in towards the body.
Split-fingered fastball/forkball: turn of the glove side to side.
Knuckleball, palmball: shows grip before throwing.

Watch every pitcher (starter and reliever) when they throw off the mound. See what they throw and how hard. Did the pitcher warm up long enough or properly? Were more fastballs thrown than curveballs? Was there a knuckleball mixed in? Assess the pitcher's, plus your own team's, strengths and weaknesses. Also, check for the pitcher having difficulty throwing strikes. Were the pitches high or low? That may carry over to the game. Lack of consistency may be mental, physical, or a problem with the actual mound.

The Work

Work on different situations and batting counts when taking BP in practice. Hitting live on the field is great so you can see where the ball travels, but batters get far more swings in the cage. Avoid having kids swinging simply at pitches down the middle. Hit strikes. On a rainy day try some competition against a teammate at the indoor batting cage. Using the pitching machine, try three outs for each hitter in a nine-inning game. Employ strategy, base hits, outs, etc. with the opponent serving as the umpire.

BP Stories

Former MLB player and Worcester, Massachusetts, native Mark Johnson was famous for hitting BP under the lights *after* Legion games. Three of my youth coaches, John Stearns, Jim Leal and Wayne Boraccini, threw BP *without* L-screens. Needless to say you didn't want to take a called strike with these guys throwing. For my final high school season I built a batting cage in my dirt cellar with old carpets and chicken wire and made my own L-screen and batting tee

(I hit .506 that season). The seniors that year all tried to schedule study hall for their final class of the day. Our principal didn't seem to notice, thank goodness, that we were outside on the field hitting BP during most of those classes.

In college Dr. John Winkin (U. Maine) took notes during our BP. University of Miami players showed up at our BP/game against Villanova. When we played the Hurricanes the next day it was as if they knew exactly where to play me. I once allowed my hitters to "swing for the fences" to show off our power and muscle. We were then totally shut down that day, which taught me a most valuable lesson: Never do anything in pregame to tick a team off.

One of the most successful high school coaches in Massachusetts history is famous for busting out the pitching machine on game day with the visiting team in attendance. He cranks the machine to about 90 mph, and most of his kids can't even come close to making contact. But what the opposition doesn't know is that his team has already hit BP. What they're seeing is an aberration and designed to make the opponent overconfident.

In our last game of the 1997 season, a line drive to the face broke my glasses and forced me to do ground rules with taped frames and gauze up my nose. But that taught me a lesson: The next time we hit in that chain-link cage, I threw BP in full catcher's equipment. Earlier that year we scrapped pregame BP at the Mass. Maritime Academy, and the kids did soft toss and drills for 30 minutes. Boy were they upset with me. But we left with a sweep.

I've coached players who built batting cages in their back yards. Plus, for those kids who work part-time at indoor batting facilities, do they work there for the money or the free swings?

My five minutes of fame came in 1995 when a photo of me throwing BP behind trash cans appeared on the front page of the *Boston Globe* sports section. I came up with the "Morgan Drill" after throwing close-range BP to Boston College's Ryan Morgan in the Cape Cod League. I got Morgan ready to hit before home games with absolute gas from a short distance away. I'd pick my spots with pinpoint control, so Morgan could time his quick hands and sweet swing for each area.

In 1997 I benched my captain for disciplinary reasons. Then I told him to redeem himself in pregame BP. He proceeded to try and take my head off with each swing. That day he launched the game-winning home run. In 1999, we played Eastern Connecticut State University, who was the defending national champion. Legendary Bill Holowaty, with 30-plus years of coaching experience, was out there, feisty as ever, and threw to the entire team. It fired me up as I took the field to throw. And I can't forget to mention area Legion coach Greg Desto, who taught himself to throw BP with *both* hands.

On a rainy day in 2003, we held an "optional" hitting practice for our Le-gion team at a local indoor cage. Every kid showed up. Two years earlier we had to continue a suspended state tournament legion game at 9:00 A.M. The game started at 11:00 P.M. the night before and was halted at 1:30 A.M. (fog). We ended up losing the morning game, so our next game was 1:00 P.M. later that day. Instead of getting some sleep or going out for breakfast, we literally hit from 10:30 A.M.-noon. And I mean hit. It was probably the most aggressive BP session I've ever been a part of. We won the 1 P.M. game, won the next day as well, and gave the eventual state and New England regional champion (Milford) all they could handle in Final Four action.

Afterthought

Pitching is an unnatural motion. The arm is suppose to go underhand, not overhand. My elbow ligament still bulges out when I throw, but I'll keep chucking until my arm falls off. When your BP pitcher needs to get really loose, apply some Atomic Balm, Flexall, and Icy Hot (pain relief solutions) as a singular mixture. It burns at first and stings in the shower, but you can throw all day. Also invest in those sweat-jackets that you see pro pitchers wearing in the dugouts.

18

Signals

"Baseball is a game of quick episodes; it is also a game of anticipation. Therefore, advance information can be invaluable."

— George Will, author of *Men at Work*

Introduction

Signals are the manager's way to influence, control, and win a game. The batter must be keyed into possible calls and strategies. Signs in baseball are given at every possible moment; even L.L. coaches give offensive signals and call the pitches. Take it from a championship coach: signal calling wins games.

Whatever the signaling method, reinforce and repeat the signs throughout the season. Write them down for the kids if need be. At Worcester State we put together a 150-page playbook that includes all of the signs, so players can review them at home (also includes fundamentals, strategy, and photos of hitter stances and swings). Reiterate their importance and the horror of missing them. Signals make baseball challenging and competitive. No team wins by simply throwing equipment on the field. You must out-think and out-hit the opposition.

What the Coach Has to Do

Have offensive and defensive signals. The coaches also call every pitch at Worcester State. The basics for offense include the sacrifice bunt, steal, hit-and-run, and squeeze bunt. The younger the team, the simpler the signals and concepts should be. Kids' attention spans aren't as developed as advanced players'. Also, kids should play and learn the game through actual competition. The more mature a player becomes, the more the need for signal calling. So don't complicate matters.

Calling plays must be thought out and executed. Try to be one pitch, and even one hitter, ahead of the action. Remember to give signals even with two outs and/or two strikes on the batter. Players should watch the entire sequence. Practice the fundamentals along with strategy. Use the plays in your arsenal, because signals do little for a team if they're left on the bench.

Lastly, to penalize mental mistakes and missed signs, put the Kangaroo Court into order. Have an assistant coach or veteran player assess monetary amounts to forgotten uniform pieces, running through stop signs, pitchers walking leadoff hitters, going 1-2-3, or whatever the team can come up with. This money can go towards the team banquet at the end of the season.

How to Signal

This all depends on you. Obviously the professional manager can't verbally call the signs, because of the roar of the crowd. At the younger levels, verbal signs do two things. First, everyone hears them. Second, there's little room for misinterpretation. The only drawback is that they may leave you without much of a voice after the game.

Give signals in the dugout or at third base. Whichever you choose, be visible to all runners and the batter. Watch the defense and how they set up. Every method must be easily interpreted. Missing a sign is a sin, especially when a player gets out because of it. Simply twirl the index finger for a review of the signals. Call a timeout if anyone is confused. Make sure the batter and base runner confirm the squeeze play with a touch system, so everyone is on the same page. A batter swinging away on the squeeze or a steal of home could be very dangerous.

Have an indicator that tips off a signal. It could be anything. Once the indicator is called, everyone knows something is on. Also use a takeoff sign to confuse the opposition (i.e. wipe across the chest). Lastly, after a foul ball ("Is the previous signal still on?") tap the brim of your hat as a way to signal that the same play is on. Finish with a clap of the hands, so players know the signals are complete for that particular play. If nothing is on, simply flick your fingers. Runners should always show the number of outs whenever they reach base and watch for signs while on the actual bag. *Other:* Longtime Westboro Massachusetts High School coach Bob Poole uses plywood boards to signal his offense. The various pieces have different colors and numbers and are flipped side to side or upside down for a particular play. It's unique, and I don't know anyone who's been able to decipher Poole's system.

Player-to-Player Signals

A basic signal for the hitter and base runner pertains to a pitch in the dirt. The hitter must signal for advancement to the next base or hold, according to how far the ball skips away. Standard operation for this play is to advance if the ball goes beyond the home-plate dirt circle. And whenever there's a scoring runner, the on-deck batter should sprint to home plate, get the bat out of the way, and indicate whether to stay up or to slide, and if to slide, where.

Hitters can also have player-to-player signals. This could apply to certain teammates or may be used during a particular game or inning. For example, two on-deck hitters notice the third baseman playing back. If able to reach base, the next batter will lay down a drag bunt on the first pitch. This way both players can anticipate the strategy and possibly move up to third base on a perfectly placed bunt down the third base line. Also, if you call for a drag bunt, base runners need to know this in order to get a good jump and be safe at the next base. Remember, whenever in doubt on the bases, and always on force plays, it's a good idea to slide.

Defensive Strategy

So much occurs on a single pitch. Coaches, hitters, base runners, and fielders are all signaling and moving. It's like a swarm of bees on a diamond, all hoping to anticipate what and where the pitcher will throw and where the batter will hit the ball. In a game the following could all be happening at once:

- Offensive team's manager giving signs to the third base coach.
- Third base coach relaying those signs to the batter and/or base runner(s).
- A hitter possibly giving signs to the base runner and vice versa.
- Catchers giving signs to the pitcher or relaying signs from the bench to the pitcher.
- Middle infielders relaying that pitch to the outfielders.
- Middle infielders relaying the signs to each other on base coverage for steal attempts.
- Catchers possibly giving signs to the pitcher and/or infielders for a possible pickoff throw.

For hitters, advance information on fielder placement can be a key for batting average and can decide the outcome of games. Here are some examples:

- Instead of playing the infield in with a base runner on third base and less than two outs, why not play back, wait for the offensive team to call its own signals, and then charge to the front of the infield grass? This puts added pressure on the batter and gives the defense the upper hand. The batter now has to make a quick adjustment in the swing and change the objective of one's job to get the runner home. This is exactly why the hitter shouldn't change his/her approach too much. Don't think just contact for the above scenario. Get a pitch to drive.
- The shortstop gives a nonverbal sign with his/her mouth to the second baseman to decide who's covering the bag on a steal attempt (open mouth:

second base covers; closed: shortstop covers).
- This should influence the offensive strategy for a hit-and-run. With a right-handed hitter up, don't assume the right side of the infield will be vacated on a steal attempt. Some teams change up the coverage, so be alert.
- Middle infielders relay the type of pitch to outfielders, who then move according to the pitch, location, and person hitting. Just as every batter should make note of the defense before every at-bat, a hitter can also adjust the swing as the ball is arriving by noticing any movement by an infielder.

Stealing Signs

To keep the opposition from trying to steal signs, change the indicator or add in a new wipe signal to cancel everything out. Assign a non-starter the task of trying to decipher the other team's signs, but don't make this a top priority. Focus on your team and what each player's job is for that particular game.

Scorebook

Do you know how to do the scorebook? You've probably done it. But could you actually coach a kid on all the proper symbols and notations? If not, instructions for the procedure and abbreviations are located at the beginning of each book.

The scorebook is a team's diary. Hire a trustworthy and intelligent baseball mind to do the recordings. Every scorebook may be a little different. Complete the team totals after each game. Write neatly in pencil since mistakes made in pen are permanent. Make copies of the pages after each game in case the book gets lost or misplaced. Those stats for opposing clubs also come in handy the following season. Lastly, remember to record RBI totals, hit-by-pitches, caught stealing, and know the proper way to calculate ERA.

No players should ever come near the scorebook person, let alone have the opportunity to question or change a marking in their favor. Also, to keep things simple for a lead or deficit use the score differential (4–1 is 3–0), not the actual score.

Statistics

Hitters love to see their names in print. Submit precise stats and game summaries (mail, phone, FAX, e-mail) to the appropriate media outlets or league office. Always know the time/date deadlines for each newspaper, for example. The higher the batting statistics, the more All-Star players a team may have. Everyone knows a .400 hitter, but how many times does anyone know or even notice a good fielding percentage? Box scores and stats focus on the offense. So continue to shoot for those awards, both during and after the season. The more notoriety to a program, the easier recruiting becomes. Remember also that someone has to vote for Coach of the Year!

Avoid allowing players to see their complete in-season statistics. Players know when they're hitting well and when they're not. Stats only cause problems and take away from the team approach to winning. Awards shouldn't be the sole reason for competition. Reinforce hard work and dedication to team ideals. Have in-season awards (i.e. Superman T-shirt) that players win per week for stellar performances on and off the field. Mike Easler let star hitters of the day parade around in his "Hit Man" jacket (his famous MLB nickname). Award a game ball to the winning pitcher. Hand out first home run balls. Take a team photo. And call out the best grades when report cards come out.

After each season award certificates or trophies at the team banquet. Don't have to many different awards, but make them count. Try MVP, Top Hitter (highest batting average), Top Pitcher (most wins or lowest ERA), Best Defense (fielding percentage), Top Rookie (best first-year player), Unsung Hero (hardest-working team player), Student-Athlete (highest grades), Sportsmanship (conduct, attitude, discipline), and Courage (player battling or coming back from an injury).

19

Work Ethic, Attitude and Winning

"It wasn't so much the record-busting that made [Pete] Rose such an appealing national icon; it was the sheer gusto with which he played the game, the belly-sliding, glove-banging intensity he brought to the ballpark every day."

— Ron Firmite, writer

Introduction

Work ethic means dedication throughout the year. With a champion named each season, every team has a shot at the title. Strive to be the best at everything, and always be prepared. Winners understand certain qualities to be successful. Know and live by them.

Work Ethic

Perfecting skills doesn't occur only at practice. It's before and after training sessions, on weekends, in poor weather, at night before bed, off the tee, in the cellar, indoors during the winter, at the weight room, on the track, and in the batting cages. Be the first one to practice and last to leave. Use Mike Piazza as motivation. The perennial All-Star catcher was a 62nd-round draft pick by the Dodgers in 1988. He hit in his own indoor cage in Philadelphia. This work has led to a thriving and potentially Hall of Fame career.

After winning Game 6 of the 1991

World Series with an extra-inning homer, Kirby Puckett was asked about the pressure and of playing the deciding Game 7 the very next day. Puckett replied, "I'll get my rest when I'm dead." Shortly after winning Game 3 of the 1996 playoffs against the Orioles, Bernie Williams did 15 minutes of abdominal exercises on the clubhouse floor (he never goes to sleep without doing his sit-ups). Rickey Henderson has been known to climb the Stairmaster machine on the highest level for some 20 minutes just before game time. Nomar Garciaparra puts himself through Navy Seal-like training each off season. Carlton Fisk used to travel with his own weight set. And Alex Rodriguez goes through a regimented batting routine every day that includes soft toss, tee, cage, and live BP.

My captain, Eric Swedberg, was swinging a bat in the weight room at nine o'clock on a Friday night during our school's holiday break. Rick Asadoorian (former number one draft pick of the Red Sox) hit balls off a tee all by himself *after* an American Legion game. Because

I didn't feel right at the plate after playing Drexel University (Pennsylvania), I walked to the nearest baseball field with my tee, bat, and a bag of balls. I hit until it got dark and walked backed to the hotel. I got two solid hits the next day.

In 1996 on our spring training trip to the Coco Expo in Florida, my assistant coach and I went out for late-night dinner. It was a chilly and rainy evening. When we got near our car, we noticed a figure under a street light in the parking lot. We walked over to find a Japanese youngster, who was on school vacation, swinging a bat. I asked him what he was doing. In broken English he said, "Went oh-fa-four today."

Dave Ford, a former UConn star and later a minor leaguer, used to hit BP with orange baseballs in the snow. In the early 1990s I gave private hitting lessons to 15-year-old Todd Brodeur of Auburn (Massachusetts). As a high school senior he shattered my school record of highest batting average in a season. Then at Trinity College (Connecticut) in 1999 he laced a game-winning single in the bottom of the ninth to beat Worcester State. I guess he listened to me all those times in the cage.

Not Just Physical Skills

Increase players' baserunning speed through countless sprints. Become better fielders by taking ground balls every day. Get kids in the batting cage. Take 100 bunts off the pitching machine. Throw a baseball through a tire. Read baseball books. Watch other teams practice. Scout an opponent. Learn the strike zone by watching MLB pitchers on TV. See how other players approach and play the game. Always keep in mind what

others are doing, and then do a little bit more. I learned so much more about hitting after meeting with Mike Easler at Fenway Park. Plus Tim Wakefield worked with my knuckleball pitcher and taught him drills to do on his own.

Hustle

What good comes from sprinting out an infield pop-up? More than meets the eye. Hustle should come naturally. It means more for outs rather than hits, because adrenaline will push a player to stretch a single into a double. And how many times does one really get to run the bases in a game — three, maybe four times? Make the most of it by running hard. In our first game of 2002, my captain hit a routine infield fly into a swirling Florida wind. The ball dropped in, and he slid safely into second base.

Hustle forces the defense into mistakes. Joe DiMaggio played with such passion because he wanted to show any first-time fans how the game should be played. As former Murdock (Massachusetts) High School coach Dave Smith said to me once, "It doesn't take any talent to hustle." And I can't help but remember dominating at an away college game. The opposing coach screamed at his team, because our guys were continually beating his players to the foul balls.

One of my former players didn't run out a foul pop-up that almost landed in fair territory. Boy, did he get an earful. From that time forward, Jeff Wood (2001–03) sprinted every ball hit — fair or foul. Even balls hit behind towards the backstop, he would run them out. He got the message, as did his teammates. Wood was named captain and made All-Conference in 2003.

Toughness

If kids play hard, injuries may happen. But lazy ballplayers accomplish nothing. Players sitting around should make your blood boil. No one plays baseball forever, so cherish every moment, and unless an injury is detrimental to the team, play with pain and S.I.U. (Suck It Up).

Ty Cobb had his tonsils removed without anesthesia before a spring training game by a doctor who was later committed to an institution. Catcher Johnny Bench took such a beating that he had trouble getting in and out of cabs. Ken Caminiti was named National League MVP in 1996. He *won* the award after an August performance in Mexico against the Mets. Suffering from dehydration and food poisoning, Caminiti started the game in sweltering heat after a night without sleep and an IV in his arm. With a meal consisting of a Snickers bar, Caminiti blasted two homers in his first two at-bats before being unwillingly taken out by manager Bruce Bochy.

Mo Vaughn won the American League MVP in 1995 despite hitting with

Pick each other up. (Bruce Baker)

a broken finger for half the season. Bobby Bonilla and Paul O'Neill both battled through hamstring pulls to lead their respective teams to World Series titles. After undergoing hip replacement surgery, Bo Jackson returned to the majors and hit a home run in his first game back.

Mike Giardi of Harvard broke his hand sliding into first base trying to beat out an infield hit. He went out the next inning and made a solid catch-and-throw at shortstop. Between games his hand was X-rayed and unfortunately put in a cast. The hustle play became the eventual winning run in a crucial conference game, but we lost our captain for the rest of the season (Giardi was still voted Ivy League Player of the Year). I tore ligaments in my wrist in 1992 on a similar play (I never missed a game). Worcester State All-American Eric Swedberg was a three-time conference Player of the Year playing with a metal plate in his ankle. Matt Heenan was All-Conference despite suffering from both a broken jaw and cheekbone. And Little Leaguer Kurt Sabacinski tore a broken fingernail off at our hitting clinic. We taped it up, and he didn't miss a station.

Matt Murton (Georgia Tech) broke his hand in Team USA action, but played through the pain and later led the Wareham Gatemen to their second consecutive Cape League Championship in 2002. Zach Smithlin (Bourne Braves) overcame surgeries to *both* wrists to have a standout senior season at Penn State, and he later signed a pro contract with St. Louis.

Attitude

Attitude reflects the inner drive and a proper approach to pressure. Respect the game for the now, past players, and those coming after you. Ballplayers shouldn't be welcomed as heroes for making practice on time. That's expected. A great attitude means taking the game day approach to drills, diving and sliding in practice, not arguing with umpires, and picking each other up. In 1982 Ralph Houk, then Red Sox manager, said of 43-year-old Carl Yastrzemski, "Nobody on this club works harder. That's why he's an inspiration to our young kids."

When players aren't at home, a winning team has kids who are at the ballfield, in the cages, at the library or study hall, in the weight room or gym, or hanging out with their teammates. I once called a recruit at home, and his mother said he was out hitting with his father. Great stuff!

As players change with age, so do their roles and expectations. Youngsters should always hustle to show others how bad they want to play (be seen but not heard). Older players or veterans should hustle to show the younger players how

the game should be played — all out. Be a role model to all of the kids. As a two-year college captain, I carried the equipment both seasons.

Athletes and coaches should also want to leave a piece of themselves behind before advancing a level of play or even finishing their career. Be it a unique quality, leadership skill, team function, or a championship team, look to be important. Work to be better than most. Have your kids come up with the team saying for huddles, choose the uniform for big games, or lead the stretches.

Attitude also focuses on winning and losing. Everybody loves a winner. Losing is difficult to swallow, but make sure the team comes first. For example, avoid a celebration after going two for three when the team lost 10–3. Learn to leave losses on the field. Life is too precious for depression caused by a single loss or slump. Never accept losing, but work so it doesn't happen again. In the 2001 Massachusetts State American Legion Final, the last out of the game was a fielder's choice hit by the Lowell star shortstop Derek Sodre. After coming to a stop down the right field line, he spun around, and sprinted to home plate to be the first person in line to shake hands.

The Team Wins

Jack Parker, who has coached the Boston University hockey program to three national championships, once remarked to a player who strolled into the locker room just before the start of practice, "If you're five minutes early ... you're late."

T.E.A.M. (Bruce Baker)

A classic line is to say, "Stop thinking about yourself." Winning teams sacrifice for each other. That not only goes for hitting the ball to the right side with a runner on second base, for example, but it also stands for staying Together, having Enthusiasm, the right Attitude, and staying Motivated all game. Ron Fraser, former University of Miami coach, insisted that his Hurricanes end practice each day by running hand in hand across the field in a chain. Fraser led eight clubs to the College World Series. And the best thing that can be said about a baseball player is that he was a great teammate.

W.I.N. (Whatever Is Necessary)

Hitting symbolizes the ultimate competition: Standing in a diamond with a single competitor. No one can throw a pick or block. A malfunctioning clock can't be blamed for a loss. Compete to win no matter what the game: wiffleball, checkers, conditioning workouts, or in the classroom. Never let up. Competition should be fun, and in adversity lies opportunity. It was said that Michael Jordan, during his attempt to play minor league baseball, was the hardest-working player on the team.

Winning is grand and scoreboard watching is fashionable during the pennant race, but do these things off the field. Distractions kill a winning attitude. Be concerned with the pitch and swing. Let the press and fans do all the talking. But sometimes a team needs a motivational lift. In 2002 we played 12th-ranked powerhouse Wartburg (Iowa) in Florida. I told the team we were going to sweep the doubleheader. We did and went on a 10-game win streak.

Tom Seaver once said, "There are only two places in this league. First place and no place." Winning should never be overemphasized. Every team wants to win, but is every team committed to being successful? Don't declare yourself number one before actually reaching that goal. Be that quiet team who methodically goes about their job. Play loose, but hustle when stepping over the chalk lines. Don't worry about the schedule or an opponent. Even if you're playing the defending champs, they have to beat *you*.

When winning a big regular-season game, don't act like you just won the World Series. Expect to win. Have a line of non-starters come out and give high fives to the starters. Shake hands with the other team and head directly to the outfield for a team meeting.

Here are some other winning qualities:

- Put the bat on the ball. Limit strike-outs, and get hits on two-strike counts and with two outs.
- Have a team saying. This gives a group an identity and personality (i.e. "No Pain No Spain"—1992 USA Olympic motto).
- Play hard every inning. Anything can happen in baseball. Especially when losing. This is the time when players have to pick up their bootstraps.
- Do the little things. This includes cheering for teammates, carrying and setting up the equipment, backing up bases, sprinting on and off the field, base coaching, running to get foul balls, and being on time. Always feel there's something to do. Love those hustlers and kids who get things done.
- Get the uniform dirty. Uniforms can be washed and stitched up, so there's no reason why shirt, pants, and socks shouldn't be filthy. A clean uniform

Act first class in victory and defeat. (Bruce Baker)

has an owner who did little to help the team win. So dive back into bases, slide into bags, leap for balls in the gap, don't be afraid of going after fly balls near the fences, and stand in against those hard throwers.

Coach's Role

Successful coaches have players who will do anything to win. Each coach has a different philosophy, but all have a will to win. Fun comes from success. Broadcast that vigor in practice, in the locker room, and on the playing field. Make sure every player knows you'll do anything for them.

Always preach winning as a team. Never rebuild; instead, reload. Lou Holtz instructed his players on how to carry him off the field in the 1988 national championship game. This wasn't being cocky — just preparing to win.

I played on playoff teams in every sport for seven straight years from L.L. all the way through high school. This in-

cluded soccer, baseball, and even street hockey. Then in college I endured four consecutive losing seasons. It wasn't until 1998 that I was surrounded by a winning club — over 10 long years. But I knew that with hard work, loyal and knowledgeable coaches, recruiting talent, and a winning attitude that success would eventually come.

Demand hustle and loyalty, but this is a two-way street. Tell the team to do everything you say and if they do, success will come. Put the responsibility on them. Believe it and do it. And it's a lot easier to be strict at first and then ease off a bit when the kids start believing in the program, as opposed to the other way around. Remember, there can only be one person in charge.

Review offensive strategy before and during competition. Don't use a lot of team huddles during a game, mostly because you have a hitter who needs to get ready and hit. Speak more on an individual basis, and let your assistants strategize and coach as well. Stay away from long and loud motivational speeches. They may do a lot for the coach, but little for the athlete.

How to Dress

Teams should carry themselves with pride, dignity and class. This begins with on-the-field antics and extends to the uniform. Round the brim of the hat for better focus. Make sure the stirrups show and don't fall down during the game. Be dressed in full uniform before stepping on the diamond, and walk from the bus/cars to the field as a team. Button the jersey. Tuck the uniform shirt in the pants. Never wear a hat backwards. Wear wristbands, taped wrists, and eye black for the right reasons. Try to look good on game day. Leave any earrings/jewelry at home, and avoid long hair. Shine the spikes. Wash/bleach the uniform, and hang clothes on a hanger to avoid wrinkles. And never show up to a game with a dirty uniform. Carry equipment in a baseball bag, so belongings never get misplaced or lost. Put your name/number on everything.

Wear the school/team colors with pride. At Worcester State we want to look and play the best. We model ourselves after winners with pinstripe game pants (New York Yankees), button-down/loose-fitting gold uniform tops (LSU Tigers), tackle twill lettering and our names stitched on the back (MLB), and have the old English "W" on our fitted hats (U. Miami). Fund-raising money (so players don't have to buy them) pays for team sweat suits and shorts (practice outfits), wool hats (for cold weather), T-shirts (with motivational sayings), and metal spikes. Our

Dress to impress. (Bruce Baker)

team deal with Ringor out of Oregon, an equipment company that specializes in baseball, includes discounts, group orders, and no charge for returns. Thus, there have been countless recruits, fans, and even opposing players who have been thoroughly impressed with our uniforms and practice attire.

John Wooden taught his basketball players at UCLA how to properly wear their socks and tie their shoes. Wooden didn't want his kids to suffer blisters or shin splints. Prepare for the unexpected. That way the team can focus on performing.

Line the helmets and bats together against the backstop each inning. Keep the dugout clean for safety and organizational reasons, and afterwards make sure it's cleaner than it was when you arrived. Talk to parents and fans only *after* games. Keep everyone in the dugout. And stand in formation for the National Anthem. To play with the best, start by appearing and acting the best. If you put your hands in the dough, be committed to making the best loaf of bread possible.

20

Dealing with Failure

"The only way to prove you're a good sport is to lose."
— Ernie Banks, Mr. Cub

Introduction

Baseball is a unique game in terms of failure. In virtually every other sport, time and situations quickly allow second chances (i.e. missed shot in basketball, dropped catch in football, or poor pass in hockey or soccer). In baseball, some hitters may have to wait three innings, or an entire game, to get another at-bat. Players must come to grips with not succeeding at every play. No batter gets a hit every time up. Mistakes and failure are part of the game.

Dealing with failure is a determining factor in success on and off the field. Maturity comes in recognizing mistakes and calmly making amends. Visual and external frustration may lead to tantrums, influence the ability to hit consistently, and may carry over to schoolwork. Common signs of frustration include: throwing of equipment, walking with the head down, or not speaking with peers and family. Make every effort to combat feelings of failure, and speak with the player and his/her parents. Avoid confronting a player directly after an out, especially a strikeout. Wait a few moments, so they can cool off. Then try to rectify the situation.

I got frustrated once in a high school preseason scrimmage. My coach said, "Look to hit that first good fastball." But I had always taken a strike. "Why?" coach Paul Fenton said. "The first one is usually the best one." I went on to hit over .500 that year.

Getting angry and throwing equipment only make that player and team look bad. A former coach once made my teammate run numerous laps around the track with a trash can on his back. He had kicked the can over the previous day after a striking out. That player, and team for that matter, never had another such outburst the rest of the season.

Things happen during the season that warrant positive reinforcement: strikeouts, injuries, illness, losing streaks, and batting slumps. Some are daily, weekly, monthly, and even seasonally. Getting into one isn't the problem; it's getting out of it with one's sanity and confidence intact.

Some players hit line drives without desirable results. Yale University employed the "Baker Shift" during the second game of our doubleheader. They moved the infield and outfield to my pull side. I adjusted my stance and hit three missiles that afternoon. All were caught by the shifting fielders. Oh well. When hitting well, don't change a thing. Those line drives will soon find holes. And what if one isn't hitting the ball hard? Here are some tips:

Pitching Wins

Though a team can't win without runs, effective and consistent pitching and defense combined will probably win you more ballgames. Because the pitcher has the upper hand in controlling the speed and flow of a game, batters fail more often than they succeed. So pitchers who throw strikes and fielders who make the routine plays will most likely be competitive in a high percentage of games. A hitter is only as good as their last game. So don't get too emotional (high or low) about a hitting streak or even a slump. Stay with the same approach. After a poor at-bat, grab the glove for defense, and when a turn comes up again, focus.

Go Back to Basics

Talk to slumping batters. Examine the grip, stance and swing. Eliminate pregame BP for a team that isn't working as hard as they should. This has worked almost every time we've gone back to just drills. And sometimes a team simply needs a rest. Review the fundamentals, watch a highlight film, and assess their swings on videotape. Bring in a former star player to speak to the team. Remember to swing down, and keep the head steady on contact. Shake up the lineup. Do whatever it takes without pushing the panic button. More important than anything else: Don't hide from a slump. Face it head on and work to correct the flaws.

In the movie *Top Gun*, Tom Cruise crashes his fighter jet, but his commanding officer instructs him to get back up flying as soon as possible. If one is allowed to reflect on the negative, one can't get back to thinking about the positive. Action is so much better than sitting around. Get out there and work. So during hitting drills, always end with a quality swing. In close-range BP fire pitches quickly in between poor cuts, so kids can't reflect on the negative. In game day BP always end with a line drive, and if a kid has a poor round, don't be afraid to throw him/her a second round to get them back on track. These all reinforce the positive and a coaching mentality that while mistakes may happen, we're going to work together to fix them.

Stay with One Stance or Bat

Too many hitters blame their stance or bat for making outs. Why do kids throw their helmet after taking a called third strike? If one didn't swing, why was it the helmet's fault? A slump is usually mental rather than physical for normally fine hitters. Don't worry about external flaws; instead focus on internal ones. Confront slumps with confidence and desire; not by switching weapons.

For example, what if a slump continues even after switching from a 28- to a 30-inch bat, or even an open stance to a closed one? Options A and B haven't worked, so will a third, fourth, or even fifth option make a difference? Probably not. Stay with what previously worked. The hitter and coach will have an easier task of fixing basic flaws or confidence problems when dealing with one bat and stance.

Dropping down a bat size for bat speed purposes is one thing. Moreover, decide if an injured player is hurting the team. Also, the coach has to make immediate decisions if a player is simply having a bad game. You never want a kid striking out a fourth time in a game, for example. Use pinch hitters if need be. The good coach not only has to be a good judge of talent, but also one for making changes during a game which is in the best interest of the team.

One Pitch, One at-Bat at a Time

Kids can break out of a slump with one swing. A slump, just as swinging well, can end and start up again. Keep the same mentality. Batting averages go up and down at roughly the same rate. Go back to concentrating on each pitch. Attempting to change the world with one swing only brings you closer to the end of it.

Each at-bat adds to the hitter's knowledge about the pitcher. If a batter sees, for example, eight to 10 pitches, fouls a couple off, and grounds out, be satisfied and proud. For that brief moment of work, he/she won the battle. Also, think about the value of drawing a walk. Most pitchers get more ticked off in walking people than they do in giving up base hits. And a slumping batter could look at it this way: Walks take away the at-bats with the possibility of making outs.

During a game, a slumping hitter's last concern should be mechanics or personal statistics. That person should concentrate on seeing the ball out of the pitcher's hand, trust their instincts, and react to a strike. Use close-range BP for improved bat speed, confidence, and reaction time. Anyone in a groove says, "I'm seeing the ball great." Streaky hitters are not concerned with proper mechanics or techniques. Their reactions simply take over. Thinking only puts more thoughts into a hitter's mind. Since it takes less than a second to swing, practice the following adage: See Ball ... Hit Ball!

Swing Hard and Be Aggressive

Slapping the ball with the intention of just making contact is fine with two strikes, but not for getting out of a slump. Swing hard and never get cheated. After an aggressive line out, realize four things: (1) Everything was correct from a mechanical standpoint, (2) have the confidence in knowing this fact, (3) use that information for later at-bats, and (4) salute the defense. The pitcher may have gotten the out, but wait until the next plate appearance.

Failure must be dealt with and confronted. Don't make excuses about the pitcher, field, bat, umpire, weather or whatever. After a poor swing, forget about it. Never shake the head in disgust, and never nod after a called strike. Have zero personality and facial expression; that goes for the batter and even the coach. A slumping hitter should also never guess at the pitch. React and think line drive up the middle.

In a six-inning game, everyone in the lineup is guaranteed at least two at-bats. Make each one count. Performance is forced upon every starter. Look for the positive in virtually every one of those negative at-bats. Kids perform so much better in a positive environment and can make amends through constructive criticism. No one enjoys just being yelled at. As a team you're all in it together, so stick together as a unit at all times. See what a kid or team does when the going gets tough. Do they have thick skin and continue to battle until the end?

Corey Davis (1999–02) was always an aggressive hitter at Worcester State, but he lost his confidence during his junior season. He went from starting as a freshman to riding the bench. But we got him a pinch hitting appearance in the 2001 ECAC New England Championship Game, and he ripped a single. He worked hard over the next summer, in the weight room, and seemed to be hitting soft toss whenever I saw him in the gym. I called him down for a talk in a fall tournament game his senior year. The batter before him had just laced a home run. I told Corey to smash another one. He looked at me dumbfounded, knowing my displeasure for swinging for the fences. What I didn't tell him was that I wanted to see the old CD-swing. Well, we did hit back-to-back home runs, later won three games in one day to clinch the tournament, and Davis was the Tournament MVP. He went on to have a spectacular spring season: .377 average, 53 RBI, 57 hits, and nine HR.

Kids should never ask out of the lineup, no matter how bad things are going. Wally Pipp asked for a day off because of a headache. His replacement, Lou Gehrig, went on to play in 2,130 consecutive games. So keep practicing and working hard. Sooner or later good things will happen!

Drag Bunt

The drag bunt is a great "slump buster." A successful drag gives the hitter an opportunity to run the bases. Use speed for an advantage. A drag bunt looks the same as a line drive single in the scorebook. Also pressure the defense by calling for the hit-and-run and/or

swinging 3–0 (usually a good pitch to hit). This gets the kids swinging and hopefully putting the ball in play. And never take a walk as a negative. Walks allow the individual a chance to steal bases and score runs.

Write Down What Works

Use a diary during the season. Go home after each game and write down what worked and what didn't work. Add the name of the pitcher, type of pitches, pitches hit or missed, where they were hit, what the count was on contact, or any pregame routines—whatever happened that day. The hitter can look back to games before a slump began, for example. You'll be surprised what kids, no matter what their age, can do in a well run, well prepared athletic environment.

Some hitters take the first pitch every at-bat and immediately get behind in the count. Why not instead zone that first pitch? Many pitchers intend to get ahead with a straight fastball so they can physically endure the whole game, especially if they have a good defense behind them. Use notebooks and hitting/pitching charts, and check for these tendencies.

Mike Easler showed me his "Hitting Scorebook." He looked for adjustments, pitching patterns, good, and poor at-bats. Some coaches use videotape analysis and spray charts. Write things down (strengths and weaknesses; things to work on), and address them during the game and especially afterwards. Look for trends. Focus on improvement. Other topics include the actual count, pitches hit, location, field placement, solid contact or not, strategy, discipline, concentration level, and team performance against particular pitchers.

Make sure to watch the *whole* swing. Most people watch the ball in flight. See where the hitter finishes, strike vs. non-strike, etc. The notebook should continue throughout a season. Use drills and make adjustments to correct any flaws. Talk about hitting or simply leave a hot hitter alone. If anything, don't go haywire with theories. And whenever giving hitting tips, do so when you're batting. Same goes for fielding tips when on defense. This way kids can concentrate better on the skills for that moment.

Remember the Good

Former LSU coach Skip Bertman posted weekly news articles on the back of the dugout. In times of frustration, players could look at these headlines and be reminded how fortunate they were to be Fightin' Tigers. LSU players were allowed 15 seconds to vent anger in the deep part of the dugout and to snap a rubber band on their wrist until they could forget their failure and get back into the game. As a Legion coach, I used to say, "Take it to the woods." This way kids could vent in the nearby wooded area without being in full view of everyone else.

Bertman also stressed the importance of taking responsibility for failures on and off the field. He wanted his players to say, "I'm better than that." Be that coach who puts an arm around a kid after he/she fails. Tell them that you still believe in them. Keep your office door open or stay after practice so kids can come and talk. And remember that a coach is only as good as his/her players.

Never Get Down

Being mentally strong has a lot to do with success. A leader and competitor can't get down. Take the same approach to batting. It may be difficult, but a winner stays positive.

Use the same number of swings in BP and/or grounders or fly balls. Never refrain from taking BP if a kid is in a slump. That's a sign of quitting. Take each moment of the game as it happens. Baseball games and seasons are too drawn out to dwell on the negative. Strive for **K.E.D.** Know you're the best. Expect the best. Do your best.

Coaching Tips

Keep hitting simple, especially during slumps. Try to have one voice. Don't have every assistant tell a kid different things. That's why coaching roles are so important. And watch out for parents who think they know it all.

In the movie *Major League*, the Indians' slugger worshiped voodoo to save himself from the wretched curveball. In real life, the curveball is hit by waiting properly and keeping the weight/hands back. But sometimes you can use some zany tips to cure the doldrums.

I've emptied the bat bag as a way to "wake up the bats." We built a small fire one day to "burn away all of the evil spirits" of that season thus far. Fix the "injured bats" by wiping them with gauze pads. Make a pyramid of bats at home plate, and have each player bang out the slumps by firing a ball into the pile. Reward bubble gum for hits. Play some fun games like stickball (when indoors use a Jugs foam ball and broom handle). Try Home Run Derby at practice (five to seven swings each; anything but a home run is an out; no running). And it's ice cream for everyone if they can come back from a huge deficit.

Believe good things can happen. (John Meany)

Then there's the "Golden Chuck Bat." In 1995 my Senior Babe Ruth team was having a tough season, and the kids weren't having a lot of fun. So I painted a wooden bat and inscribed G.C.B. on it. Each hitter threw the bat as far as possible, the only time throwing of equipment was allowed. Who could toss it the farthest? Fling it to the heavens. Laugh the slump off by having a ball; sorry, throwing a bat. They did just that. I saw one of my players from that team just last year, and he still remembered what this stunt did for the morale of the squad that summer.

Lastly, here are some sayings to use during the good and even bad times: "Figure it out." "Get it done." "Don't tell me...show me." "Don't ask questions." "No excuses." "Don't say if or ask why." "If you're down one...score two." "No 1-2-3's." "Never go easy." "You may lose a battle, but the goal is to win the war." And whenever there's a negative always try and come back with a positive!

21

Running a Hitting Clinic

"You gotta be a man to play baseball for a living. But you gotta have a lot of little boy in you."

—Roy Campanella, Hall of Fame catcher

Introduction

The following chapter provides tips, suggestions, and ideas for running a hitting clinic. The Worcester State Hitting Clinic runs for three days in our gym during the February school vacation. The sessions are two hours each for the separate age groups: first eight- to 11-followed by 12- to 17-year-olds. I hire a staff of local high school and college coaches as well as my own players. It's become the top hitting clinic in our area. Former campers have gone on to state high school championships, and the College World Series, and three kids played on the Jesse Burkett team, who were U.S. Finalists at the 2002 L.L. World Series.

Overview on How to Start

First pick a time frame or week and reserve the facility. If it's weeklong, register the clinic with the state board of health. Design, print, and mail out a brochure. Hire a coaching staff, trainer and counselors. Generate a namebase and put kids into even teams according to age. Purchase equipment and T-shirts. Type up the daily schedule on a com-

puter, and back everything up on disk. Set time limits for each activity. Start with a registration and an opening ceremony. Figure out a plan for snacks/meals and injuries. Use drills, stations, and try indoor games if applicable. Work hard and have fun. Hand out awards and evaluations on the final day. Pay off the bills and salaries, and start advertising for next year.

Other important items include having a specific time frame and sticking to it. Get more done in less time. Stretch and run beforehand. Make the sessions a progression. Continually review and teach new skills. Talk and work with every kid. Be a hands-on coach. Build camaraderie through partner and group work. At the end of the day remind everyone of the next day's activities. Take attendance each day. Write down activities that worked and those that didn't. If outside always have a rain schedule. Update and revise every year.

Clinic Notes from A-to-Z

Account: Establish a budget, and write up an expense account. Figure in apparel (T-shirts and/or hats), equipment, facility reservation, snacks/meals, awards, salaries, mailings and miscellaneous. Photocopy all registration forms and checks. Open a separate checking account (all of our money goes into the baseball fund-raising account). Have a cutoff date to guarantee a child's spot, but try not to turn anyone away (avoid initial deposits). Copy all receipts, because they may be used for tax deduction purposes.

Brochure: Create a first-class flyer. Print plenty of extras. Devise a set of mailing labels on disk. Send out a bulk mail through a mailing service. Ask area youth league presidents for addresses of the kids. Include photos of the director, facilities, and the kids themselves. On the cover include the clinic name, years of existence, location, age limits, for boys and/or girls, and an address, phone, FAX number, and email address. List facility information, philosophy, and a quote from the director. Provide session dates and times, costs, cutoff date, tuition inclusions (T-shirt/hat, snacks/meals, giveaways, photos, certificate and evaluation), check-in and pick-up times, registration procedures, and the awards ceremony. The player application should include spaces/lines for all biographical information, years of attendance, T-shirt size, week(s) attending (multiple weeks), parent names, phone numbers, an emergency contact, and how one found out about it. Send along a confirmation notice, or a phone call, upon receipt of payment.

Encourage kids to join their friends on teams via the mail registration. Include a standard release waiver, and spaces/lines for a signature and date, medical information and/or health problems,

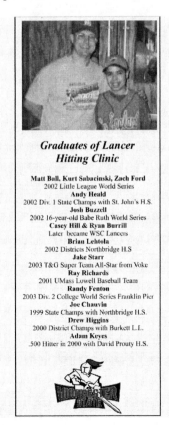

Graduates of Lancer Hitting Clinic

Matt Ball, Kurt Sabacinski, Zach Ford
2002 Little League World Series
Andy Heald
2002 Div. 1 State Champs with St. John's H.S.
Josh Buzzell
2002 16-year-old Babe Ruth World Series
Casey Hill & Ryan Burrill
Later became WSC Lancers
Brian Lehtola
2002 Districts Northbridge H.S
Jake Starr
2003 T&G Super Team All-Star from Voke
Ray Richards
2001 UMass Lowell Baseball Team
Randy Fenton
2003 Div. 2 College World Series Franklin Pier
Joe Chauvin
1999 State Champs with Northbridge H.S.
Drew Higgins
2000 District Champs with Burkett L.L.
Adam Keyes
.500 Hitter in 2000 with David Prouty H.S.

HIT CLINIC APPLICATION FORM
(please print)

NAME_____
ADDRESS_____
CITY_____ STATE___ ZIP_____
SCHOOL_____
AGE & GRADE_____ /_____
T-SHIRT (Circle): ADULT S M L XL
PARENT'S NAME_____
HOME/WORK PHONE_____ /_____
EMERGENCY CONTACT(S) & PHONE(S)

_____

Any medical conditions or physical limitations which your child has which could impede his or her ability to safely participate in the Clinic must be listed below. If none, check here:_____

I agree to allow the staff and trainer of the Clinic to treat my child in the event of any ordinary injury while at the Clinic. In the event of any emergency I understand that the emergency contact phone number(s) listed on this application will be called. In the event no contact can be made, I authorize the Clinic to proceed as necessary. I release the Clinic from liability associated with injury or accident while at the Clinic.

PARENT'S SIGNATURE:_____

Camp fee is $70.00 for the 3-day session.
Please send payment in full ASAP to reserve your child's place. Payment confirms your child's registration. For Q's call the WSC Baseball Office at 508-929-8852 or dbaker1@worcester.edu. If you need another flyer(s), email Coach Baker to receive 1 online.

MAKE CHECKS PAYABLE TO:
WSC Athletic Trust Fund - Hit Clinic

Cut out this form and send with payment to:
Worcester State College, Dirk Baker - Baseball
486 Chandler Street, Worcester, MA 01602-2597

How did you hear about the clinic - OR
Name(s) you want your child to be grouped with?

9th ANNUAL

WORCESTER
State College

2004

HITTING CLINIC

February 16 - 17 - 18

Monday, Tuesday, Wednesday

Ages 8-11 (9-11 a.m.)
&
Ages 12-17 (11 a.m.-1 p.m.)

At Worcester State College
508-929-8852
WSC Baseball Office

THE CLINIC'S PURPOSE

Get a jump-start on the spring baseball season! WSC offers the Top Hitting Clinic in Central Mass. with one of the best staffs anywhere. The aim is to teach the essentials of hitting while emphasizing an overall understanding of what Ted Williams called, *"The toughest thing to do in all of sports."* Kids will be separated into 2 groups: ages 8-11 and 12-17. Each camper will be taught the fundamentals of the swing and shown dozens of drills. The hitter will be prepared to enter his/her spring season. They'll leave the clinic a harder worker, with better hitting skills, and more confidence. All sessions are designed for individual improvement. Clinic structure will allow equal time for instruction and enjoyment. Older players will be guided towards pursuing baseball at the college level & beyond.

CLINIC FACILITIES

Worcester State's indoor practice facility is located in the school's gymnasium. There will be access to video and lecture rooms. A video on hitting will be shown each day. Every camper will receive a *Lancer Baseball T-shirt* & WSC media guide. Hitters will use the batting cage, multiple soft toss nets, *Jugs* machines, state-of-art training devices, and dozens of bats, indoor baseballs, tees, and helmets. Every hitter is guaranteed 200+ swings a day. Like we say at WSC, *"We Hit 'Till Our Hands Bleed."*

SAFETY

We pride ourselves on the organization and safety of the clinic. To ensure for that, all drills and activities are led by a coach. Instead of the regular hardball, hitters will make use of balls with a rubberized coating as well as tennis balls, whiffle balls, and tape balls. We also have numerous water stations, and snacks will be provided each day. Access to the WSC athletic medical room will be provided, and a trainer will be on hand.

WSC HAS THE LONGEST RUNNING HITTING CLINIC IN CENTRAL MASS.

ARRIVAL

Campers should be dropped off and picked up inside the WSC gymnasium (last building on right). Check-in and check-out will be directly inside the front doors. In case of bad weather, we will make every effort to hold the clinic. Assume it's on, or call the Baseball Office at 508-929-8852 & listen to the recorded message.

GROUPS

Group 1 (ages 8-11) and Group 2 (ages 12-17).
Note if you want your child moved up or down a group, or paired with another child.
Kids are put into teams and stay with that group all week.

DAYS

MON. 9-11am (Group 1) & 11am-1pm (Group 2)
TUES. 9-11am (Group 1) & 11am-1pm (Group 2)
THUR. 9-11am (Group 1) & 11am-1pm (Group 2)
Note that Monday is a Holiday.
On Day 1 Arrive 30 Min. Early For Check-In.

SAMPLE OF SESSIONS

Grip	**Stance**
Stride and Swing	**Bat Speed**
Hand-eye Coordination	**Mental Preparation**
Confidence Building	**Game Strategy**
Bunting	**Practice Habits & Drills**
Switch Hitting	**Team Hitting Swings**
Wrist Hitting	**Home Run Derby**
Increasing Batting Average	**How to Beat the Pitcher**

Each child must bring:
* Glove & Sneakers
* Own Bat (if you have one)
* Batting Gloves (if you have them)
NOTE: Write Your Name On All Personal Items!

PAYMENT

Fee is $70.00. Enrollment is limited & accepted on a first-come first-serve basis.

Try to send the payment **1 week prior** to the start of the clinic. **$10 discount** for multiple family members (i.e. $130 for brothers). Return the application ASAP.

DIRECTOR: DR. DIRK BAKER

Dirk Baker is in his 9th year as Head Coach at Worcester State College. WSC WENT 27-7 IN 2003, made the NCAA Tournament in 2002 and has led the MASCAC Conference in hitting 5 years running from 1998-2002. They were nationally ranked (#30) in 2002 when they went 33-9. He has won the most games of any coach in school history, and also has the highest winning %. In 1996, WSC's Jason Akana led the NCAA in batting, and Eric Swedberg '02 was a 3-time Div. 3 All-American. Swedberg also played in the Cape Cod Baseball League. Baker wrote a book on "150 Baseball Games for Kids" to be sold at the clinic. He also self-published 2 other books on baseball. His playing accomplishments include leading Central Mass. in batting and RBI in 1987 while at Auburn High, and then being a New England and North Atlantic Conference All-Star at Boston University. He set school records for home runs and walks in 1991. Baker graduated in 1998 with his Ed.D. from BU and teaches 2 courses at WSC.

COACHING STAFF

Mike O'Brien, WSC Asst. Baseball Coach

John McGuirk, No. Middlesex H.S. Coach

Neal Portnoy, WSC Asst. Baseball Coach

Matt Heenan, WSC Asst. Baseball Coach

Eric Swedberg, WSC 3-time All-American

Steve Coyle, Mgr. Worcester Giants

Ron Silvestri, Voke Coach - 2000 District Champs

Mike Farrell, Tantasqua Head Coach

Jessica Kirk, WSC Head Athletic Trainer

The player/coach ratio will be about 8:1.
Lancer Baseball Players will assist each day.

---

credit card info, check payable to, and the address. Leave space for a "staff use only" section. Some overnight camps/clinics require a separate medical form (proof of a physical) which may be sent upon receipt of the application. Include a basic daily schedule with times, and sample skill sessions and specialties. Provide a director biography, staff listing and titles, child-to-coach ratio, family discounts, scholarships (possibly an essay contest), and successes of former campers. One side (address and bulk stamp included) should be left blank for mailing purposes. Advertise on the radio, in newspapers and magazines, on campus e-mail, and in athletic media guides. Hang and dole out brochures at schools and L.L. sign-ups plus youth, summer, and high school games.

The brochure needs to explain everything to limit the flow of calls with questions about dates/times, costs, etc. Have clinic information on the school website (also include a sign-up form), and leave periodic information on the voice mail (i.e. openings, clinic full, and ways to receive a brochure). And remember to provide driving/parking directions as well. For multiple clinics (use different-colored paper for each), have these printed up together and as soon as possible. Once I have my mailing labels, I send all of my clinic brochures as one (December, February, April and June) in a prestamped bulk mail envelope. Many of the campers attend all four. I love doing clinics, and it's great for recruiting purposes.

Competition: Preach participation and enjoyment over scoring and winning. Stress teamwork over individual performances. Ask the kids to try every-thing. Play a game of ping-pong or rac-quetball at lunchtime (if applicable). Utilize the counselors into skills demon-strations. Conclude each day with an en-joyable activity, so the kids are left joy-ously tired. Try to attract every kid back the next year.

Day 1: Start early with a meeting for both the coaches and counselors. Go over the printed schedule. Then have the kids check in at the various stations: at-tendance/payment, team names, T-shirt, labeling equipment, etc. Have a video playing when people walk in. Set a time frame for registration. Sell any extra T-shirts, but make sure kids get the size they signed up for. Attract a current or former professional player to speak on the first day. Make a brief introduction to the parents and kids. Boast of the years of coaching experience and academic/athletic success of the counselors. Eval-uate the kids, and possibly videotape (which they keep) them each day. Use baseball cards and bubble gum as daily prizes. On the final day have a closing ceremony. Bring every child up for their evaluation packet, photos (team and in-dividual), and signed certificate. Award an autographed ball by pulling a name from a hat. Ask an MLB public relations department to donate leftover promo-tional items. Pick out a kid for each age group with the best attitude or sports-manship.

Equipment: Use all types of balls and bats. Encourage kids to bring their own bats and batting gloves. Use the tee for purposes of making contact. Batters should wear helmets. Make an equip-ment inventory checklist. Clearly label all equipment, both personal and team (write names on hats and gloves, and put tape on bats). Mark bags with athletic

tape according to team names or age groups. For example: red bags for the Red Sox (ages seven to eight), blue bags for Blue Jays (nine to 10), black bags for Pirates (11 to 12), and green bags for A's (13 to 17). Avoid using hard balls if at all possible. Have the kids set up the equip-ment/stations to start as well as put everything away at the end of each day. Issue a time-limit contest for such tasks.

My preferred hitting equipment in-cludes: Diamond regulation baseballs, Jugs foam and dimpled balls, Easton In-crediball, Worth RIF Ball (Reduced In-jury Factor), Safe-T-Ball, deBeer Mush Ball, Wiffle ball, Nerf ball, Rag Ball, and Rawlings Radar Ball; Easton aluminum bats and Thunderstick, Louisville Slug-ger wooden bats, Wiffle bat, and the Bratt's Bat; Jugs or ATEC pitching ma-chine, Lefebvre or Tuffy batting tee, Short-stroke Trainer, and ATEC soft toss nets; Rawlings helmets, Easton equipment bags, and Franklin batting gloves. Sepa-rate the team equipment in different bags and buckets (i.e. bats, helmets, catcher's gear, and the many sets of balls). *Note*: When ordering bats for your own team give a sporting goods catalog to the kids, so they can pick out the ones they want. And make sure you have these equip-ment vitals: top-quality game bats, com-fortable helmets, and plenty of practice baseballs.

Facilities: Utilize all of the areas at your disposal: the gym, class and video rooms, pool, Astroturf, football field, dugouts and diamonds. Use the PA sys-tem. Rake the fields before and after playing. Stress respect of the facilities and especially the bathrooms. No food, soda, sunflower seeds, or gum allowed. Throw the drinking cups away.

Goals: Skills should be explained, demonstrated, corrected and repeated.

Work on the "fun" in fundamentals. Kids should listen and follow the rules. Include everyone. Emphasize the game and not the score. Encourage hustle and teamwork. Stress improvement. Remember to smile, and don't be afraid to laugh.

Hitting: Assign a number to everyone. That number becomes a person's spot in the batting order. Have one on-deck batter at a time with everyone else sitting down in the dugout or bench area. For example, kids not hitting sit on the pull-out bleachers. Avoid batting the best players at the top of the lineup to ensure for equal opportunities. Also try (1) alphabetizing A to Z or Z to A (last name, first name, etc.), (2) by height, (3) position (pitcher bats first, catcher second, etc.), (4) reversing the batting order each day, or (5) team captains grabbing the bat with fist-over-fist to see who hits first. For creativity try switch hitting, or make everything a fair ball (except foul tips). Use 3-and-2 counts. Let a toddler stay up until he/she makes contact. Play stickball or bunt with the Thunderstick bat. Use the tee or soft toss (to stress a particular skill) in the actual games as well. When organizing a team-swinging drill in a circle (for safety purposes), put tape on the gym floor (chalk in the parking lot) to distinguish individual "spots."

Indoor Schedule: For the outdoor clinic, always plan for inclement weather. If a session is postponed for snow, for example, issue a credit to a future clinic (i.e. to avoid refunds). A rain format depends upon the number of kids, gym size, and indoor facilities. Think about lengthening the snack/lunch period or having extra pool time. Show a highlight or bloopers video. Try a mental preparation/relaxation exercise (confidence building through visualization) with everyone lying down with their eyes closed. Do a "Stump the Coach" trivia extravaganza. Try the "Izzy Wright" (Is He Right?) rulebook quiz. Have a question-answer period. Hold a bubble-blowing contest. Show the kids how to properly mold a hat, break in a glove, and wear a uniform. Play the "Alphabet Game" by picking a major leaguer's last name which begins with the letter "A" and so on (go in reverse order for double names such as Andy Ashby). Have a chalkboard session on scorebook symbols and interpretations. Teach the art of signals (verbal and nonverbal). Play wiffleball, pepper or flip. Do soft toss or tee work with tape balls. Try a massive Simon Says or Red Light/Green Light game. For the hardy during a warm rain storm, go back outside and try a home run trot around the bases complete with a dive into the plate (best for end of the day). When balls get wet, dry them in an industrial size dryer.

Jersey: Print up a quality T-shirt. Create a colorful and distinctive design or logo. That T-shirt is free advertising for your clinic, school or program. Distribute the shirts according to the size marked on the application form. Make sure every coach, counselor, and staff member receives a T-shirt. Always print up extra. Give shirts out to key personnel such as athletic department staff, janitors, groundscrew, and kitchen workers. Established clinics can print up adjustable hats, sweatshirts, or polo shirts for the coaches. Have a day where kids can dress up in uniform of their own local team or favorite professional club. Attract a sporting goods sponsor (i.e. for every 100 T-shirts get one bat free), and print their business logo on the back or sleeve. Some companies run clinic deals where you buy a pair of cleats and get turf shoes at half price.

Kinesiology: This term means the study of body movement. Get the kids loose, stretched, and ready to go. Exercises are designed to improve skills and promote better overall health. Stress flexibility and a proper warmup. Start with a light jog. Progress into stretching and calisthenics. Work together in a circle. Have different leaders each day. Include stretches for the arms, shoulders, wrists, fingers, hips, legs (hamstrings and quadriceps), back, groin and neck. Use calisthenics to increase the range of motion (i.e. jumping jacks, toe touches, bunny hops, low squats, lateral lunges, high knees, backward kicks, skips and carioca). Have conditioning as a separate station. Samples include pick-ups and quick-feet exercises, wall-sits, swinging a weighted bat, squeezing tennis balls, push-ups, sit-ups, reverse dips, jump rope, and medicine ball work. *Other:* Mimic the swing by pulling a stretch cord attached to a door knob.

Lunch: Have a specific area for eating (i.e. lunch, snack times, and freeze pop breaks). Stick to the time schedule for these breaks. Get out of the sun and sit down. Set up tables, chairs and barrels. Ask if anyone is allergic to the foods being handed out. Explain the procedure for serving, sitting and cleanup. Relax while watching a video. Do snacks (granola bars or crackers) in the morning and popsicles in the afternoon. Buy food/gum in bulk from a wholesale club.

Making Teams: Arrange kids in a line and have them count off "1-2, 1-2." Each number is a team. For four teams count off, "1-2-3-4" and so on. Try 10-versus 11-year-olds, for example. Try switching teams so kids can interact with other people. Total participation is the key. Have everyone hit in each station. Assign people to retrieve foul balls,

coach the bases, or keep score. For games, use more than three outfielders, designate people to warm up the outfielders, starting pitcher, clean up the dugout (bats and helmets), or throw balls to the first baseman and center fielder after each inning. Name a head cheerleader or a bench/bullpen coach.

Names: Put name tags on people and equipment. Use first names or nicknames. Try a name game for everyone to get to know each other. As a way to meet new people, toss gloves into a pile. Tell kids to pick out a different glove and go speak to that glove's owner for a few minutes.

Outs: Instead of playing three outs per inning, let everyone bat before changing sides (see how many runs they score). Use six outs in a group hitting game. Encourage catches off of the gym walls and ceilings. In most cases enforce cooperation rather than elimination.

Positions: For factors of confidence, play without gloves when using a wiffle, tennis, foam, or Nerf ball. Try rotating positions each inning for games; simply move up or down a number for each fielding area. Bench players not in the original defensive alignment should bat first. Base coaches should be substitutes or the last two people making outs from the previous inning. Coaches/counselors should throw all batting practice and in the games themselves. When coaches pitch have a kid stand either left or right of the rubber, and let this player field comebackers. Record the alignment of players each day, so children get to play every position.

Quick Rules: The quicker the rules the faster an activity starts. Use the E.D.D. format: "Explain. Demonstrate. Do." When speaking make sure kids look at you with both eyes. Never speak until there is complete quiet. Ask kids to repeat the rules. Review skills after stations and games. Hand out pamphlets on the fundamentals. Explain confusing rules and plays such as batter/catcher interference, the hit-and-run, infield fly, illegal pitch, force outs, dead ball, and a dropped third strike versus caught foul tips (high school and up). Make any hazards "out of play." Have a clipboard, pen and watch (preferably with a stopwatch function). Use a whistle or horn to switch stations (make sure the kids put all bats down). Set up exact time limits and follow the daily schedule. Allow for stretching, warmup, time to and from stations, and questions. Record game results, and chart progress for evaluations and awards. Alter the traditional rules by allowing fielders behind the fence, in foul territory, or behind the backstop. Concessions for age should be made for field size, regulation ball and bat sizes, leading, sliding, length of base paths, and plate-to-mound distances. Make creative indoor rules such as home runs off of the basketball backboard or triples that hit specific banners hanging in the gym.

Runs: Instead of running around the bases, offensive teams can do any of the following together before the defensive team records an out or gets the ball back to the pitcher. Try sprinting wall to wall, pushups, sit-ups, or jumping jacks. Skip, hop, or run hand in hand with a partner. Allow more than one runner per base. To get more people involved, start each inning with any number of kids on the base(s). Substitute cones as bases. Use a manual scoreboard or count out loud to keep track of points. Run the bases in reverse (never have the kids run backwards), in different order, or vary the direction according to where the ball

is hit. For batting points, use line drives/ground balls over fly balls. Deduct points for swings-and-misses.

Safety: Safety is the number one priority in any playing environment. Warm up and condition the kids properly. Review the boundaries. Pinpoint any hazards such as rocks, holes, or sharp edges on the backstop or fences. Avoid dangerous situations altogether. No running up or down steps. Check for untied shoes. Wear cleats outdoors. No lollipops. Remove watches and jewelry. Note that regulation balls, thrown bats, and stationary bases can be very dangerous. Use batting helmets and full catcher's equipment, including a protective cup. Make sure the first-aid kit is fully stocked. Know where the trainer/nurse is located and/or nearest phone. Respond to injuries quickly and responsibly. Clean cuts up fast. Young bones break easily, so listen to the kids when they get hurt. Never move anyone who is unconscious. Inform the medical staff of all injuries. A registered nurse or certified trainer should always be on call. Hats and sunscreen should be mandatory for any hot-weather setting. Have water at every field or station. Be able to notice dehydration and heat stroke. On "3-H Days" (hazy, hot and humid) get into the shade, hose the kids down, or head to the pool early. Have a record of child medical conditions (i.e. asthma, seizures, diabetes, allergies, bee stings, etc.). Toddlers should go with a coach to the bathroom. Have a lifeguard maintain pool protocol. Take attendance each morning, before and after lunch, and before kids leave for the day. Assign a designated area for kids to stay until they are picked up. Lastly, every coach should be certified in first aid and CPR.

The Pitcher: Have the coaches and

counselors do the majority of pitching. Be consistent in velocity. Throw breaking balls (older players), or alter the count (quickens the game). Use a pitching machine in the cage.

Umpire: Every game should have an umpire and strict rules. Encourage questions beforehand. Use a clicker to keep track of balls, strikes and outs. Any arguing or questioning of calls should result in a lost run for that particular team.

Variety: Clinics are great for the coaches and counselors too. Adults want to learn new drills and rekindle old friendships. Encourage the staff to get involved with stations they have little or no experience in. Challenge the kids to learn new skills, and help those less talented. Ask coaches to wear their school T-shirts and the many varieties of minor and MLB caps. Bring along wooden bats and the fungo. Dare to do what no clinic has done before. Take a day trip to a nearby minor league game (group ticket deal). Document the many moments on video. Analyze kids' swings on video, and show them action photographs of the major leaguers.

Work: While a clinic is fun for the kids, it's also work for the coaches. Coaches should run the teams, stations and games. Have the counselors umpire, throw BP, and feed the pitching machines. Start each day with a theme. Let the staff offer game day scenarios, fundamentals and drills. Devise a salary scale, and tell each staff member his/her paycheck amount before day one. Increase pay for exemplary work, years of service, and inflation. Include stipends for gas (commuters) and dorm supervisors (overnight). Award checks on the final day. Pay staff generously. A clinic is only as good as the people who work at them. This includes directors/assistant directors, coaches/counselors, trainers/nurses, and guest speakers. Worcester State players receive their payments via meal money on the Florida trip. Send information on designer letterhead to the staff during the year (include a phone/mail directory). Notify them months ahead of time about the clinic dates and times.

X: Never put a "X" through a kid in relation to effort. Everyone deserves a chance to perform, especially since they're paying to attend your clinic. Discipline is another story. For effective learning to occur, the coach must have control of the playing environment. Be fair and consistent, and never pick favorites. Be courteous and polite. Foul language is forbidden by everyone. Use positive reinforcement. Avoid using running as punishment. Threats rarely work, but taking away what kids enjoy most (games) can be very effective in controlling rambunctious youngsters. Notice if a kid is just having a bad day or isn't feeling well. Talk to them and find out what's wrong. Troublemakers may surface, so deal with them swiftly and decisively. Avoid holding a grudge, but know that "one bad apple can ruin the crop."

Yard: Play on the big or little diamonds. Drive vans to local fields. Create multiple diamonds on the Astroturf or football field. Organize small stations. Divide the gym area into multiple stations: video, cage, soft toss, bunting, and Home Run Derby, for example. Assemble batting tunnels and mini-cages in areas out of the way. Run stations in the parking lot.

Zs: A key to athletic performance is a good night's sleep. Encourage the kids to be early, wear the clinic T-shirt, and eat a good breakfast. For overnight clinics assign two counselors per floor with two to four kids per room. Have a lights-out policy (depends on age) and an orientation on day one (i.e. rules, emergency procedures, and locations of the cafeteria, nurse's station, and pay phone). Coaches should stay in separate quarters. A suggested clothing list includes: fan, pillow, sleeping bag, pajamas, watch, alarm clock, sneakers, shoes, socks, underwear, pants, shorts, shirts, sweats, bathing suit, jacket, rain coat, laundry bag, shower shoes, towel, toiletries (soap, toothpaste, deodorant, etc.), sunscreen, bug repellant, all baseball/softball gear including glove, bat, hat, game pants and cleats, equipment bag, water bottle, reading materials, Walkman, headphones and CDs, pen, notebook, postcards, stamps, flashlight and money. Label clothes and equipment appropriately.

Sample of Daily Sessions

The Worcester State Hitting Clinic has been run every winter since 1996. I hire about 10 coaches, and my players work in increments between their classes. We attract over 100 kids from L.L. to high school. Each session lasts two hours each. This way kids work hard the entire period plus you can get two groups into the gym for four hours (WSC varsity teams use the gym in the afternoon). Stations are 15 minutes each, and kids rotate from activity to activity. Because we only have one gym, we try to maximize our space along with two classrooms. For notes on how to run some of the stations and games, see the previous chapters. Here's how we run it:

Day 1

Group 1

8:00–8:55 A.M.: Coaches meeting, sign-in procedure, T-shirts, trivia/video in gym.

9:00–9:10 A.M.: Coach bios, intro counselors/trainer, review policies and procedures, quick stretch.

9:10–9:30 A.M.: Hitting Fundamentals (bat size, grip, stance).

9:35–9:50 A.M.: Station 1

Counselor: Red Sox—Watching video in classroom with snacks (end of gym).

Coaches: Marlins—Bunting (front of the gym).

Coaches: Braves—Double-barrel BP in cage with tennis balls (middle of the gym).

Coach: Dodgers—HR Derby (far end of the gym).

Counselor: Yankees—Review of MLB Hitter Photos in classroom (in gym lobby).

9:50–10:05 A.M.: Station 2

Counselor: Dodgers—Watching video in classroom with snacks (end of gym).

Coaches: Yankees—Bunting (front of the gym).

Coaches: Marlins—Double-barrel BP in cage with tennis balls (middle of the gym).

Coach: Braves—HR Derby (far end of the gym).

Counselor: Red Sox—Review of MLB Hitter Photos in classroom (in gym lobby).

10:05–10:20 A.M.: Station 3

Counselor: Braves—Watching video in classroom with snacks (end of gym).

Coaches: Red Sox—Bunting (front of the gym).

Coaches: Yankees—Double-barrel BP in cage with tennis balls (middle of the gym).

Coach: Marlins—HR Derby (far end of the gym).

Counselor: Dodgers—Review of MLB Hitter Photos in classroom (in gym lobby).

10:20–10:35 A.M.: Station 4

Counselor: Marlins—Watching video in classroom with snacks (end of gym).

Coaches: Dodgers—Bunting (front of the gym).

Coaches: Red Sox—Double-barrel BP in cage with tennis balls (middle of the gym).

Coach: Yankees—HR Derby (far end of the gym).

Counselor: Braves—Review of MLB Hitter Photos in classroom (in gym lobby).

10:35–10:50 A.M.: Station 5

Counselor: Yankees—Watching video in classroom with snacks (end of gym).

Coaches: Braves—Bunting (front of the gym).

Coaches: Dodgers—Double-barrel BP in cage with tennis balls (middle of the gym).

Coach: Red Sox—HR Derby (far end of the gym).

Counselor: Marlins—Review of MLB Hitter Photos in classroom (in gym lobby).

10:50–11:00 A.M.: Organize equipment, review day and intro for Day 2, kids leave with parents.

Group 2

10:30–11:00 A.M.: Clinic Director handles sign-ins and T-shirts for Group 2.

11:00–11:10 A.M.: Coach bios, intro counselors/trainer, review policies and procedures, quick stretch.

11:10–11:30 A.M.: Hitting Fundamentals (bat size, grip, stance).

11:35–11:50 A.M.: Station 1

Counselor: Red Sox—Watching video in classroom with snacks (end of gym).

Coaches: Marlins—Bunting (front of the gym).

Coaches: Braves—Double-barrel BP in cage with tennis balls (middle of the gym).

Coach: Dodgers—HR Derby (far end of the gym).

Counselor: Yankees—Review of MLB Hitter Photos in classroom (in gym lobby).

11:50–12:05 P.M.: Station 2

Counselor: Dodgers—Watching video in classroom with snacks (end of gym).

Coaches: Yankees—Bunting (front of the gym).

Coaches: Marlins—Double-barrel BP in cage with tennis balls (middle of the gym).

Coach: Braves—HR Derby (far end of the gym).

Counselor: Red Sox—Review of MLB Hitter Photos in classroom (in gym lobby).

12:05–12:20 P.M.: Station 3

Counselor: Braves—Watching video in classroom with snacks (end of gym).

Coaches: Red Sox—Bunting (front of the gym).

Coaches: Yankees—Double-barrel BP in cage with tennis balls (middle of the gym).

Coach: Marlins—HR Derby (far end of the gym).

Counselor: Dodgers—Review of MLB Hitter Photos in classroom (in gym lobby).

12:20–12:35 P.M.: Station 4

Counselor: Marlins—Watching video in classroom with snacks (end of gym).

Coaches: Dodgers—Bunting (front of the gym).

Coaches: Red Sox—Double-barrel BP in cage with tennis balls (middle of the gym).

Coach: Yankees—HR Derby (far end of the gym).

Counselor: Braves—Review of MLB Hitter Photos in classroom (in gym lobby).

12:35–12:50 P.M.: Station 5

Counselor: Yankees—Watching video in classroom with snacks (end of gym).

Coaches: Braves—Bunting (front of the gym).

Coaches: Dodgers—Double-barrel BP in cage with tennis balls (middle of the gym).

Coach: Red Sox—HR Derby (far end of the gym).

Counselor: Marlins—Review of MLB Hitter Photos in classroom (in gym lobby).

12:50–1:00 P.M.: Organize equipment, review day and intro for Day 2, kids leave with parents.

Day 2

Group 1

8:30–9:00 A.M.: Attendance and sign-in procedures, coaches man stations, video/trivia in gym.

9:00–9:05 A.M.: Welcome, review of Day 1, intro for Day 2, quick stretch.

9:10–9:30 A.M.: Review of the stride and swing, All-Swing Drill.

9:35am–9:50 A.M.: Station 1

Counselor: Red Sox—Watching video in classroom with snacks (end of gym).

Coaches: Marlins—Soft toss with tennis or tape balls (front of gym).

Coaches: Braves—Double-barrel BP in cage with tennis balls (middle of gym).

Coach: Dodgers—HR Derby or Line Drive Contest (far end of gym).

Counselors: Yankees—Tees (front of gym).

9:50–10:05 A.M.: Station 2

Counselor: Dodgers—Watching video in classroom with snacks (end of gym).

Coaches: Yankees—Soft toss with tennis or tape balls (front of gym).

Coaches: Marlins—Double-barrel BP in cage with tennis balls (middle of gym).

Coach: Braves—HR Derby or Line Drive Contest (far end of gym).

Counselors: Red Sox—Tees (front of gym).

10:05–10:20 A.M.: Station 3

Counselor: Braves—Watching video in classroom with snacks (end of gym).

Coaches: Red Sox—Soft toss with tennis or tape balls (front of gym).

Coaches: Yankees—Double-barrel BP in cage with tennis balls (middle of gym).

Coach: Marlins—HR Derby or Line Drive Contest (far end of gym).

Counselors: Dodgers—Tees (front of gym).

10:20–10:35 A.M.: Station 4

Counselor: Marlins—Watching video in classroom with snacks (end of gym).

Coaches: Dodgers—Soft toss with tennis or tape balls (front of gym).

Coaches: Red Sox—Double-barrel BP in cage with tennis balls (middle of gym).

Coach: Yankees—HR Derby or Line Drive Contest (far end of gym).

Counselors: Braves—Tees (front of gym).

10:35–10:50 A.M.: Station 5

Counselor: Yankees—Watching video in classroom with snacks (end of gym).

Coaches: Braves—Soft toss with tennis or tape balls (front of gym).

Coaches: Dodgers—Double-barrel BP in cage with tennis balls (middle of gym).

Coach: Red Sox—HR Derby or Line Drive Contest (far end of gym).

Counselors: Marlins—Tees (front of gym).

10:50–11:00 A.M.: Organize equipment, review day and intro for Day 3, kids leave with parents.

Group 2

10:30–11:00 A.M.: Clinic director handles attendance and sign-in procedures, video/trivia in lobby.

11:00–11:05 A.M.: Welcome, review of Day 1, intro for Day 2, quick stretch.

11:05–11:15 A.M.: Coach lecture on Work Ethic.

11:20–11:35 A.M.: Review of the stride and swing, All-Swing Drill.

11:35–11:50 A.M.: Station 1

Counselor: Red Sox—Watching video in classroom with snacks (end of gym).

Coaches: Marlins—Soft toss with tennis or tape balls (front of gym).

Coaches: Braves—Double-barrel BP in cage with tennis balls (middle of gym).

Coach: Dodgers—HR Derby or Line Drive Contest (far end of gym).

Counselors: Yankees—Tees (front of gym).

11:50–12:05 P.M.: Station 2

Counselor: Dodgers—Watching video in classroom with snacks (end of gym).

Coaches: Yankees—Soft toss with tennis or tape balls (front of gym).

Coaches: Marlins—Double-barrel BP in cage with tennis balls (middle of gym).

Coach: Braves—HR Derby or Line Drive Contest (far end of gym).

Counselors: Red Sox—Tees (front of gym).

12:05–12:20 P.M.: Station 3

Counselor: Braves—Watching video in classroom with snacks (end of gym).

Coaches: Red Sox—Soft toss with tennis or tape balls (front of gym).

Coaches: Yankees—Double-barrel BP in cage with tennis balls (middle of gym).

Coach: Marlins—HR Derby or Line Drive Contest (far end of gym).

Counselors: Dodgers—Tees (front of gym).

12:20–12:35 P.M.: Station 4

Counselor: Marlins—Watching video in classroom with snacks (end of gym).
Coaches: Dodgers—Soft toss with tennis or tape balls (front of gym).
Coaches: Red Sox—Double-barrel BP in cage with tennis balls (middle of gym).
Coach: Yankees—HR Derby or Line Drive Contest (far end of gym).
Counselors: Braves—Tees (front of gym).

12:35–12:50 P.M.: Station 5

Counselor: Yankees—Watching video in classroom with snacks (end of gym).
Coaches: Braves—Soft toss with tennis or tape balls (front of gym).
Coaches: Dodgers—Double-barrel BP in cage with tennis balls (middle of gym).
Coach: Red Sox—HR Derby or Line Drive Contest (far end of gym).
Counselors: Marlins—Tees (front of gym).
12:50–1:00 P.M.: Organize equipment, review day and intro for Day 3, kids leave with parents.

Day 3

Group 1

8:30–9:00 A.M.: Attendance/sign-in, deposit checks, confirm staff addresses/amounts for payment.
9:00–9:05 A.M.: Welcome, review of Day 2, intro for Day 3, quick stretch.
9:05–9:25 A.M.: All-Swing and Top-hand-release Drills, Wrist Hitting, and Hitting Specialties.

9:30–9:45 A.M.: Station 1

Counselor: Red Sox—Watching video in classroom with snacks (end of gym).
Coaches: Marlins—Pepper (front of gym).
Coaches: Braves—Double-barrel BP in cage with tennis balls (middle of gym).
Coach: Dodgers—HR Derby (far end of gym).
Counselors: Yankees—Soft toss (1-hand) and tee (front of gym).

9:45–10:00 A.M.: Station 2

Counselor: Dodgers—Watching video in classroom with snacks (end of gym).
Coaches: Yankees—Pepper (front of gym).
Coaches: Marlins—Double-barrel BP in cage with tennis balls (middle of gym).
Coach: Braves—HR Derby (far end of gym).
Counselors: Red Sox—Soft toss (1-hand) and tee (front of gym).

10:00–10:15 A.M.: Station 3

Counselor: Braves—Watching video in classroom with snacks (end of gym).
Coaches: Red Sox—Pepper (front of gym).
Coaches: Yankees—Double-barrel BP in cage with tennis balls (middle of gym).
Coach: Marlins—HR Derby (far end of gym).
Counselors: Dodgers—Soft toss (1-hand) and tee (front of gym).

10:15–10:30 A.M.: Station 4

Counselor: Marlins—Watching video in classroom with snacks (end of gym).
Coaches: Dodgers—Pepper (front of gym).

Coaches: Red Sox — Double-barrel BP in cage with tennis balls (middle of gym).

Coach: Yankees — HR Derby (far end of gym).

Counselors: Braves — Soft toss (1-hand) and tee (front of gym).

10:30–10:45 A.M.: Station 5

Counselor: Yankees — Watching video in classroom with snacks (end of gym).

Coaches: Braves — Pepper (front of gym).

Coaches: Dodgers — Double-barrel BP in cage with tennis balls (middle of gym).

Coach: Red Sox — HR Derby (far end of gym).

Counselors: Marlins — Soft toss (1-hand) and tee (front of gym).

10:45–11:00 A.M.: Organize equipment, review clinic, thank coaches and counselors. Hand out brochures for future clinics, WSC baseball media guides, pamphlets on hitting fundamentals, prizes and Sportsmanship Awards, kids leave with parents.

Group 2

10:30–11:00 A.M.: Clinic director handles attendance and sign-in procedures, video/trivia in lobby.

11:00–11:05 A.M.: Welcome, review of Day 2, intro for Day 3, quick stretch.

11:05–11:15 A.M.: Coach lecture on What the Pitcher is Trying to Accomplish.

11:20–11:35 A.M.: All-Swing and Top-hand-release Drills, Wrist Hitting, and Hitting Specialties.

11:35–11:50 A.M.: Station 1

Counselor: Red Sox — Watching video in classroom with snacks (end of gym).

Coaches: Marlins — Pepper (front of gym).

Coaches: Braves — Double-barrel BP in cage with tennis balls (middle of gym).

Coach: Dodgers — HR Derby (far end of gym).

Counselors: Yankees — Soft toss (1-hand) and tee (front of gym).

11:50–12:05 P.M.: Station 2

Counselor: Dodgers — Watching video in classroom with snacks (end of gym).

Coaches: Yankees — Pepper (front of gym).

Coaches: Marlins — Double-barrel BP in cage with tennis balls (middle of gym).

Coach: Braves — HR Derby (far end of gym).

Counselors: Red Sox — Soft toss (1-hand) and tee (front of gym).

12:05–12:20 P.M.: Station 3

Counselor: Braves — Watching video in classroom with snacks (end of gym).

Coaches: Red Sox — Pepper (front of gym).

Coaches: Yankees — Double-barrel BP in cage with tennis balls (middle of gym).

Coach: Marlins — HR Derby (far end of gym).

Counselors: Dodgers — Soft toss (1-hand) and tee (front of gym).

12:20–12:35 P.M.: Station 4

Counselor: Marlins — Watching video in classroom with snacks (end of gym).

Coaches: Dodgers — Pepper (front of gym).

Coaches: Red Sox — Double-barrel BP in cage with tennis balls (middle of gym).

Coach: Yankees—HR Derby (far end of gym).

Counselors: Braves—Soft toss (1-hand) and tee (front of gym).

12:35–12:50 P.M.: Station 5

Counselor: Yankees—Watching video in classroom with snacks (end of gym).

Coaches: Braves—Pepper (front of gym).

Coaches: Dodgers—Double-barrel BP in cage with tennis balls (middle of gym).

Coach: Red Sox—HR Derby (far end of gym).

Counselors: Marlins—Soft toss (1-hand) and tee (front of gym).

12:50–1:00 P.M.: Organize equipment, review clinic, thank coaches and counselors. Hand out brochures for future clinics, WSC baseball media guides, pamphlets on hitting fundamentals, prizes and Sportsmanship Awards, kids leave with parents.

1:00–1:30 P.M.: Put all equipment away, clean gym and classrooms, check under bleachers, and review inventory. Add new names to mailing list, revise schedule for next year, issue checks/payment forms, and buy lunch for staff.

Index